Further praise for *The Revolt of the Elites and the Betrayal of Democracy*

"Christopher Lasch spent a lifetime raising his eloquent voice on behalf of the liberty, civic responsibility, and good sense of ordinary people. His contribution was prophetic in the truest sense: calling us back to the first principles of democratic life and forward to a more just society unafraid to argue about the moral meaning of individual and social choices. It is a blessing that he left *The Revolt of the Elites and the Betrayal of Democracy*, which is both a brilliant dissection of the failures of liberals, conservatives, and radicals, and an invitation to a more responsible and fruitful approach to public life. All who come to this book will be challenged and inspired."
—E. J. Dionne, Jr.

"*The Revolt of the Elites and the Betrayal of Democracy* ranges provocatively [and] insightfully." —Robert H. Bork, *National Review*

"A full-spirited attack on the threats to American democratic culture . . . ." —*Chronicle of Higher Education*

"In *The Revolt of the Elites*, Mr. Lasch sets forth a provocative thesis. He argues that the same upper-middle-class elites 'who control the international flow of money and information . . . and thus set the terms of public debate' have paradoxically 'lost faith in the values, or what remains of them, of the West.' " —Dennis Farney, *Wall Street Journal*

"*In The Revolt of the Elites*, Lasch offers a powerful critique of American democracy that calls for a new populist program combining liberal and conservative remedies to restore its health." —Peter H. Stone, *Philadelphia Inquirer*

"This brilliant, clear-eyed work . . . examines how the American impulse toward political equality has been frustrated in the workplace and wider culture . . . ." —Paul Baumann, *Newsday*

"Lasch is so pithy and cogent that he produces the kind of book that makes you want to corner friends and read it aloud to them." — starred *Booklist*

"This posthumous contribution makes us sense the loss of Christopher Lasch ever more strongly. He had the real capacity to tell the truth, to speak plainly with subtlety, and to challenge the smug thinking into which so many privileged Americans fall with uncanny regularity. This is an important and disturbing book, even if one doesn't agree with it." —Leon Botstein

OTHER BOOKS BY CHRISTOPHER LASCH

The American Liberals and the Russian Revolution (1962)

The New Radicalism in America (1965)

The Agony of the American Left (1969)

The World of Nations (1973)

Haven in a Heartless World (1977)

The Culture of Narcissism (1979)

The Minimal Self (1984)

The True and Only Heaven (1991)

THE
Revolt *of*
the Elites

and the Betrayal of Democracy

CHRISTOPHER LASCH

W. W. NORTON & COMPANY
NEW YORK LONDON

The text of this book is composed in Janson
with the display set in Janson
composition and manufacturing by the Maple-Vail Book
Manufacturing Group.
Book design by Chris Welch

Portions of chapter 4 appeared in "A Reply to Jeffrey Isaac," *Salmagundi*, Winter 1992. Reprinted by permission. Chapter 5 appeared in different form as "Communitarianism or Populism?" *New Oxford*, May 1992. Copyright © 1992 New Oxford Review. Reprinted with permission from the New Oxford Review (1069 Kains Ave., Berkeley, CA 94706). Chapter 6 appeared in different form as "Preserving the Mild Life," *Pittsburgh History*, Summer 1991. Copyright © 1991 by the Historical Society of Western Pennsylvania. Chapter 7 appeared in different form as "Civic Wrongs," *Tikkun*, vol. 6, no. 2. Reprinted from *Tikkun Magazine*, a bimonthly Jewish Critique of Politics, Culture and Society. Chapter 8 appeared in different form as "The Great Experiment: Where Did It Go Wrong?" in *Beyond Cheering and Bashing*, edited by James Seaton and William K. Buckley. Reprinted by permission of Popular Press. Chapter 9 appeared in different form as "Journalism, Publicity and the Lost Art of Argument," *Media Studies Journal*, Spring 1990. Reprinted with permission. Chapter 10 appeared in different form as "Politics and Culture: Academic Pseudo-radicalism," *Salmagundi*, Winter 1991. Reprinted by permission. Portions of Chapter 11 appeared in "For Shame," "*New Republic*, August 10, 1992. Reprinted by permission. Chapter 12 appeared in different form as "The Saving Remnant," *New Republic*, November 19, 1990. Reprinted by permission. Chapter 13 appeared in different form as "The Soul of Man Under Secularism," *New Oxford Review*, July–August 1991. Copyright © 1991 New Oxford Review. Reprinted with permission from the New Oxford Review (1069 Kains Ave., Berkeley CA 94706).

ISBN 0-393-31371-9

W.W. Norton & Company, Inc., 500 Fifth Avenue, New York, N. Y. 10110
W.W Norton & Company Ltd., 10 Coptic Street, London WC1A 1PU

5 6 7 8 9 10

For Robert Westbrook

Contents

III   THE DARK NIGHT OF THE SOUL

A c k n o w l e d g m e n t s

S ince this book was written under trying circumstances, I am more than usually indebted to others
for advice and assistance. My daughter Betsy did
much of the typing and contributed a good deal of invaluable editorial assistance, at the expense of her own work.
Suzanne Wolk also sacrificed her own work in order to type
large sections of the manuscript. Nell, my wife, undertook
to teach me, at this late date, the uses of a word processor;
without this helpful machine, which would have remained
inaccessible to me without her guidance, this book could
not have been completed in the allotted time. Her arduous
labors also included copy-editing and correcting my far
from perfect drafts.

Robert Westbrook, Richard Fox, William R. Taylor,
William Leach, and Leon Fink read the manuscript
in whole or in part. No doubt I am forgetting others who

read the title essay and offered encouragement at a critical juncture. Finally, I am indebted to my editor, Henning Gutmann, for his unfailingly helpful advice and encouragement.

Some of the chapters in this book appeared, in different form, in various periodicals: "The Abolition of Shame" and "Philip Rieff and the Religion of Culture" in the *New Republic;* "Communitarianism or Populism?" and "The Soul of Man under Secularism" in the *New Oxford Review;* "Racial Politics in New York" in *Tikkun;* "Conversation and the Civic Arts" in *Pittsburgh History;* "The Lost Art of Argument" in the *Gannett Center Journal;* "Does Democracy Deserve to Survive?" and "Academic Pseudo-radicalism" in *Salmagundi.* All of these pieces have been extensively revised. Since they appeared for the most part in rather obscure journals of opinion, I trust that most of my readers will find them unfamiliar in any case.

THE

Revolt *of* *the* Elites

and the Betrayal of Democracy

One

Introduction

The Democratic Malaise

ost of my recent work comes back in one way or another to the question of whether democracy has a future. I think a great many people are asking themselves the same question. Americans are much less sanguine about the future than they used to be, and with good reason. The decline of manufacturing and the consequent loss of jobs; the shrinkage of the middle class; the growing number of the poor; the rising crime rate; the flourishing traffic in drugs; the decay of the cities—the bad news goes on and on. No one has a plausible solution to these intractable problems, and most of what passes for political discussion doesn't even address them. Fierce ideological battles are fought over peripheral issues. Elites, who define the issues, have lost touch with the people. (See chapter 2, "The Revolt of the Elites.") The unreal, artificial character of our politics reflects their insulation from the common life, together with a secret conviction that the real problems are insoluble.

George Bush's wonderment, when he saw for the first time an electronic scanning device at a supermarket check-out counter, revealed, as in a flash of lightning, the chasm that divides the privileged classes from the rest of the nation. There has always been a privileged class, even in America, but it has never been so dangerously isolated from its surroundings. In the nineteenth century wealthy families were typically settled, often for several generations, in a given locale. In a nation of wanderers their stability of residence provided a certain continuity. Old families were recognizable as such, especially in the older seaboard cities, only because, resisting the migratory habit, they put down roots. Their insistence on the sanctity of private property was qualified by the principle that property rights were neither absolute nor unconditional. Wealth was understood to carry civic obligations. Libraries, museums, parks, orchestras, universities, hospitals, and other civic amenities stood as so many monuments to upper-class munificence.

No doubt this generosity had a selfish side: It advertised the baronial status of the rich, attracted new industries, and helped to promote the home city against its rivals. Civic boosterism amounted to good business in an age of intense competition among cities, each aspiring to preeminence. What mattered, however, was that philanthropy implicated elites in the lives of their neighbors and in those of generations to come. The temptation to withdraw into an exclusive world of their own was countered by a lingering awareness, which in some circles survived even the riotous self-indulgence of the Gilded Age, that "all have derived benefits from their ancestors," as Horace Mann put it in 1846, and that therefore, "all are bound, as by an oath, to transmit those benefits, even in an improved condition, to posterity." Only an "isolated, solitary being, . . . having no relations to a community around him," could subscribe to the "arrogant doctrine of absolute ownership," according to Mann, who spoke not only for himself but for a considerable body of opinion in the older cities, in much of New England, and in New England's cultural dependencies in the Old Northwest.

Thanks to the decline of old money and the old-money ethic of civic responsibility, local and regional loyalties are sadly attenuated today. The mobility of capital and the emergence of a global market contribute to the same effect. The new elites, which include not only corporate managers but all those professions that produce and manipulate information—the lifeblood of the global market—are far more cosmopolitan, or at least more restless and migratory, than their predecessors. Advancement in business and the professions, these days, requires a willingness to follow the siren call of opportunity wherever it leads. Those who stay at home forfeit the chance of upward mobility. Success has never been so closely associated with mobility, a concept that figured only marginally in the nineteenth-century definition of opportunity (chapter 3, "Opportunity in the Promised Land"). Its ascendancy in the twentieth century is itself an important indication of the erosion of the democratic ideal, which no longer envisions a rough equality of condition but merely the selective promotion of non-elites into the professional-managerial class.

Ambitious people understand, then, that a migratory way of life is the price of getting ahead. It is a price they gladly pay, since they associate the idea of home with intrusive relatives and neighbors, small-minded gossip, and hidebound conventions. The new elites are in revolt against "Middle America," as they imagine it: a nation technologically backward, politically reactionary, repressive in its sexual morality, middlebrow in its tastes, smug and complacent, dull and dowdy. Those who covet membership in the new aristocracy of brains tend to congregate on the coasts, turning their back on the heartland and cultivating ties with the international market in fast-moving money, glamour, fashion, and popular culture. It is a question whether they think of themselves as Americans at all. Patriotism, certainly, does not rank very high in their hierarchy of virtues. "Multiculturalism," on the other hand, suits them to perfection, conjuring up the agreeable image of a global bazaar in which exotic cuisines, exotic styles of dress, exotic music, exotic tribal customs can be savored indiscriminately, with no questions asked and no commitments required. The new elites are at home only in transit, en route to a high-level conference, to the grand opening of a new franchise, to an international film festival, or to an undiscovered resort. Theirs is essentially a tourist's view of the world—not a perspective likely to encourage a passionate devotion to democracy.

IN THE TRUE AND ONLY HEAVEN, I tried to recover a tradition of democratic thought—call it populist, for lack of a better term—that has fallen into disuse. One reviewer surprised me by complaining that the book had nothing to say about democracy (a misunderstanding I have laid to rest, I trust, in chapter 4, "Does Democracy Deserve to Survive?"). That he could miss the point of the book in this way tells us something about the current cultural climate. It shows how confused we are about the meaning of democracy, how far we have strayed from the premises on which this country was founded. The word has come to serve simply as a description of the therapeutic state. When we speak of democracy today, we refer, more often than not, to the democratization of "self-esteem." The current catchwords—diversity, compassion, empowerment, entitlement—express the wistful hope that deep divisions in American society can be bridged by goodwill and sanitized speech. We are called on to recognize that all minorities are entitled to respect not by virtue of their achievements but by virtue of their sufferings in the past. Compassionate attention, we are told, will somehow raise their opinion of themselves; banning racial epithets and other forms of hateful speech will do wonders for their morale. In our preoccupation with words, we have lost sight of the tough realities that cannot be softened simply by flattering people's self-image. What does it profit the residents of the South Bronx to enforce speech codes at elite universities?

In the first half of the nineteenth century most people who gave any thought to the matter assumed that democracy had to rest on a broad distribution of property. They understood that extremes of wealth and poverty would be fatal to the democratic experiment. Their fear of the mob, sometimes misinterpreted as aristocratic disdain, rested on the observation that a degraded laboring class, at once servile and resentful, lacked the qualities of mind and character essential to democratic citizenship. Democratic habits, they thought—self-reliance, responsibility, initiative— were best acquired in the exercise of a trade or the management of a small holding of property. A "competence," as they called it, referred both to property itself and to the intelligence and enterprise required by its management. It stood to reason, therefore, that democracy worked best when property was distributed as widely as possible among the citizens.

The point can be stated more broadly: Democracy works best when men and women do things for themselves, with the help of their friends and neighbors, instead of depending on the state. Not that democracy should be equated with rugged individualism. Self-reliance does not mean self-sufficiency. Self-governing communities, not individuals, are the basic units of democratic society, as I argue in chapters 5 ("Populism or Communitarianism?"), 6 ("Conversation and the Civic Arts"), and 7 ("Racial Politics in New York"). It is the decline of those communities, more than anything else, that calls the future of democracy into question. Suburban shopping malls are no substitute for neighborhoods. The same pattern of development has been repeated in one city after another, with the same discouraging results. The flight of population to the suburbs, followed by the flight of industry and jobs, has left our cities destitute. As the tax base shrivels, public services and civic amenities disappear. Attempts to revive the city by constructing convention centers and sports facilities designed to attract tourists merely heighten the contrast between wealth and poverty. The city becomes a bazaar, but the luxuries on display in its exclusive boutiques, hotels, and restaurants are beyond the reach of most of the residents. Some of those residents turn to crime as the only access to the glittering world seductively advertised as the American dream. Those with more modest aspirations, meanwhile, are squeezed out by high rents, gentrification, and misguided policies intended to break up ethnic neighborhoods that allegedly stand in the way of racial integration.

POPULISM, AS I understand it, was never an exclusively agrarian ideology. It envisioned a nation not just of farmers but of artisans and tradesmen as well. Nor was it implacably opposed to urbanization. In the fifty years preceding World War I, the rapid growth of cities, the influx of immigrants, and the institutionalization of wage labor presented democracy with a formidable challenge, but urban reformers like Jane Addams, Frederic C. Howe, and Mary Parker Follett were confident that democratic institutions could be adapted to the new conditions of urban life. Howe caught the essence of the so-called progressive movement when he referred to the city as the "hope of democracy." Urban neighborhoods, it appeared, re-created the conditions of small-town life with which democracy had been associated in the nineteenth century. The city fostered new forms of association in its own right, notably the labor union, together with a lively civic spirit.

The conflict between town and country, exploited by nativist demagogues who depicted the city as a sink of iniquity, was largely illusory. The best minds have always understood that town and country are complementary and that a healthy balance between them is an important precondition of the good society. It was only when the city became a megalopolis, after World War II, that this balance broke down. The very distinction between town and country became meaningless when the dominant form of settlement was no longer urban or rural, much less a synthesis of the two, but a sprawling, amorphous conglomeration without clearly identifiable boundaries, public space, or civic identity. Robert Fishman has argued persuasively that the new pattern can no longer be adequately described even as suburban since the suburb, formerly a residential annex of the city, has now taken over most of its functions. Cities retain a residual importance as the home of large law firms, advertising agencies, publishing companies, entertainment enterprises, and museums, but the middle-class neighborhoods that sustained a vigorous civic culture are rapidly disappearing. Mere remnants, our cities are increasingly polarized; upper-middle-class professionals, together with the service workers who cater to their needs, maintain a precarious hold on the high-rent districts and barricade themselves against the poverty and crime threatening to engulf them.

N O N E O F T H I S bodes well for democracy, but the outlook becomes even darker if we consider the deterioration of public debate. Democracy requires a vigorous exchange of ideas and opinions. Ideas, like property, need to be distributed as widely as possible. Yet many of the "best people," as they think of themselves, have always been skeptical about the capacity of ordinary citizens to grasp complex issues and to make critical judgments. Democratic debate, from their point of view, degenerates all too easily into a shouting match in which the voice of reason seldom makes itself heard. Horace Mann, wise in so many things, failed to see that political and religious controversy is educative in its own right and therefore tried to exclude divisive issues from the common schools (chapter 8, "The Common Schools"). His eagerness to avoid sectarian quarrels is understandable enough, but it left a legacy that may help to explain the bland, innocuous, mind-numbing quality of public education today.

American journalism has been shaped by somewhat similar reservations about the reasoning powers of ordinary men and women (chapter 9, "The Lost Art of Argument"). According to Walter Lippmann, one of the pioneers of modern journalism, the "omnicompetent citizen" was an anachronism in the age of specialization. In any case, most citizens, he thought, cared very little about the substance of public policy. The purpose of journalism was not to encourage public debate but to provide experts with the information on which to base intelligent decisions. Public opinion, Lippmann argued in opposition to John Dewey and other veterans of the progressive movement, was a weak reed. It was shaped more by emotion than by reasoned judgment. The very concept of a public was suspect. The public idealized by the progressives, a public capable of the intelligent direction of public affairs, was a "phantom." It existed only in the minds of sentimental democrats. "The public interest in a problem," Lippmann wrote, "is limited to this: that there shall be rules. . . . The public is interested in law, not in the laws; in the method of law, not in the substance." Substantive questions could safely be left to experts, whose access to scientific knowledge immunized them against the emotional "symbols" and "stereotypes" that dominated public debate.

Lippmann's argument rested on a sharp distinction between opinion and science. Only the latter, he thought, could claim to be objective. Opinion, on the other hand, rested on vague impressions, prejudices, and wishful thinking. This cult of professionalism had a decisive influence on the development of modern journalism. Newspapers might have served as extensions of the town meeting. Instead they embraced a misguided ideal of objectivity and defined their goal as the circulation of reliable information—the kind of information, that is, that tends not to promote debate but to circumvent it. The most curious feature in all this, of course, is that although Americans are now drowning in information, thanks to newspapers and television and other media, surveys regularly report a steady decline in their knowledge of public affairs. In the "age of information" the American people are notoriously ill informed. The explanation of this seeming paradox is obvious, though seldom offered: Having been effectively excluded from public debate on the grounds of their incompetence, most Americans no longer have any use for the information inflicted on them in such large amounts. They have become almost as incompetent as their critics have always claimed—a reminder that it is debate itself, and debate alone, that gives rise to the desire for usable information. In the absence of democratic exchange, most people have no incentive to master the knowledge that would make them capable citizens.

THE MISLEADING DISTINCTION between knowledge and opinion reappears, in a somewhat different form, in the controversies that have recently convulsed the university (chapter 10, "Academic Pseudo-radicalism"). These controversies are bitter and inconclusive because both sides share the same unacknowledged premise: that knowledge has to rest on indisputable foundations if it is to carry any weight. One faction—identified with the left although its point of view bears little resemblance to the tradition it claims to defend—takes the position that the collapse of "foundationalism" makes it possible for the first time to see that knowledge is merely another name for power. The dominant groups—white Eurocentric males, in the usual formulation—impose their ideas, their canon, their self-serving readings of history on everybody else. Their power to suppress competing points of view allegedly enables them to claim for their own particularistic ideology the status of universal, transcendent truth. The critical demolition of foundationalism, according to the academic left, exposes the hollowness of these claims and enables disfranchised groups to contest the prevailing orthodoxy on the grounds that it serves only to keep women, homosexuals, and "people of color" in their place. Having discredited the dominant world view, minorities are in a position to replace it with one of their own or at least to secure equal time for black studies, feminist studies, gay studies, Chicano studies, and other "alternative" ideologies. Once

knowledge is equated with ideology, it is no longer necessary to argue with opponents on intellectual grounds or to
enter into their point of view. It is enough to dismiss them
as Eurocentric, racist, sexist, homophobic—in other words,
as politically suspect.

Conservative critics of the university, understandably
uneasy with this sweeping dismissal of Western culture,
can find no way of defending it except by appealing to the
very premise the collapse of which invites the attack on the
classics: that acknowledgment of certain axiomatic principles is the precondition of reliable knowledge. Unfortunately for their cause, it is impossible, at this late date, to
resurrect the absolutes that once seemed to provide secure
foundations on which to build dependable structures of
thought. The quest for certainty, which became an obsessive theme in modern thought when Descartes tried to
ground philosophy in indubitable propositions, was misguided to begin with. As John Dewey pointed out, it distracted attention from the real business of philosophy, the
attempt to arrive at "concrete judgments . . . about ends
and means in the regulation of practical behavior." In their
pursuit of the absolute and immutable, philosophers took a
disparaging view of the time-bound and contingent. "Practical activity," as Dewey put it, became in their eyes
"intrinsically an inferior sort of thing." In the world view
of Western philosophy, knowing came to be split off from
doing, theory from practice, the mind from the body.

The lingering influence of this tradition colors the conservative critique of the university. Foundationalism, conservatives argue, provides the only defense against moral and
cultural relativism. Either knowledge rests on immutable
foundations or men and women are free to think whatever
they please. "Things fall apart; the center cannot hold;/mere
anarchy is loosed upon the world." Conservatives never tire

of quoting Yeats's lines in order to show what happens when axiomatic principles lose their authority. The trouble in academia, however, derives not from the absence of secure foundations but from the belief (shared, it must be repeated, by both parties to this debate) that in their absence the only possible outcome is a skepticism so deep that it becomes indistinguishable from nihilism. That this is not, in fact, the only possible outcome would have been abundantly clear to Dewey, and the revival of pragmatism as an object of historical and philosophical study—one of the few bright spots in an otherwise dismal picture—holds out some hope of a way out of the academic impasse.

THE QUEST FOR certainty has more than merely academic interest. It also enters into the heated controversy over the public role of religion. Here again both sides often turn out to share the same premise, in this case that religion provides a rock of security in an unpredictable universe. It is the collapse of the old certainties, according to critics of religion, that makes it impossible (impossible, at least, for those exposed to the corrosive influence of modernity) to take religion seriously. Defenders of religion tend to argue from the same premise. Without a set of unquestioned dogmas, they say, people lose their moral bearings. Good and evil become more or less indistinguishable; everything is permitted; old injunctions are defied with impunity.

Such arguments are advanced not only by evangelical preachers but occasionally by secular intellectuals troubled by the threat of moral anarchy (chapter 12, "Philip Rieff and the Religion of Culture"). With good reason, these intellectuals deplore the privatization of religion, the disappearance of religious issues from public discussion. Their case is weakened, however, by a couple of serious flaws. In the first place, it is impossible to revive religious belief simply because it serves a useful social purpose. Faith issues from the heart; it cannot be summoned up on demand. In any case, religion cannot be expected to provide a comprehensive, definitive code of conduct that settles every dispute and resolves every doubt. It is this very assumption, curiously enough, that leads to the privatization of religion. Those who want to keep religion out of public life argue that religious belief, in the nature of things, commits the believer to indisputable dogmas that lie beyond the reach of rational argument. They too, these skeptics, see religion as a body of ironclad dogmas the faithful are forbidden to question. The same qualities that make religion attractive to those who regret its decline—the security that it allegedly provides against doubt and confusion, the comfort adherents allegedly derive from an airtight system that leaves nothing unexplained—make it repulsive to the secular mind. Opponents of religion argue further that it necessarily fosters intolerance, since those who embrace it imagine themselves to be in possession of absolute, exclusive truths irreconcilable with other truth claims. Given the opportunity, they will invariably seek to make everyone else conform to their own ways. The cultured despisers of religion suspect that religious tolerance, in short, is a contradiction in terms—a fact seemingly borne out by the long history of religious warfare.

No doubt this disparaging view of religion, which has been with us for a long time, contains more than a little truth. Still, it misses the religious challenge to complacency, the heart and soul of faith (chapter 13, "The Soul of Man under Secularism"). Instead of discouraging moral inquiry, religious prompting can just as easily stimulate it by calling attention to the disjunction between verbal profession and practice, by insisting that a perfunctory observance of prescribed rituals is not enough to assure salvation, and by encouraging believers at every step to question their own motives. Far from putting doubts and anxieties to rest, religion often has the effect of intensifying them. It judges those who profess the faith more harshly than it judges unbelievers. It holds them up to a standard of conduct so demanding that many of them inevitably fall short. It has no patience with those who make excuses for themselves—an art in which Americans have come to excel. If it is ultimately forgiving of human weakness and folly, it is not because it ignores them or attributes them exclusively to unbelievers. For those who take religion seriously, belief is a burden, not a self-righteous claim to some privileged moral status. Self-righteousness, indeed, may well be more prevalent among skeptics than among believers. The spiritual discipline against self-righteousness is the very essence of religion.

Because a secular society does not grasp the need for such a discipline, it misunderstands the nature of religion: to console but, first of all, to challenge and confront. From a secular point of view, the overriding spiritual preoccupation is not self-righteousness but "self-esteem" (chapter 11, "The Abolition of Shame"). Most of our spiritual energy is devoted precisely to a campaign against shame and guilt, the object of which is to make people "feel good about themselves." The churches themselves have enlisted in this therapeutic exercise, the chief beneficiaries of which, in theory at least, are the victimized minorities that have been systematically deprived of self-esteem by a vicious history of oppression. What these groups need, according to the prevailing consensus, is the spiritual consolation provided by the dogmatic assertion of their collective identity. They are encouraged to recover their ancestral heritage, to revive discarded rituals, and to celebrate a mythical past in the name of history. Whether or not this bracing account of their distinctive past actually meets accepted standards of historical interpretation is a secondary consideration; what matters is whether it contributes to the positive self-image that allegedly makes for "empowerment." The same benefits misleadingly associated with religion—security, spiritual comfort, dogmatic relief from doubt—are thought to flow from a therapeutic politics of identity. In effect, identity politics has come to serve as a substitute for religion— or at least for the feeling of self-righteousness that is so commonly confused with religion.

These developments shed further light on the decline of democratic debate. "Diversity"—a slogan that looks attractive on the face of it—has come to mean the opposite of what it appears to mean. In practice, diversity turns out to legitimize a new dogmatism, in which rival minorities take shelter behind a set of beliefs impervious to rational discussion. The physical segregation of the population in self-enclosed, racially homogeneous enclaves has its counterpart in the balkanization of opinion. Each group tries to barricade itself behind its own dogmas. We have become a nation of minorities; only their official recognition as such is lacking to complete the process.* This parody of "community"—a term much in favor but not very clearly understood—carries with it the insidious assumption that all members of a given

---

*The vagueness of the concept makes it impossible for policy makers to agree on a list of designated minorities entitled to compensation for a history of oppression. Social scientists first began to speak of minorities, in the current sense of the term, during the New Deal era. It referred to groups that had been "singled out . . . for differential and unequal treatment," in the words of Louis Wirth. Whereas national minorities in Europe were generally denounced as aggressive and warlike, American minorities were seen as victims rather than predators. From the beginning, minority status thus gave those able to claim it a certain moral and political leverage. If "the mere fact of being generally hated . . . is what

group can be expected to think alike. Opinion thus becomes a function of racial or ethnic identity, of gender or sexual preference. Self-selected minority "spokespersons" enforce this conformity by ostracizing those who stray from the party line—black people, for instance, who "think white."

---

defines a minority group," as Arnold and Caroline Rose explained, the moral advantage invariably lay with the "minority" (even if it made up a statistical majority of the population). Pressure to expand the category, with a consequent loss of precision, has proved irresistible. By the seventies it included not only various racial and ethnic groups but women (except when they were verbally distinguished by the meaningless formula "women and minorities"), homosexuals, and groups (e.g., the deaf) formerly treated by social scientists as "deviant."

Justice Lewis Powell declared in the *Bakke* case (1978), the Supreme Court's definitive but muddled statement in the matter of affirmative action, that "the United States had become a nation of minorities." He admitted, however, that the term was hopelessly imprecise. Any group that could "lay claim to a history of prior discrimination" could assert its minority status and its entitlement to the newly created "rights" conferred by the courts in their expansive interpretation of affirmative action. It was equally clear, however, that "not all of these groups" could "receive preferential treatment," for then "the only 'majority' left would be the new *minority* of white Anglo-Saxon Protestants." How was it to be decided, in that case, exactly which groups were eligible for compensatory treatment? It would be hard to quarrel with Powell's conclusion that "there is no principled basis of deciding which groups would merit 'heightened judicial solicitude' and which would not."

In spite of its obvious imprecision, the minority concept has had enormous influence on social policy. Searching public debate could only strengthen popular opposition to affirmative action and the notion of minorities that undergirds it. In the absence of such a debate, government officials find themselves in the unenviable position of attempting to enforce policies unsupported by any semblance of a social consensus. Philip Gleason, in a thoughtful review of the minority concept, observes that "differential treatment . . . surely requires more explicit recognition and debate than it has so far received"—an understatement, if there ever was one.

How much longer can the spirit of free inquiry and open debate survive under these conditions?

MICKEY KAUS, a *New Republic* editor, has advanced an interpretation of the democratic malaise, under the provocative and slightly misleading title *The End of Equality*, that has a great deal in common with the interpretation advanced in these pages.* According to Kaus, the most serious threat to democracy, in our time, comes not so much from the maldistribution of wealth as from the decay or abandonment of public institutions in which citizens meet as equals. Equality of income, he argues, is less important than the "more attainable" goal of social or civic equality. He reminds us that foreign observers used to marvel at the lack of snobbery, deference, and class feeling in America. There was "nothing oppressed or submissive" about the American worker, Werner Sombart wrote in 1906. "He carries his head high, walks with a lissom stride, and is as open and cheerful in his expression as any member of the middle class." A few years later R. H. Tawney noted that America was "marked indeed by much economic inequality, but it is also marked by much social equality." It is this culture of self-respect, according to Kaus, that we are in danger of losing.

The trouble with our society, from this point of view, is not just that the rich have too much money but that their

---

*Kaus's title is ambiguous because it is not altogether clear whether he proposes to abandon the struggle against inequality or whether the proper goal or object ("end") of an egalitarian society, as he sees it, is a rich civic life accessible to all, not a leveling of incomes. The second reading turns out to be the right one. This does not, however, rule out the possibility that a measure of economic equality is one important means or precondition to the end of civic equality.

money insulates them, much more than it used to, from the common life. The "routine acceptance of professionals as a class apart" strikes Kaus as an ominous development. So does their own "smug contempt for the demographically inferior." Part of the trouble, I would add, is that we have lost our respect for honest manual labor. We think of "creative" work as a series of abstract mental operations performed in an office, preferably with the aid of computers, not as the production of food, shelter, and other necessities. The thinking classes are fatally removed from the physical side of life—hence their feeble attempt to compensate by embracing a strenuous regimen of gratuitous exercise. Their only relation to productive labor is that of consumers. They have no experience of making anything substantial or enduring. They live in a world of abstractions and images, a simulated world that consists of computerized models of reality—"hyperreality," as it has been called—as distinguished from the palpable, immediate, physical reality inhabited by ordinary men and women. Their belief in the "social construction of reality"—the central dogma of postmodernist thought—reflects the experience of living in an artificial environment from which everything that resists human control (unavoidably, everything familiar and reassuring as well) has been rigorously excluded. Control has become their obsession. In their drive to insulate themselves against risk and contingency—against the unpredictable hazards that afflict human life—the thinking classes have seceded not just from the common world around them but from reality itself.

The culture wars that have convulsed America since the sixties are best understood as a form of class warfare, in which an enlightened elite (as it thinks of itself) seeks not so much to impose its values on the majority (a majority perceived as incorrigibly racist, sexist, provincial, and xenophobic), much less to persuade the majority by means of rational public debate, as to create parallel or "alternative" institutions in which it will no longer be necessary to confront the unenlightened at all.

According to Kaus, public policy should seek not to undo the effects of the market (which inevitably promotes inequality of income) but to limit its scope—"to restrict the sphere of life in which money matters." Drawing on Michael Walzer's *Spheres of Justice*, he argues that the goal of civic liberalism, as distinguished from "money liberalism," is "to create a sphere of life in which money is devalued, to prevent those who have money from concluding they are superior." Walzer is similarly concerned to limit the "extraction not only of wealth but of prestige and influence from the market," as he puts it. He treats the problem of justice as a problem of boundaries and "boundary revision." Money, even more than other good things like beauty, eloquence, and charm, has a tendency to "seep across boundaries" and to buy things that should not be for sale: exemption from military service; love and friendship; political office itself (thanks to the exorbitant cost of political campaigns). The principle of equality is best served, Walzer maintains, not by ensuring an equal distribution of income but by setting limits to the imperialism of the market, which "transforms every social good into a commodity." "What is at issue," he writes, ". . . is the dominance of money outside its sphere."*

There is much wisdom in these words, and those who value democracy would do well to heed them. But it is

---

*Similar concerns were raised, much earlier, in the work of sociologists loosely affiliated with the progressive movement, especially in Charles Horton Cooley's *Social Process*, published in 1907. The "pecuniary motive," Cooley wrote, "excludes such vast provinces of life that we equally important to remember—what neither Walzer nor Kaus would deny in the last analysis—that economic inequality is intrinsically undesirable, even when confined to its proper sphere. Luxury is morally repugnant, and its incompatibility with democratic ideals, moreover, has been consistently recognized in the traditions that shape our political culture. The difficulty of limiting the influence of wealth suggests that wealth itself needs to be limited. When money talks, everybody else is condemned to listen. For that reason a democratic society cannot allow unlimited accumulation. Social and civic equality presuppose at least a rough approximation of economic equality. A "plurality of spheres," as Walzer calls it, is eminently desirable, and we should do everything possible to enforce the boundaries among them. But we also need to remember that boundaries are permeable, especially where money is concerned, that a moral condemnation of great wealth must inform any defense of the free market, and that moral condemnation must be backed up with effective political action.

In the old days Americans agreed, at least in principle, that individuals cannot claim entitlement to wealth far in excess of their needs. The persistence of this belief, even though it is admittedly only an undercurrent in the celebration of wealth that now threatens to drown all competing values, offers some hope that all is not yet lost.

---

may well wonder at the extent of our trust in the market process." As he saw it, "Pecuniary values fail to express the higher life of society." The counterweight to the market was to be found in activities undertaken for their own sake and not for the sake of extrinsic rewards—in art, workmanship, and professionalism. "The pleasure of creative work and the sharing of this by those who appreciate the product, . . . unlike the pleasure of possessing things we win from others, . . . increases the more we share it, taking us out of the selfish atmosphere of every-day competition."

Part I

The Intensification of Social Divisions

The Revolt of
the Elites

Once it was the "revolt of the masses" that was held to threaten social order and the civilizing traditions of Western culture. In our time, however, the chief threat seems to come from those at the top of the social hierarchy, not the masses. This remarkable turn of events confounds our expectations about the course of history and calls long-established assumptions into question.

When José Ortega y Gasset published *The Revolt of the Masses*, first translated into English in 1932, he could not have foreseen a time when it would be more appropriate to speak of a revolt of elites. Writing in the era of the Bolshevik Revolution and the rise of fascism, in the aftermath of a cataclysmic war that had torn Europe apart, Ortega attributed the crisis of Western culture to the "political domination of the masses." Today it is the elites, however—those who control the international flow of money and information, preside over philanthropic foundations and institutions of higher learning, manage the instruments of cultural production and thus set the terms of public debate—that have lost faith in the values, or what remains of them, of the West. For many people the very term "Western civilization" now calls to mind an organized system of domination designed to enforce conformity to bourgeois values and to keep the victims of patriarchal oppression—women, children, homosexuals, people of color—in a permanent state of subjection.

From Ortega's point of view, one that was widely shared at the time, the value of cultural elites lay in their willingness to assume responsibility for the exacting standards without which civilization is impossible. They lived in the service of demanding ideals. "Nobility is defined by the demands it makes on us—by obligations, not by rights." The mass man, on the other hand, had no use for obligations and no understanding of what they implied, "no feeling for [the] great historical duties." Instead he asserted the "rights of the commonplace." At once resentful and self-satisfied, he rejected "everything that is excellent, individual, qualified, and select." He was "incapable of submitting to direction of any kind." Lacking any comprehension of the fragility of civilization or the tragic character of history, he lived unthinkingly in the "assurance that tomorrow [the world] will be still richer, ampler, more perfect, as if it enjoyed a spontaneous, inexhaustible power of increase." He was concerned only with his own well-being and looked forward to a future of "limitless possibilities" and "complete freedom." His many failings included a "lack of romance in his dealings with women." Erotic love, a demanding ideal in its own right, had no attraction for him. His attitude toward the body was severely practical: He made a cult of physical fitness and submitted to hygienic regimens that

promised to keep it in good repair and to extend its longev-
ity. It was, above all, however, the "deadly hatred of all
that is not itself" that characterized the mass mind, as
Ortega described it. Incapable of wonder or respect, the
mass man was the "spoiled child of human history."

All these habits of mind, I submit, are now more characteristic of the upper levels of society than of the lower or
middle levels. It can hardly be said that ordinary people
today look forward to a world of "limitless possibility."
Any sense that the masses are riding the wave of history
has long since departed. The radical movements that dis-
turbed the peace of the twentieth century have failed one
by one, and no successors have appeared on the horizon.
The industrial working class, once the mainstay of the
socialist movement, has become a pitiful remnant of itself.
The hope that "new social movements" would take its place
in the struggle against capitalism, which briefly sustained
the left in the late seventies and early eighties, has come to
nothing. Not only do the new social movements—feminism, gay rights, welfare rights, agitation against racial discrimination—have nothing in common, but their only
coherent demand aims at inclusion in the dominant structures rather than at a revolutionary transformation of
social relations.

It is not just that the masses have lost interest in revolution; their political instincts are demonstrably more conservative than those of their self-appointed spokesmen and
would-be liberators. It is the working and lower middle
classes, after all, that favor limits on abortion, cling to the
two-parent family as a source of stability in a turbulent
world, resist experiments with "alternative lifestyles," and
harbor deep reservations about affirmative action and other
ventures in large-scale social engineering. More to Ortega's
point, they have a more highly developed sense of limits

than their betters. They understand, as their betters do not, that there are inherent limits on human control over the course of social development, over nature and the body, over the tragic elements in human life and history. While young professionals subject themselves to an arduous schedule of physical exercise and dietary controls designed to keep death at bay—to maintain themselves in a state of permanent youthfulness, eternally attractive and remar-riageable—ordinary people, on the other hand, accept the body's decay as something against which it is more or less useless to struggle.

Upper-middle-class liberals, with their inability to grasp the importance of class differences in shaping attitudes toward life, fail to reckon with the class dimension of their obsession with health and moral uplift. They find it hard to understand why their hygienic conception of life fails to command universal enthusiasm. They have mounted a cru-sade to sanitize American society: to create a "smoke-free environment," to censor everything from pornography to "hate speech," and at the same time, incongruously, to extend the range of personal choice in matters where most people feel the need of solid moral guidelines. When con-fronted with resistance to these initiatives, they betray the venomous hatred that lies not far beneath the smiling face of upper-middle-class benevolence. Opposition makes humanitarians forget the liberal virtues they claim to uphold. They become petulant, self-righteous, intolerant. In the heat of political controversy, they find it impossible to conceal their contempt for those who stubbornly refuse to see the light—those who "just don't get it," in the self-satisfied jargon of political rectitude.

Simultaneously arrogant and insecure, the new elites, the professional classes in particular, regard the masses with mingled scorn and apprehension. In the United

States, "Middle America"—a term that has both geographical and social implications—has come to symbolize everything that stands in the way of progress: "family values," mindless patriotism, religious fundamentalism, racism, homophobia, retrograde views of women. Middle Americans, as they appear to the makers of educated opinion, are hopelessly shabby, unfashionable, and provincial, ill informed about changes in taste or intellectual trends, addicted to trashy novels of romance and adventure, and stupefied by prolonged exposure to television. They are at once absurd and vaguely menacing—not because they wish to overthrow the old order but precisely because their defense of it appears so deeply irrational that it expresses itself, at the higher reaches of its intensity, in fanatical religiosity, in a repressive sexuality that occasionally erupts into violence against women and gays, and in a patriotism that supports imperialist wars and a national ethic of aggressive masculinity.

THE GENERAL COURSE of recent history no longer favors the leveling of social distinctions but runs more and more in the direction of a two-class society in which the favored few monopolize the advantages of money, education, and power. It is undeniable, of course, that the comforts of modern life are still distributed far more widely than they were before the Industrial Revolution. It was this democratization of comfort that Ortega had in mind when he spoke of the "rise of the historical level." Like many others, Ortega was struck by the unheard-of abundance generated by the modern division of labor, by the transformation of luxuries into necessities, and by the popularization of standards of comfort and convenience formerly confined to the rich. These facts—the material fruits of modernization—are not in question. In our time, however, the democratization of abundance—the expectation that each generation would enjoy a standard of living beyond the reach of its predecessors—has given way to a reversal in which age-old inequalities are beginning to reestablish themselves, sometimes at a frightening rate, sometimes so gradually as to escape notice.

The global disparity between wealth and poverty, the most obvious example of this historic reversal, has become so glaring that it is hardly necessary to review the evidence of growing inequality. In Latin America, Africa, and large parts of Asia, the sheer growth in numbers, together with the displacement of rural populations by the commercialization of agriculture, has subjected civic life to unprecedented strains. Vast urban agglomerations—they can scarcely be called cities—have taken shape, overflowing with poverty, wretchedness, disease, and despair. Paul Kennedy projects twenty of these "megacities" by 2025, each with a population of eleven million or more. Mexico City will already have more than twenty-four million inhabitants by the year 2000, São Paulo more than twenty-three million, Calcutta sixteen million, Bombay fifteen-and-a-half million. The resulting strain on housing, sanitation, transportation, and other civic facilities can easily be foreseen, but the hellish conditions likely to follow defy the most doom-ridden imagination. Even now the devastation is so great that the only available response to the sensational scenes of squalor and starvation with which people are daily regaled by the media is one less of indignation than of helpless indifference.

As the collapse of civic life in these swollen cities continues, not only the poor but the middle classes will experience conditions unimaginable a few years ago. Middle-class standards of living can be expected to decline throughout what is all too hopefully referred to as the developing world. In a country like Peru, once a prosperous nation with reasonable prospects of evolving parliamentary institutions, the middle class for all practical purposes has ceased to exist. A middle class, as Walter Russell Mead reminds us in his study of the declining American empire *Mortal Splendor*, "does not appear out of thin air." Its power and numbers "depend on the overall wealth of the domestic economy," and in countries, accordingly, where "wealth is concentrated in the hands of a tiny oligarchy and the rest of the population is desperately poor, the middle class can grow to only a limited extent. . . . [It] never escapes its primary role as a servant class to the oligarchy." Unfortunately this description now applies to a growing list of nations that have prematurely reached the limits of economic development, countries in which a rising "share of their own national product goes to foreign investors or creditors." Such a fate may well await unlucky nations, including the United States, even in the industrial world.

It is the crisis of the middle class, and not simply the growing chasm between wealth and poverty, that needs to be emphasized in a sober analysis of our prospects. Even in Japan, the very model of successful industrialization in the last two or three decades, public opinion polls conducted in 1987 revealed a growing belief that the country could no longer be described as middle-class, ordinary people having failed to share in the vast fortunes accumulated in real estate, finance, and manufacturing.

THE CHANGING CLASS structure of the United States presents us, sometimes in exaggerated form, with changes that are taking place all over the industrial world. People in the upper 20 percent of the income structure now control half the country's wealth. In the last twenty years they alone have experienced a net gain in family income. In the brief years of the Reagan administration alone, their share of the national income rose from 41.6 percent to 44 percent. The middle class, generously defined as those with incomes ranging from fifteen to fifty thousand dollars a year, declined from 65 percent of the population in 1970 to 58 percent in 1985. These figures convey only a partial, imperfect impression of momentous changes that have taken place in a remarkably short period of time. The steady growth of unemployment, now expanded to include white-collar workers, is more revealing. So is the growth of the "contingent labor force." The number of part-time jobs has doubled since 1980 and now amounts to a quarter of available jobs. No doubt this massive growth of part-time employment helps to explain why the number of workers covered by retirement plans, which rose from 22 percent to 45 percent between 1950 and 1980, slipped back to 42.6 percent by 1986. It also helps to explain the decline of union membership and the steady erosion of union influence. All these developments, in turn, reflect the loss of manufacturing jobs and the shift to an economy increasingly based on information and services.

In 1973 a high school graduate would have earned an average income (in 1987 dollars) of $32,000. By 1987 high school graduates, if they were lucky enough to find steady employment at all, could expect to make less than $28,000—a decline of 12 percent. High school dropouts could still make almost $20,000 a year in 1973, on the average; by 1987 this figure had fallen by 15 percent to a new low of $16,000. Even a college education in itself no longer assures affluence: in the same period the average earnings of college graduates increased only from $49,500 to $50,000.

Affluence these days—or for many Americans mere survival, for that matter—requires the additional income provided by women's participation in the labor force. The prosperity enjoyed by the professional and managerial classes, which make up most of the upper 20 percent of the income structure, derives in large part from the emerging marital pattern inelegantly known as assortative mating—the tendency of men to marry women who can be relied on to bring in income more or less equivalent to their own. Doctors used to marry nurses, lawyers and executives their secretaries. Now upper-middle-class men tend to marry women of their own class, business or professional associates with lucrative careers of their own. "What if the $60,000 lawyer marries another $60,000 lawyer," Mickey Kaus asks in his book *The End of Equality*, "and the $20,000 clerk marries a $20,000 clerk? Then the difference between their incomes suddenly becomes the difference between $120,000 and $40,000," and "although the trend is still masked in the income statistics by the low average wages of women," Kaus adds, "it's obvious to practically everyone, even the experts, that something like this is in fact happening." It is unnecessary, incidentally, to seek much further for an explanation of feminism's appeal to the professional and managerial class. Female careerism provides the indispensable basis of their prosperous, glamorous, gaudy, sometimes indecently lavish way of life.

THE UPPER MIDDLE class, the heart of the new professional and managerial elites, is defined, apart from its rapidly rising income, not so much by its ideology as by a way of life that distinguishes it, more and more unmistakably, from the rest of the population. Even its feminism—that is, its commitment to the two-career family—is a matter more of practical necessity than of political conviction.

Efforts to define a "new class" composed of public administrators and policy makers, relentlessly pushing a program of liberal reforms, ignore the range of political opinions among the professional and managerial elites. These groups constitute a new class only in the sense that their livelihoods rest not so much on the ownership of property as on the manipulation of information and professional expertise. Their investment in education and information, as opposed to property, distinguishes them from the rich bourgeoisie, the ascendancy of which characterized an earlier stage of capitalism, and from the old proprietary class—the middle class in the strict sense of the term—that once made up the bulk of the population.

Since they embrace a wide variety of occupations—brokers, bankers, real estate promoters and developers, engineers, consultants of all kinds, systems analysts, scientists, doctors, publicists, publishers, editors, advertising executives, art directors, moviemakers, entertainers, journalists, television producers and directors, artists, writers, university professors—and since they lack a common political outlook, it is also inappropriate to characterize managerial and professional elites as a new ruling class. Alvin Gouldner, in one of the most convincing attempts to anatomize the "new class," found the unifying element in their "culture of critical discourse," but even though this formulation captures an essential feature of the secular, analytical attitude that now prevails in the higher circles, it exaggerates the intellectual component in the culture of the new elites and their interest in the rationalization of life, just as it minimizes their continuing fascination with the capitalist market and their frenzied search for profits.

A more salient fact is that the market in which the new elites operate is now international in scope. Their fortunes are tied to enterprises that operate across national boundaries. They are more concerned with the smooth functioning of the system as a whole than with any of its parts. Their loyalties—if the term is not itself anachronistic in this context—are international rather than regional, national, or local. They have more in common with their counterparts in Brussels or Hong Kong than with the masses of Americans not yet plugged into the network of global communications.

Robert Reich's category of "symbolic analysts" serves, apart from its syntactical incoherence, as a useful, empirical, and rather unpretentious description of the new class. These are people, as Reich describes them, who live in a world of abstract concepts and symbols, ranging from stock market quotations to the visual images produced by Hollywood and Madison Avenue, and who specialize in the interpretation and deployment of symbolic information. Reich contrasts them with the two other principal categories of labor: "routine production workers," who perform repetitive tasks and exercise little control over the design of production, and "in-person servers," whose work also consists of routine, for the most part, but "must be provided person-to-person" and therefore cannot be "sold worldwide." If we allow for the highly schematic and necessarily imprecise character of these categories, they correspond closely enough to everyday observation to give us a fairly accurate impression not only of the occupational structure but of the class structure of American society, since the "symbolic analysts" are clearly rising while the other categories, which make up 80 percent of the population, are declining in wealth and status.

A more serious objection than imprecision is Reich's extravagantly flattering portrait of the "symbolic analysts." In his eyes, they represent the best and brightest in American life. Educated at "elite private schools" and "high-quality suburban schools, where they are tracked through advanced courses," they enjoy every advantage their doting parents can provide.

> Their teachers and professors are attentive to their academic needs. They have access to state-of-the-art scientific laboratories, interactive computers and video systems in the classroom, language laboratories, and high-tech school libraries. Their classes are relatively small; their peers are intellectually stimulating. Their parents take them to museums and cultural events, expose them to foreign travel, and give them music lessons. At home are educational books, educational toys, educational videotapes, microscopes, telescopes, and personal computers replete with the latest educational software.

These privileged young people acquire advanced degrees at the "best [universities] in the world," the superiority of which is proved by their ability to attract foreign students in great numbers. In this cosmopolitan atmosphere they overcome the provincial folkways that impede creative thought, according to Reich. "Skeptical, curious, creative," they become problem solvers par excellence, equal to any challenge. Unlike those who engage in mind-numbing routines, they love their work, which engages them in lifelong learning and endless experimentation.

Unlike old-fashioned intellectuals, who tend to work by themselves and to be jealous and possessive about their ideas, the new brain workers—producers of high-quality "insights" in a variety of fields ranging from marketing and finance to art and entertainment—operate best in teams. Their "capacity to collaborate" promotes "system thinking"—the ability to see problems in their totality, to absorb the fruits of collective experimentation, and to "discern larger causes, consequences, and relationships." Since their work depends so heavily on "networking," they settle in "specialized geographical pockets" populated by people like them. These privileged communities—Cambridge, the Silicon Valley, Hollywood—become "wondrously resilient" centers of artistic, technical, and promotional enterprise. They represent the epitome of intellectual achievement, in Reich's admiring view, and of the good life conceived as the exchange of "insights," "information," and professional gossip. The geographical concentration of knowledge producers, once it reaches a critical mass, incidentally provides a market for the growing class of "in-person servers" who cater to their needs.

> It is no accident that Hollywood is home to a conspicuously large number of voice coaches, fencing trainers, dancing instructors, performers' agents, and suppliers of photographic, acoustic and lighting equipment. Also found in close proximity are restaurants with precisely the right ambience favored by producers wooing directors and directors wooing screenwriters, and everyone in Hollywood wooing everyone else.

Universal admission to the class of "creative" people would best meet Reich's ideal of a democratic society, but since this goal is clearly unattainable, the next best thing, presumably, is a society composed of "symbolic analysts" and their hangers-on. The latter are themselves consumed with dreams of stardom but are content, in the meantime, to live in the shadow of the stars waiting to be discovered and are symbiotically united with their betters in a continuous search for marketable talent that can be compared, as Reich's imagery makes clear, only with the rites of courtship. One might add the more jaundiced observation that the circles of power—finance, government, art, entertainment—overlap and become increasingly interchangeable. It is significant that Reich turns to Hollywood for a particularly compelling example of the "wondrously resilient" communities that spring up wherever there is a concentration of "creative" people. Washington becomes a parody of Tinseltown; executives take to the airwaves, creating overnight the semblance of political movements; movie stars become political pundits, even presidents; reality and the simulation of reality become more and more difficult to distinguish. Ross Perot launches his presidential campaign from the "Larry King Show." Hollywood stars take a prominent part in the Clinton campaign and flock to Clinton's inaugural, investing it with the glamour of a Hollywood opening. TV anchors and interviewers become celebrities; celebrities in the world of entertainment take on the role of social critics. The boxer Mike Tyson issues a three-page open letter from the Indiana prison where he is serving a six-year term for rape, condemning the president's "crucifixion" of assistant attorney general for civil rights nominee Lani Guinier. The starstruck Rhodes Scholar Robert Reich, prophet of the new world of "abstraction, system thinking, experimentation, and collaboration," joins the Clinton administration in the incongruous capacity of secretary of labor, administrator, in other words, of the one category of employment ("routine production") that has no future at all (according to his own account) in a society composed of "symbolic analysts" and "in-person servers."

ONLY IN A world in which words and images bear less and less resemblance to the things they appear to describe would it be possible for a man like Reich to refer to himself, without irony, as secretary of labor or to write so glowingly of a society governed by the best and brightest. The last time the "best and brightest" got control of the country, they dragged it into a protracted, demoralizing war in Southeast Asia, from which the country has still not fully recovered. Yet Reich seems to believe that a new generation of Whiz Kids can do for the faltering American economy what Robert McNamara's generation failed to do for American diplomacy: to restore, through sheer brainpower, the world leadership briefly enjoyed by the United States after World War II and subsequently lost not, of course, through stupidity so much as through the very arrogance—the "arrogance of power," as Senator William Fulbright used to call it—to which the "best and brightest" are congenitally addicted.

This arrogance should not be confused with the pride characteristic of aristocratic classes, which rests on the inheritance of an ancient lineage and on the obligation to defend its honor. Neither valor and chivalry nor the code of courtly, romantic love, with which these values are closely associated, has any place in the world view of the best and brightest. A meritocracy has no more use for chivalry and valor than a hereditary aristocracy has for brains. Although hereditary advantages play an important part in the attainment of professional or managerial status, the new class has to maintain the fiction that its power rests on intelligence alone. Hence it has little sense of ancestral gratitude or of an obligation to live up to responsibilities inherited from the past. It thinks of itself as a self-made elite owing its privileges exclusively to its own efforts. Even the concept of a republic of letters, which might be expected to appeal to elites with such a large stake in higher education, is almost entirely absent from their frame of reference. Meritocratic elites find it difficult to imagine a community, even a community of the intellect, that reaches into both the past and the future and is constituted by an awareness of intergenerational obligation. The "zones" and "networks" admired by Reich bear little resemblance to communities in any traditional sense of the term. Populated by transients, they lack the continuity that derives from a sense of place and from standards of conduct self-consciously cultivated and handed down from generation to generation. The "community" of the best and brightest is a community of contemporaries, in the double sense that its members think of themselves as agelessly youthful and that the mark of this youthfulness is precisely their ability to stay on top of the latest trends.

ORTEGA AND OTHER critics described mass culture as a combination of "radical ingratitude" with an unquestioned belief in limitless possibility. The mass man, according to Ortega, took for granted the benefits conferred by civilization and demanded them "peremptorily, as if they were natural rights." Heir of all the ages, he was blissfully unconscious of his debt to the past. Though he enjoyed advantages brought about by the general "rise in the historic level," he felt no obligation either to his progenitors or to his progeny. He recognized no authority outside himself, conducting himself as if he were "lord of his own existence." His "incredible ignorance of history" made it possible for him to think of the present moment as far superior to the civilizations of the past and to forget, moreover, that contemporary civilization was itself the product of centuries of historical development, not the unique achievement of an age that had discovered the secret of progress by turning its back on the past.

These habits of mind, it would seem, are more accurately associated with the rise of meritocracy than with the "revolt of the masses." Ortega himself admitted that the "prototype of the mass man" was the "man of science"—the "technician," the specialist, the "learned ignoramus" whose mastery of "his own tiny corner of the universe" was matched only by his ignorance of the rest. But the process in question does not derive simply from the replacement of the old-fashioned man of letters by the specialist, as Ortega's analysis implies; it derives from the intrinsic structure of meritocracy itself. Meritocracy is a parody of democracy. It offers opportunities for advancement, in theory at least, to anyone with the talent to seize them, but "opportunities to rise," as R. H. Tawney points out in *Equality*, "are no substitute for a general diffusion of the means of civilization," of the "dignity and culture" that are needed by all "whether they rise or not." Social mobility does not undermine the influence of elites; if anything, it helps to solidify their influence by supporting the illusion that it rests solely on merit. It merely strengthens the likelihood that elites will exercise power irresponsibly, precisely because they recognize so few obligations to their predecessors or to the communities they profess to lead. Their lack of gratitude disqualifies meritocratic elites from the burden of leadership, and in any case, they are less interested in leadership than in escaping from the common lot—the very definition of meritocratic success.

The inner logic of meritocracy has seldom been more rigorously exposed than in Michael Young's dystopic vision in his *The Rise of the Meritocracy, 1870–2033*, a work written in the tradition of Tawney, G. D. H. Cole, George Orwell, E. P. Thompson, and Raymond Williams. Young's narrator, a historian writing in the fourth decade of the twenty-first century, approvingly chronicles the "fundamental change" of the century and a half beginning around 1870: the redistribution of intelligence "between the classes." "By imperceptible degrees an aristocracy of birth has turned into an aristocracy of talent." Thanks to industry's adoption of intelligence testing, the abandonment of the principle of seniority, and the growing influence of the school at the expense of the family, "the talented have been given the opportunity to rise to the level which accords with their capacities, and the lower classes consequently reserved for those who are also lower in ability." These changes coincided with a growing recognition that economic expansion was the "overriding purpose" of social organization and that people ought to be judged by the single test of how much they increase production. Meritocracy, in Young's description, rests on a mobilized economy driven by the compulsion to produce.

The recognition that meritocracy is more efficient than heredity was not enough, in itself, to inspire or justify a "psychological change on the vast scale that the economy required." Indeed, "The hereditary principle would never have been overthrown," continues Young's narrator, ". . . without the aid of a new religion—and that religion was socialism." Socialists, "mid-wives of progress," contributed to the eventual triumph of meritocracy by encouraging large-scale production, by criticizing the family as the nursery of acquisitive individualism, and, above all, by ridiculing hereditary privilege and the "current criterion of success." ("It's not what you know but who you are that counts.") "The main body of socialists were far more critical of the inequality due to unearned than to earned income—the stereotype was of the rich man who had inherited a fortune from his father." In Young's world, only a handful of sentimental egalitarians condemned inequality as such and "quaintly spoke of the 'dignity of labour' as though manual and mental work were of equal worth." These same sentimentalists clung to the delusion that a system of common schools, because it promoted a "common culture," was an essential component of a democratic society. Fortunately their "over-optimistic belief in the educability of the majority" did not survive the test of experience, as Sir Hartley Shawcross noted in 1956: "I do not know a single member of the Labour Party, who can afford to do so, who does not send his children to a public school [i.e., to what would be called a private school in the United States]." A doctrinaire belief in equality collapsed in the face of the practical advantages of an educational system that "no longer required the clever to mingle with the stupid."

Young's imaginative projection of postwar trends in Great Britain sheds a great deal of light on similar trends in the United States, where a seemingly democratic system of elite recruitment leads to results that are far from democratic: segregation of social classes; contempt for manual labor; collapse of the common schools; loss of a common culture. As Young describes it, meritocracy has the effect of making elites more secure than ever in their privileges (which can now be seen as the appropriate reward of diligence and brainpower) while nullifying working-class opposition. "The best way to defeat opposition," Young's historian observes, "is [by] appropriating and educating the best children of the lower classes while they are still young." The educational reforms of the twentieth century "enabled the clever child to leave the lower class . . . and to enter into a higher class into which he was fitted to climb." Those who were left behind, knowing that "they have had every chance," cannot legitimately complain about their lot. "For the first time in human history the inferior man has no ready buttress for his self-regard."

It should not surprise us, then, that meritocracy also generates an obsessive concern with "self-esteem." The new therapies (sometimes known collectively as the recovery movement) seek to counter the oppressive sense of failure in those who fail to climb the educational ladder, while leaving the existing structure of elite recruitment—acquisition of educational credentials—intact. Since the sense of failure no longer appears to have any rational basis, it presumably requires therapeutic attention. Without much conviction, therapists send the message that the failure of academic misfits, the homeless, the unemployed, and other losers is no fault of their own: that the cards are stacked against them, that tests measuring academic achievement are culturally biased, and that academic achievement has become hereditary, in effect, since the upper middle classes pass on to their children the accumulated advantages that virtually guarantee advancement. As Young observes, people on the left (like their opponents on the right) are happiest when attacking hereditary privilege. They ignore the real objection to meritocracy—that it drains talent away from the lower classes and thus deprives them of effective leadership—and content themselves with dubious arguments to the effect that education does not live up to its promise of fostering social mobility. If it did, they seem to imply, no one would presumably have any reason to complain.

A N A R I S T O C R A C Y O F talent—superficially an attractive ideal, which appears to distinguish democracies from societies based on hereditary privilege—turns out to be a contradiction in terms: The talented retain many of the vices of aristocracy without its virtues. Their snobbery lacks any acknowledgment of reciprocal obligations between the favored few and the multitude. Although they are full of "compassion" for the poor, they cannot be said to subscribe to a theory of noblesse oblige, which would imply a willingness to make a direct and personal contribution to the public good. Obligation, like everything else, has been depersonalized; exercised through the agency of the state, the burden of supporting it falls not on the professional and managerial class but, disproportionately, on the lower-middle and working classes. The policies advanced by new-class liberals on behalf of the downtrodden and oppressed—racial integration of the public schools, for example—require sacrifices from the ethnic minorities who share the inner cities with the poor, seldom from the suburban liberals who design and support those policies.

To an alarming extent the privileged classes—by an expansive definition, the top 20 percent—have made themselves independent not only of crumbling industrial cities but of public services in general. They send their children to private schools, insure themselves against medical emergencies by enrolling in company-supported plans, and hire private security guards to protect themselves against the mounting violence against them. In effect, they have removed themselves from the common life. It is not just that they see no point in paying for public services they no longer use. Many of them have ceased to think of themselves as Americans in any important sense, implicated in America's destiny for better or worse. Their ties to an international culture of work and leisure—of business, entertainment, information, and "information retrieval"—make many of them deeply indifferent to the prospect of American national decline. In Los Angeles the business and professional classes now see their city as the "gateway" to the Pacific Rim. Even if the rest of the country is on the verge of collapse, they say, the West Coast "just can't stop growing no matter what," in the words of Tom Lieser, an economist at Security Pacific. "This is fantasy land and nothing will be able to put a stop to that." Joel Kotkin, a business writer who moved to Los Angeles in the mid-seventies and immediately became one of the city's leading boosters, agrees that the coastal economy is exempt from the "great angst of the Atlantic world." Recent hard times in California have not notably diminished this optimism.

In the borderless global economy, money has lost its links to nationality. David Rieff, who spent several months in Los Angeles collecting material for his book *Los Angeles: Capital of the Third World*, reports that "at least two or three times a week, . . . I could depend on hearing someone say that the future 'belonged' to the Pacific Rim." The movement of money and population across national borders has transformed the "whole idea of place," according to Rieff. The privileged classes in Los Angeles feel more kinship with their counterparts in Japan, Singapore, and Korea than with most of their own countrymen.

The same tendencies are at work all over the world. In Europe referenda on unification have revealed a deep and widening gap between the political classes and the more humble members of society, who fear that the European Economic Community will be dominated by bureaucrats and technicians devoid of any feelings of national identity or allegiance. A Europe governed from Brussels, in their view, will be less and less amenable to popular control. The international language of money will speak more loudly than local dialects. Such fears underlie the reassertion of ethnic particularism in Europe, while the decline of the nation-state weakens the only authority capable of holding ethnic rivalries in check. The revival of tribalism, in turn, reinforces a reactive cosmopolitanism among elites.

Curiously enough, it is Robert Reich, notwithstanding

his admiration for the new class of "symbolic analysts," who provides one of the most penetrating accounts of the "darker side of cosmopolitanism." Without national attachments, he reminds us, people have little inclination to make sacrifices or to accept responsibility for their actions. "We learn to feel responsible for others because we share with them a common history, . . . a common culture, . . . a common fate." The denationalization of business enterprise tends to produce a class of cosmopolitans who see themselves as "world citizens, but without accepting . . . any of the obligations that citizenship in a polity normally implies." But the cosmopolitanism of the favored few, because it is uninformed by the practice of citizenship, turns out to be a higher form of parochialism. Instead of supporting public services, the new elites put their money into the improvement of their own self-enclosed enclaves. They gladly pay for private and suburban schools, private police, and private systems of garbage collection; but they have managed to relieve themselves, to a remarkable extent, of the obligation to contribute to the national treasury. Their acknowledgment of civic obligations does not extend beyond their own immediate neighborhoods. The "secession of the symbolic analysts," as Reich calls it, provides us with a particularly striking instance of the revolt of elites against the constraints of time and place.

THE WORLD OF the late twentieth century presents a curious spectacle. On the one hand, it is now united, through the agency of the market, as it never was before. Capital and labor flow freely across political boundaries that seem increasingly artificial and unenforceable. Popular culture follows in their wake. On the other hand, tribal loyalties have seldom been so aggressively promoted. Religious and ethnic warfare breaks out in one country after another: in India and Sri Lanka; in large parts of Africa; in the former Soviet Union and the former Yugoslavia.

It is the weakening of the nation-state that underlies both these developments—the movement toward unification and the seemingly contradictory movement toward fragmentation. The state can no longer contain ethnic conflicts, nor, on the other hand, can it contain the forces leading to globalization. Ideologically nationalism comes under attack from both sides: from advocates of ethnic and racial particularism but also from those who argue that the only hope of peace lies in the internationalization of everything from weights and measures to the artistic imagination.

The decline of nations is closely linked, in turn, to the global decline of the middle class. Ever since the sixteenth and seventeenth centuries, the fortunes of the nation-state have been bound up with those of the trading and manufacturing classes. The founders of modern nations, whether they were exponents of royal privilege like Louis XIV or republicans like Washington and Lafayette, turned to this class for support in their struggle against the feudal nobility. A large part of the appeal of nationalism lay in the state's ability to establish a common market within its boundaries, to enforce a uniform system of justice, and to extend citizenship both to petty proprietors and to rich merchants, alike excluded from power under the old regime. The middle class understandably became the most patriotic, not to say jingoistic and militaristic, element in society. But the unattractive features of middle-class nationalism should not obscure its positive contributions in the form of a highly developed sense of place and a respect for historical continuity—hallmarks of the middle-class sensibility that can be appreciated more fully now that middle-class culture is everywhere in retreat. Whatever its faults, middle-class nationalism provided a common ground, common standards, a common frame of reference without which society dissolves into nothing more than contending factions, as the Founding Fathers of America understood so well—a war of all against all.

Three

Opportunity in the Promised Land

Social Mobility or the Democratization of Competence?

The new managerial and professional elites, for reasons I have tried to make clear, have a heavy investment in the notion of social mobility—the only kind of equality they understand. They would like to believe that Americans have always equated opportunity with upward mobility, that "the opportunity for social mobility for everyone is the very fabric of the 'American Dream,' " as Lloyd Warner wrote in 1953. But a careful look at the historical record shows that the promise of American life came to be identified with social mobility only when more hopeful interpretations of opportunity had begun to fade, that the concept of social mobility embodies a fairly recent and sadly impoverished understanding of the "American Dream," and that its ascendancy, in our own time, measures the recession of the dream and not its fulfillment.

If social mobility describes what Americans have always believed in, as Warner claimed, why did the term take so long to come into common use? Only five years earlier the editors of *Life* magazine, in an article based on Warner's studies of social stratification, still had to speak of social mobility in quotation marks, as if referring to a technical term of art unfamiliar to the general public.* Did this coinage commend itself merely as an academic refinement of an older idiom, a new and slightly pretentious way of talking about a long-established ideal of economic opportunity?

The significance neither of the phrase itself nor of the timing of its appearance can be dismissed so easily. It entered everyday speech in the wake of the Great Depression, when the hierarchical structure of American society could no longer be ignored. It conveyed both apprehension and reassurance. On the one hand, it confirmed the reality of class distinctions—something "every American knows but frequently forgets," as the editors of *Life* explained. On the other hand, it held out the hope that class barriers were not insurmountable. In *Life*'s words, "this phenomenon of social 'mobility'—the opportunity to move rapidly upward

---

*"A Sociologist Looks at an American Community," *Life* (Sept. 12, 1949), pp. 108–18. After explaining "how social standing is scored" according to Warner's "mathematical yardstick," this article proceeds to illustrate the six social classes found in Rockford, Illinois—one of the communities analyzed in Warner's monograph *Democracy in Jonesville*. The tone of the piece, which concludes with the interview with Warner quoted below, can be gathered from *Life*'s account of Sam Sygulla, a semiskilled worker who lived in a trailer, who never graduated from high school, and whose "scores" placed him "at the bottom of the ladder." In spite of these disadvantages, "he has dreams," *Life* reported. "If he . . . can overcome his educational handicap, Sam will have begun the slow but feasible climb upward."

through the levels of society—is the distinguishing characteristic of U.S. democracy and the thing for which it is famous and envied throughout the world." Social mobility, Warner told the editors, was the "saving grace" of a hierarchically ordered world. This reassuring note ended his interview, which was otherwise full of the forebodings that run through all his work.

His research raised the possibility that older "channels" of upward mobility were "drying up," as the editors put it. Higher education, not the most efficient or equitable "conveyor belt" for ambition, had taken their place; elsewhere Warner called it "not only the royal road but perhaps the only road to success." It was a road, to be sure, that only a few could hope to travel. Indeed, the educational system appeared to deflate working-class aspirations more often than it nurtured and rewarded them. These "findings," Warner admitted, furnished something less than "categorical encouragement to those of us who would like to believe that, since the occupational route no longer is as free as it once was, education is providing an adequate substitute." Still, most Americans continued to believe in the existence of equal opportunity, even if social research did not necessarily support such a belief. The "dream," as Warner described it, appeared to have a life of its own; it had become a necessary illusion, the persistence of which reconciled people to inequality and softened the otherwise troubling contradiction between egalitarian ideology and the hierarchical division of labor required by modern industry. As long as "workers generally believe that opportunity is available for those who really wish to try and . . . have the necessary brains and talent," their "faith in the present system," as Warner put it, would survive everyday disappointments. It was a good thing, his analysis seemed to imply, that workers seldom read sociology, which might have called their faith into question.*

The same considerations that led Warner and *Life*'s publisher, Henry Luce, to celebrate the popular belief in upward mobility have led writers on the left to deplore it. As Warner pointed out, workers who no longer believe in mobility "blame the system" instead of blaming themselves. For the American left it is precisely this failure to blame the system that has historically thwarted the development of working-class radicalism. Having internalized the myth of the self-made man, workers have too often sacrificed solidarity to the illusory hope of individual advancement. Worse, they have accepted a failure to advance as a moral judgment on their own lack of ambition or intelligence. Studies that document the persistence of these attitudes—among others, E. Wight Bakke's investigation of unemployed workers during the Depression, the Lynds' study of Muncie, Indiana, *Middletown in Transition*, and Ely Chinoy's well-known monograph *Automobile Workers and the American Dream*—have achieved canonical status on the left, even though many of them were written from a centrist point of view, because they seem to indict the "folk gospel" of "opportunity and success," as Chinoy called it, as a major

---

*E. A. Ross, one of the founders of American sociology, once urged his colleagues, in something of the same spirit, not to be too quick to "lift the veil" protecting popular illusions from scientific scrutiny. The beliefs that held society together—the "ideals and affirmations elaborated in the social mind"—were not to be "bawled from every housetop." The "wise sociologist" would "venerate a moral system too much"—even if it consisted entirely of superstitions—"to uncover its nakedness." He would address himself, moreover, not to the man in the street but to "teachers, clergymen, editors, law-makers, and judges." The "secret of order" must not fall into the wrong hands.

source of false consciousness among American workers.*

According to Chinoy, the "guilt and self-depreciation" with which workers reconciled themselves to their lowly position kept them from adopting goals more realistic than the pursuit of individual success: security and safety on the job, "general wage increases," and the "enrichment of leisure activities." For commentators further to the left it was the labor movement's failure to mount a frontal attack on the problem of inequality that betrayed the continuing influence of the self-help ideology. There was general agreement, however, on the central proposition that the American dream had always been equated with "opportunities for vertical mobility," in Chinoy's words—with a "widely affirmed tradition" that held out "golden opportunities . . . to able and ambitious men without regard to their original station in life."†

---

*"Middletown's working class," according to the Lynds, did not "think of itself as different" from the business class. It adhered to the "same symbols" of success. It was "caught up" in the same "tradition of a rising standard of living and lured by the enticements of salesmanship." The habit of muddling along, "in season and out, with a job or without," underlay "the large degree of unconsciousness as to class that was such a marked characteristic of Middletown's working class even in the sixth year of a great depression."

What the left makes of such findings is exemplified by Michael Lerner's argument to the effect that "self-blaming" is the most important obstacle to working-class militancy. "Workers come to feel that the problems they face are their own failures to adjust to the given reality." The "self-blaming approach," which militates against "righteous indignation against oppression," is unfortunately "rooted deep in the unconscious, and it is hard to dislodge." See also William Ryan's *Blaming the Victim*.

† Stanley Aronowitz advances the familiar argument that the "stultification of American working class consciousness"—the workers' failure to "grasp the fact that [their] own exploitation at the point of production results from systemic causes"—reflects the availability of "opportunities

THE ASSUMPTION THAT opportunity has always meant what it means today calls for historical examination. Yet most historians have confined their attention to the question of whether mobility rates have increased or declined over time. They would have been better advised to subject the concept itself to historical analysis. Like "modernization," "stratification," "status anxiety," and other dubious additions to the historian's stock of organizing ideas, the concept of social mobility has a history that needs to inform any attempt to grapple with the questions it raises or to reformulate those questions in the interest of conceptual clarity. Overawed by the institutional prestige of the social sciences, historians have been satisfied, for the most part, merely to imitate them. Historical studies of stratification have thus tended to strengthen the unexamined assumption that opportunity has always been identified, in the United States, with social mobility.

Carl Siracusa's study of nineteenth-century perceptions of industrialism and its impact on economic opportunity, *A Mechanical People*, shows how this assumption has infected even the most sensitive and painstaking work in the historical discipline. Along with many other historians influenced, almost unavoidably, by the political culture of the left, Siracusa wants to know why Americans were so reluctant to acknowledge the rise of a permanent class of wage laborers, why they clung to the "image of the respectable

---

within the system" and, more specifically, the "different access" to those opportunities among "different ethnic groups." Revolutionary consciousness founders on the "exquisite sense of the promise of American life deeply embedded among the foreign-born." But although "the myth of social mobility has not been shattered," it is increasingly difficult, according to Aronowitz, to believe that "hard work, education, and the inevitability of American expansion can produce success."

worker," as he calls it, and embraced "Horatio Algerism" as their national creed. By 1850, after all, "opportunities for upward mobility were fading rapidly," even though "in modern terms, the rate of social mobility was high," and the growth of industrial poverty should have put an end to the delusion that more than a handful of wage earners could ever work their way up the social ladder to wealth and respectability. The persistence of this "fantastic concoction" of wishful thinking, this readiness to believe the "unbelievable," strikes Siracusa as a "puzzle" or "mystery" that can be explained, insofar as it can be explained at all, only by "fear of the unknown," by a tendency to judge industrialism by its material benefits alone, and by the need to believe that the United States was somehow exempt from the fate of other nations. The belief in equal opportunity, which Siracusa equates with upward mobility, represented a "sweeping epidemic of social blindness," a "massive failure of social awareness and imagination."

According to Siracusa, Americans clung to an utterly unrealistic conception of society as a ladder, which anyone with energy and ambition could hope to climb, whereas it should have been apparent that those at the top had pulled up the ladder after them. But this imagery fails to capture the full range of nineteenth-century social thought. Robert Rantoul thought he was stating the obvious when he told an audience of workingmen that "society, as you very well know, is divided into two classes—those who do something for their living, and those who do not." These terms, staples of nineteenth-century political discourse, did not necessarily refer to the privileged classes at the top of the social scale and the hardworking but impoverished masses at the bottom. The class of "idlers" included vagabonds and beggars as well as bankers and speculators, while the category of productive workers, as Rantoul defined it, was broad enough to include not only those who worked with their hands but anyone who "superintends the employment of capital which diligence and prudence have enabled him to acquire." In the language of nineteenth-century producerism, "labor" and "capital" did not mean what they mean to us. The term "capitalist" was reserved for those who, producing nothing, lived off speculative profits, while the "laboring class," as a Democratic party broadside explained, referred to "the producers of wealth; the yeomanry who till the soil; mechanics, manufacturers, operatives, traders, whose labor sustains the state." Whigs no less than Jacksonian Democrats took an expansive view of the "working classes," defined by Levi Lincoln as the "practical agriculturist and husbandman, the manufacturer, and the mechanic." Rufus Choate considered it appropriate to speak of the "laborious, trading, and business portions of the community" in the same breath. Daniel Webster claimed that "nine tenths of the whole people belong to the laborious, industrious, and productive classes." They typically owned a little capital, he said, but not so much "as to render them independent without personal labor." Those who "combine capital with their labor" were referred to interchangeably as working-class and middle-class. According to William Henry Channing, the middle class (the "Ruling Power in this Republic") included the "Professional, Commercial, Manufacturing, Mechanical, Agricultural orders"—people "content with small means" and imbued with "habits of self-help" acquired "in the rough schools of labor."

Such descriptions of the social order were invariably played off against the hierarchical class system that prevailed in older countries. The force of the contrast depended on the claim that most Americans owned a little property and worked for a living, not that it was easier for

Americans to start from the bottom and rise to the top. In Europe the laboring classes allegedly lived on the verge of destitution, but it was not only their poverty that staggered Americans but their exclusion from civic life, from the world of learning and culture—from all the influences that stimulate intellectual curiosity and broaden people's intellectual horizons. As Americans saw it, the European working class was not merely impoverished but virtually enslaved. In societies composed of "permanent and distinct classes," in the words of the *Boston Post*, the "laboring man" was expected to remain "patient over his toils, from the settled conviction that he can never go beyond his circle, and can never change the laws that govern him."

To our ears, such a statement sounds like a plea for a class system in which it is possible to climb out of the laboring class into a higher class, but the context suggests that "going beyond his circle" referred to the opportunity to mingle on an equal footing with persons from all realms of life, to gain access to larger currents of opinion, and to exercise the rights and duties of citizenship. Foreign observers noted, often with disapproval, that ordinary Americans had opinions on every imaginable subject and that few of them seemed to have any sense of their proper place, but it was this very lack of deference, as Americans saw it, that defined a democratic society—not the chance to rise in the social scale so much as the complete absence of a scale that clearly distinguished commoners from gentlemen. The American Revolution had made subjects into citizens, and the "difference," as David Ramsay of South Carolina pointed out at the time, was "immense." Subjects looked "up to a master," whereas citizens were "so far equal, that none have hereditary rights superior to others." After the Revolution the distinction between gentlemen and commoners no longer had any meaning in America.

"Patrician and plebeian orders are unknown," wrote Charles Ingersoll in 1810. "There is no populace. . . . What in other countries is called the populace, a compost heap, whence germinate mobs, beggars, and tyrants, is not to be found in the towns; and there is no peasantry in the country. Were it not for the slaves of the south, there would be one rank."

Historians aware of the increasing inequalities introduced by the market are tempted to dismiss such claims as ignorant or insincere. In our own time money has come to be regarded as the only reliable measure of equality, and we therefore find it difficult to credit nineteenth-century impressions of America as an egalitarian society. But such impressions derived not merely from the distribution of wealth or economic opportunity but, above all, from the distribution of intelligence and competence. Citizenship appeared to have given even the humbler members of society access to the knowledge and cultivation elsewhere reserved for the privileged classes. Opportunity, as many Americans understood it, was a matter more of intellectual than of material enrichment. It was their restless curiosity, their skeptical and iconoclastic turn of mind, their resourcefulness and self-reliance, their capacity for invention and improvisation that most dramatically seemed to differentiate the laboring classes in America from their European counterparts.

The contrast struck foreign as well as native observers. For Michel Chevalier, in many ways the most astute of all visitors from abroad, it was the key to the whole democratic experiment. In America the "great discoveries of science and art" were "exposed to the vulgar gaze and placed within the reach of all." The mind of a French peasant, according to Chevalier, was full of "biblical parables" and "gross superstition," whereas the American farmer had been "initiated" into the "conquests of the human mind" that began with the Reformation. "The great scriptural traditions are harmoniously combined in his mind with the principles of modern science as taught by Bacon and Descartes, with the doctrine of moral and religious independence proclaimed by Luther, and with the still more recent notions of political freedom." The common people in America, in comparison with those in Europe, were "more fit to take a part in public affairs." They did not "need to be governed" since they were able to govern themselves. Full of "self-respect," they worked more efficiently as well; the wealth of America testified not merely to its abundance of natural resources but to the superior energy and intelligence of the laboring classes.

W HEN AMERICANS INSISTED, with one voice, that labor was the source of all value, they were not simply repeating a theoretical truism. The labor theory of value was more than an abstract principle of political economy in a country where labor's contribution to the general well-being took the form of mind as well as muscle. American mechanics, it was said, "are not untaught operatives, but an enlightened, reflective people, who not only know how to use their hands, but are familiar with principles." Mechanics' magazines returned to this theme again and again, praising the "independent and industrious American mechanic," whose mind was "free" and whose heart was "unwarped by prejudice." These publications were not alone in celebrating the virtues of American artisans and farmers or in tracing their mental energy, in the last analysis, to the effects of citizenship. Samuel Griswold Goodrich, known to his readers as Peter Parley, held that "liberty, civil and social," gave rise to a "universal spirit of improvement," which could be found "in the humblest as well as in the highest classes."

In view of his reputation as an early promoter of the success ideology in its crudest form, it is important to note that Goodrich emphasized the intelligence and virtue of ordinary men and women, not their ability to climb out of the laboring class into a higher class. He disagreed, he said, with those "refined persons" who "despise labor, and especially manual labor, as ungenteel." Nothing was "more despicable" than the "doctrine that labor is degrading"; "where such ideas prevail, rottenness lies at the foundation of society." Like Chevalier, Goodrich was struck by the contrast between the "rude, ignorant, servile" peasants he encountered in his travels on the European continent and the "intelligence and refinement" displayed by their American counterparts. In Europe the "power, genius, and intelligence of each country" were "centralized in the capital," whereas "power and privilege" in the United States were diffused throughout the country, "over the whole people." The condition of the "toiling million" furnished the most reliable measure of a nation's health. The "mechanics and laborers" of Europe lived amid scenes of "ignorance, squalidness, and degradation." In America, where a "general sentiment of equality" leveled the "distinctions of wealth and condition," they lived "on their own lands" and were "independent in their circumstances," and they had therefore acquired the "habit of forming their own opinions from their own reflections."

It was not altogether clear whether it made any sense, under these conditions—conditions widely regarded as typical as late as the Civil War—to speak of a laboring class at all. The reluctance to use the term (or the willingness to use it only in a comprehensive sense that included most of the population) appears indefensible in retrospect, but for that very reason it is important not to lose sight of the ideal underlying this aversion. Americans were admittedly slow to admit the emergence of a "class of our fellow men doomed to toil through life as mere workmen at wages," as Orestes Brownson described them in 1840. Forty years later and with much less justification, they could still "deny that there are any fixed classes in America," as the Christian Socialist Jesse Jones noted with some impatience. When he spoke of "our laboring or wage *classes*," Jones found that "this phrase is distasteful to many true-hearted Americans." He himself characterized wage labor as an "un-American" institution. In his view, however, it was no longer possible, without courting the charge of willful blindness or special pleading, to deny that "a fixed, hopeless, proletariat, wage class is the very foundation of our industrial system." At the same time he respected the "noble feeling from which this denial springs"—the feeling, which was also his own, that "the capitalists and the toilers must be one."

Looking back from our present vantage point, we are less inclined than Jones was to make any kind of allowance for those who argued that "there is no such thing among us as an hereditary working class," as the *Boston Daily Advertiser* put it in 1867. How could William Lloyd Garrison and Wendell Phillips, abolitionists acutely sensitive to injustice, dismiss criticism of wage labor as a "disgusting" form of "cant," an insult to the "intelligence of every sane man"? How can we possibly credit Phillips's claim, in 1847, that the term "would be utterly unintelligible to an audience of laboring people, as applied to themselves"? Who can respect his contention that "the laborers are neither wronged nor oppressed" and that in any case, the ballot gave them the means of self-defense? It is hard to avoid the feeling that Americans had come to rely far too heavily on self-serving comparisons with Europe, and later with the South under slavery, in their attempt to uphold an idealized image of the laboring classes under capitalism, classes ostensibly free but increasingly subject to the degrading effects of wage labor.

The "errors" to which he objected, Phillips said—the "false doctrines" encapsulated in phrases like "wages slavery" and "white slavery"—derived from the habit of "looking at American questions through European spectacles"— that is, from ignoring the contrast between the old world and the new. "In the old world, absurd and unjust institutions . . . oppress first and most cruelly the class, the weakest, whose only wealth is its labor." In America, on the other hand, workingmen had the chance to become "capitalists" by means of "economy, self-denial, temperance, education, and moral character."* But the evils introduced by industrialism into the northern United States could not be disposed of by citing greater evils elsewhere in the world. Without minimizing the contrasts so often invoked by nineteenth-century commentators on the class structure of American society, we can hardly fail to detect a slackening of moral realism and resolve in this increasingly

---

*In their eagerness to distinguish wage labor from slavery, writers in the *Liberator* did not stop with the claim that wage labor was a temporary condition from which the worker could "rise to a higher social position." They combined this line of argument with a defense of the market in labor as such. The wage earner was not exploited or degraded. "May he not choose his employer? May he not contract for wages? May he not change his occupation, whenever he can improve his condition? . . . Does he not own himself?" From this point of view, "the evil in society is not that labor receives wages, but that the wages given are not generally in proportion to the value of the labor performed." It was the abolitionist fringe, not the free-soil center, that came close to articulating a full-blown market ideology.

unconvincing celebration of free labor, a willingness to confuse the ideal with the reality.

What concerns us here, however, is the nature of the ideal itself, which is so easily misunderstood. That ideal was nothing less than a classless society, understood to mean not only the absence of hereditary privilege and legally recognized distinctions of rank but a refusal to tolerate the separation of learning and labor. The concept of a laboring class was objectionable to Americans because it implied not only the institutionalization of wage labor but the abandonment of what many of them took to be the central promise of American life: the democratization of intelligence. Even Henry Adams, not usually thought of as a tribune of the people, voiced this aspiration through one of the characters in his novel *Democracy*, who clearly spoke for Adams himself: "Democracy asserts the fact that the masses are now raised to higher intelligence than formerly. All our civilization now aims at this mark." A laboring class, then, implied as its necessary antithesis a learned and leisure class. It implied a social division of labor that recalled the days of priestcraft, when the clerical monopoly of knowledge condemned lay people to illiteracy, ignorance, and superstition. To have broken that monopoly—the most pernicious of all restraints on trade, since it interfered with the circulation not just of commodities but of ideas—was widely regarded as the crowning achievement of the democratic revolution. The reintroduction of a kind of clerical hegemony over the mind would undo that achievement, reviving the old contempt for the masses and the contempt for everyday life that was the hallmark of priestly societies. It would re-create the most obnoxious feature of class societies, the separation of learning from everyday experience.

Some such considerations, I think, explain why Orestes Brownson, who in 1840 was almost alone in his contention that industrialization had fostered the class divisions Americans feared, combined his trenchant analysis of wage labor with a seemingly arbitrary and irrelevant attack on priesthood. This aspect of Brownson's argument puzzles his interpreters today. Just when his analysis seems about to carry him to conclusions that anticipate those of Marx, Brownson veers off in an unexpected direction. Instead of attributing inequality to the appropriation of surplus value by the dominant class, he blames it on the power exercised by "sacerdotal corporations" over the life of the mind—an "idiosyncratic" and downright "silly" line of argument, according to Siracusa. But there was method in Brownson's seeming madness, even if he never unfolded its implications very systematically. Priesthood embodied the "principle of authority," he explained. Its existence was incompatible with the "authority of reason" and "freedom of mind." The "destruction of the priestly order, in every practical sense of the word priest," was therefore the "first step to be taken towards elevating the laboring classes."

In a closely related essay written the previous year, ignored by historians who admire "The Laboring Classes" but miss the direction of Brownson's argument, he pointed out that Horace Mann's educational reforms, far from democratizing intelligence, would create a modern form of priesthood by setting up an educational establishment empowered to impose the "opinions now dominant" on the common schools. "We may as well have a religion established by law," Brownson maintained, "as a system of education" that would serve, like all priestly hierarchies, merely as the "most effectual means possible of checking pauperism and crime, and making the rich secure in their possessions." The "old priestly office" having been "abolished," Mann and his allies aimed to revive it, in effect, by promoting the school at the expense of the press, the lyceum, and other agencies of popular education. By giving the school system exclusive control over education, Mann's reforms encouraged a division of cultural labor that would weaken the people's capacity to educate themselves. The teaching function would be concentrated in a class of professional specialists, whereas it ought to be diffused throughout the whole community. An educational establishment was just as dangerous as a priestly or military establishment. Its advocates had forgotten that children were best "educated in the streets, by the influence of their associates, . . . by the passions and affections they see manifested, the conversations to which they listen, and above all by the general pursuits, habits, and moral tone of the community." In 1841 Brownson returned to this theme in an essay that made his underlying concerns even more explicit. The "mission of this country," he argued, was "to raise up the laboring classes, and make every man really free and independent." That objective was completely inconsistent with a "division of society into workingmen and idlers, employers and operatives"—a "learned class and an unlearned, a cultivated class and an uncultivated, a refined class and a vulgar."

T H E S A M E K I N D of thinking informed Abraham Lincoln's highly suggestive critique of the "mud-sill theory" of society, the implications of which ranged far beyond the immediate political context—the slavery controversy—that gave rise to it. Proslavery apologists used this phrase in their polemics against the system of wage labor introduced into the North by industrialism. Wage labor, they argued, was far more cruel than slavery since employers acknowledged no responsibility to feed and clothe hired laborers, whereas slaveowners could not escape their paternal obligations (if only because they needed to maintain the value of their investment in human property). It was a measure of Lincoln's political gifts that he understood that this was the strongest argument for slavery and had to be confronted head-on. He also understood that the most effective rebuttal was to expose the argument's premise: that every civilization has to rest on one or another form of forced, degraded labor. The mud-sill theorists, he said, assumed

> that nobody labors, unless someone else, owning capital, somehow, by the use of that capital, induces him to it. Having assumed this, they proceed to consider whether it is best that capital shall *hire* laborers, and thus induce them to work by their own consent; or *buy* them, and drive them to it without their consent. Having proceeded so far they naturally conclude that all laborers are necessarily either *hired* laborers, or *slaves*. They further assume that whoever is once a *hired* laborer, is fatally fixed in that condition for life; and thence again that his condition is as bad as, or worse than that of a slave. This is the "mud-sill" theory.

Lincoln did not quarrel with his opponents' disparaging view of wage labor. He took the position, however, that "in these Free States, a large majority are neither *hirers* nor *hired*." There was no "such thing, as the free hired laborer being fixed to that condition for life." Wage labor in the North, insofar as it existed at all, served as a temporary condition leading to proprietorship. "The prudent, penniless beginner in the world, labors for wages awhile, saves a surplus with which to buy tools or land, for himself, then labors on his own account another while, and at length hires another new beginner to help him."* It is tempting to read Lincoln's idealized description of northern society—a description that reflects his experience in the West, where industrialism had not yet taken root—as a typical statement of the belief in what later came to be called social mobility. Ely Chinoy cites Lincoln's argument as a "classic expression" of the "small-business tradition," which equated opportunity with "vertical mobility." For Richard Hofstadter, who quotes the same passages (repeated by Lincoln himself on several different occasions), the "belief in opportunity for

---

*Lincoln first laid out this argument in a speech to the Wisconsin State Agricultural Society in September 1859. He repeated the heart of this address on the important occasion of his first annual message to Congress, December 3, 1861—one of his first attempts, as president, to provide a philosophical rationale for the Union cause.

The work of recent scholars makes it harder than it used to be to dismiss this kind of talk as wishful thinking. During the first half of the nineteenth century, according to Christopher Clark, "wage work," at least in the Connecticut River valley, "was intermittent. Families used their own labor whenever they could. While many men hired out their labor from time to time, . . . they were not fully dependent on doing so." They entered the labor market as a means of shoring up the household economy, which still rested on the "direct exchange of goods or work" and not on cash exchange. The labor market, Clark argues, was "shaped by familial concerns and had not yet become dominated by a large class of workers with nothing to sell but their labor." Wage labor also "reflected the seasonal character of farming and rural manufacturing"; people sometimes hired out their labor when there was no other work to be done.

Writing of his boyhood in Ridgefield, Connecticut, in the years before the War of 1812, Samuel Griswold Goodrich recalled that "every family lived as much as possible within itself." Since "money was scarce," wages were usually paid in kind. "Our servants . . . were of the neighborhood, generally the daughters of respectable farmers and mechanics. . . . Servitude implied no degradation."

for the self-made man" was the "key to his entire career." Eric Foner regards a belief in "social mobility and economic growth" as the heart of the free-labor ideology advanced by Lincoln and other members of his party. Lincoln's position allegedly reflected his "capitalist values," although Foner adds that the "objective of social mobility," as Lincoln and other free-soilers saw it, was "not great wealth, but the middle-class goal of economic independence."

The important question, however, is whether it makes sense to identify "independence" with social mobility in any sense of the term. When Lincoln argued that advocates of free labor "insisted on universal education," he did not mean that education served as a means of upward mobility. He meant that citizens of a free country were expected to work with their heads as well as their hands. Mud-sill theorists, on the other hand, held that "labor and education are incompatible." They condemned the education of working people as "useless" and "dangerous." It was a "misfortune," in their view, that workers "should have heads at all." Advocates of free labor took the position, in rebuttal, that "heads and hands should cooperate as friends; and that [each] particular head, should direct and control that particular pair of hands."

The issue is not whether Lincoln's description of northern society was altogether accurate but whether it reflected a "middle-class capitalistic" ideal, as Foner calls it. Foner recommends Brownson's essay on the laboring classes as a corrective to the "ideology of mobility" advanced by Lincoln, an ideology that allegedly minimized the obstacles to mobility. I am more impressed by what Lincoln and Brownson had in common: their shared understanding of the democratic experiment and its significance. Like Brownson, Lincoln held that democracy abrogated the "old rule" that "educated people did not perform manual labor" and thus severed the historic links among learning, leisure, and inherited wealth. "Hereditary property," Brownson argued, was impossible to reconcile with democracy; it was an "anomaly in our American system, which must be removed, or the system itself will be destroyed." Although Lincoln did not join Brownson in calling for its abolition, he assumed, I think, that inherited wealth would have little practical importance in a democracy of small property holders. He probably took it for granted that the absence of large fortunes, together with legal restrictions on primogeniture and entail, made it difficult for parents to pass on their own social standing to their children, quite apart from the cultural expectation that everyone ought to work for a living and that inherited advantages encouraged laziness and irresponsibility.

Recent scholarship suggests that a growing shortage of land set practical limits on parents' ability to bequeath property to their children. "The best most families could hope to do," writes Christopher Clark, ". . . was to reserve substantial property for one or two sons and make arrangements to give other children a start in the world through gifts, apprenticeships, or education." Lincoln's "prudent, penniless beginner" should be taken as a description of those "other children," barred from inheritance by circumstances and forced to rely on their own resources. His frame of reference was closer to the yeoman ideal than to the entrepreneurial, let alone to that of Horatio Alger. We should think of his "beginner" not as a child of poverty seeking to make his way up the social scale but as the "honorable character" celebrated in working-class magazines—the son of a "husbandman or artisan," "nurtured in the Common School or the Village Academy," whose "mind is free" and whose "heart is unwarped by prejudice," and whose object in life was "neither poverty nor riches."* The vision of the ideal democrat as a self-respecting artisan or agrarian in "his own workshop, . . . his own house," in the words of George Henry Evans, found legislative expression in the Homestead Act of 1862, which Lincoln hoped would give "every man" the "means and opportunity of bettering his condition." In the same speech in which he recommended the homestead policy on these grounds, Lincoln referred to "working men" as the "basis of all governments"—a pretty good indication that he conceived of property as a means not of escaping from labor but of realizing its full potential.

The aim of the Homestead Act, according to Foner, was "to aid the poor in achieving economic independence, to raise them into the middle class," and thus to promote "geographical and social mobility." No doubt some politicians and publicists took this view of its significance, yet the deeper symbolism of the homestead appealed to the need for roots, not to the spirit of restless ambition—to the desire for a connection with the land, for the permanence and stability that have always been threatened, nowhere more aggressively than in the United States, by the competing appeal of the market. The hope behind the Homestead Act, as Wendell Berry puts it in *The Unsettling of America*, was that "as many as possible should share in the ownership of

---

*The Alger hero himself bears a good deal of resemblance to this working-class ideal. Alger's protagonists typically spring from the country, not from the slums, although they come to the city to seek their fortunes. They are respectable young men deprived of an inheritance by the improvidence of the older generation or by chicanery or greed. Alger's emphasis falls not so much on the ascent "from rags to riches" as on the reclamation of a rightful inheritance. Even the Alger myth, then, does not conform very well to the twentieth-century ideal of upward social mobility.

the land and thus be bound to it by economic interests, by the investment of love and work, by family loyalty, by memory and tradition." In his 1859 speech to the Wisconsin Agricultural Society, the source of most of the statements I have been discussing, Lincoln upheld a norm of intensive agriculture diametrically opposed to the wasteful, migratory habits of those who saw land merely as a source of speculative profit. He condemned the "ambition for broad acres," which encouraged "careless, half performed, slovenly work." He spoke highly of the "effect of thorough cultivation upon the farmer's own mind." He said that it would prove an "exhaustless source of profitable enjoyment" to a "mind, already trained to thought, in the country school, or higher school." Nurture, not acquisition, was the burden of his exhortation.

I T   W O U L D   B E foolish to deny that competing versions of the good life appealed to many Americans in the nineteenth century. Those who spoke for the union of manual and mental employments recognized the seductive lure of wealth and fashion, the growing contempt for manual labor, and the desire to inspire envy instead of settling for respect. But it was only when the hierarchical structure of American society became unmistakable that opportunity came to be widely associated with the achievement of superior standing in an increasingly stratified, money-mad, and class-conscious society. By the end of the nineteenth century the "dignity of labor" had become an empty phrase, uttered without conviction on ritual occasions. The "laboring classes" no longer referred to the vast majority of self-reliant, self-respecting citizens; the term now referred to a permanent class of hirelings, escape from which appeared to be the only compelling definition of opportunity.

It is significant that "social mobility" entered the academic vocabulary around this time, in the context of uneasiness about the closing of the frontier. The Census Bureau's announcement, in 1890, that the country no longer "had a frontier of settlement" almost immediately took on enormous symbolic importance. This "brief official statement," wrote Frederick Jackson Turner, marked the "closing of a great historic movement." It gave new urgency to debates about the "social question." More than any other development, the closing of the frontier forced Americans to reckon with the proletarianization of labor, the growing gulf between wealth and poverty, and the tendency of each to become hereditary.

In Turner's writings, which did so much to fix the "significance of the frontier" in the American mind, an older interpretation of democracy appeared side by side with one that was only now coming to seem familiar. Summing up the "contributions of the West to American democracy" in 1903, Turner gave a new twist to the idea of opportunity so long associated with the frontier. "Western democracy through the whole of its earlier period tended to the production of a society of which the most distinctive feature was the freedom of the individual to rise under conditions of social mobility, and whose ambition was the liberty and well-being of the masses." The last phrase preserved some of the older meaning of democracy, but the rest of the sentence—which included the earliest use of the term "social mobility" that I have so far been able to find—identified the "well-being of the masses" not with the democratization of intelligence and virtue but with the opportunity to "rise" in the social scale.

In the same tangled paragraph, however, Turner spoke of the influence of the school system in creating a "larger body of intelligent plain people than can be found elsewhere in the world." Even this formulation, with its emphasis on schooling, marked a retreat from the democratic ideal of a population educated by practical experience and the exercise of citizenship, but it still made the condition of "plain people" the test of a democratic society. It implied, moreover, that material prosperity was by no means the only measure of the "well-being of the masses" or even the most important measure. Turner closed his essay by suggesting that the West's lasting contribution to democracy was the "vision of hope" that man would "grow to the full measure of his own capacity"—not exactly the kind of vision that would have commended itself to those who took their moral bearings from the Alger myth.

A N E S S A Y B Y James Bryant Conant, published in the *Atlantic* less than forty years later, provides another bench mark in the redefinition of opportunity. As president of Harvard, Conant presided over the transformation of a genteel university into the foremost stronghold of meritocracy. For our purposes the significance of his essay, "Education for a Classless Society: The Jeffersonian Tradition," lies in its attempt to link meritocracy to the tradition invoked in its subtitle. The essence of Jeffersonian democracy, as Conant saw it, was the determination to replace an aristocracy of wealth with an aristocracy of talent, not to weaken the principle of aristocracy itself. Conant stripped away all the rich associations that had once clustered around the ideal of a "classless society." The phrase no longer referred to a democracy of small property owners, to the union of mental and manual labor, to the educative and character-forming discipline of practical experience in the management of property and the exercise of citizenship, or to the hope that man would "grow to the full measure of his own capacity." It referred simply to the absence of hereditary privilege, to the "paramount importance" of "careers open to all through higher education." Lincoln, like Jefferson, construed opportunity in this way, according to Conant. The tradition articulated by these men was "summed up" in Turner's observation about "social mobility," which Conant quoted approvingly as the "heart of my argument." A "high degree of social mobility," he asserted, was the "essence of a classless society." Democracy did not require a "uniform distribution of the world's goods," a "radical equalization of wealth." What it required was a "continuous process by which power and privilege may be automatically redistributed at the end of each generation."

Having equated opportunity with upward mobility, Conant raised the question that inheres in the very concept: Was the rate of mobility slowing down? His answer was equally predictable: Thanks to the "passing of the frontier" and the "coming of modern industrialism," the United States had developed a "hereditary aristocracy of wealth." The only way of "restoring social mobility" was to make the school system a substitute for the frontier, a "vast engine" for the redistribution of opportunity. Public education, Conant thought, had "potentialities of which we little dream." It could serve as a "new type of social instrument," provided, of course, that it was redesigned with social purposes clearly in mind. The goal was to steer young people into careers suitable to their abilities. Sophisticated "testing methods," together with a "much more conscientious and discriminating form of educational guidance," would enable the school system to weed out manual workers from brain workers. A "diversified" system of education would guarantee that the professions were recruited "from every economic level," but it would also discourage unrealistic expectations. Only a minority was qualified for professional work. "Parents who expect miracles . . . must be reminded of the limitations imposed by nature." No one expected an athletic coach to make a "football hero" out of an "undersized" young man with "awkward legs," and there was no reason to ask teachers to work similar wonders in the classroom.

It would be hard to find a better example than Conant's essay of the paltry view of democracy that has come to prevail in our time. In the name of the "Jeffersonian tradition," which envisioned a community of intelligent, resourceful, responsible, and self-governing citizens, Conant proposed merely to ensure the circulation of elites. He saw in democracy nothing more than a system for recruiting leaders. His program—"social mobility through education"—contained the additional irony that although it presupposed a rigorous separation of manual and mental labor and a hierarchy of social status in which those who worked with their hands ranked at the bottom, it was conceived as a way of achieving a "classless society."* Without any sense of the intrinsic absurdity of his undertaking, Conant tried to bring together ideas drawn from utterly incompatible realms of discourse. His mixing "social mobility" and a "classless society" makes mixing oil and water look like child's play.

Historically the concept of social mobility was clearly articulated only when people could no longer deny the exis-

---

*Conant tried to convince himself that a "diversified" system of education would somehow contribute to the "building up of more than one 'elite.' " Excellence would be recognized in many areas, not just in the professions. His overriding concern with the recruitment of professionals, however, gave the game away.

tence of a degraded class of wage earners tied to that condition for life—only when the possibility of a classless society, in other words, was decisively abandoned. The notion that egalitarian purposes could be served by the "restoration" of upward mobility betrayed a fundamental misunderstanding. High rates of mobility are by no means inconsistent with a system of stratification that concentrates power and privilege in a ruling elite. Indeed, the circulation of elites strengthens the principle of hierarchy, furnishing elites with fresh talent and legitimating their ascendancy as a function of merit rather than birth.

The truth is that our society is at once "highly stratified and highly mobile," in the words of Wendell Berry. There is little evidence that rates of vertical mobility have declined. On the contrary, a vast body of social research points fairly consistently to the conclusion that rates of mobility have remained more or less constant ever since the Civil War.* During that same period of time, however, the concentration of corporate power, the decline of small-scale production, the separation of production from consumption, the growth of the welfare state, the professionalization of knowledge, and the erosion of competence, responsibility, and citizenship have made the United States into a society in which class divisions run far more deeply than they

---

*See, for example, Seymour Martin Lipset and Reinhard Bendix, *Social Mobility in an Industrial Society* (1959); Harmut Kaelble, *Social Mobility in the 19th and 20th Centuries* (1983); Edward Pessen, ed., *Three Centuries of Social Mobility in America* (1974); Peter Blau and Otis D. Duncan, *The American Occupational Structure* (1967); Alan C. Kerckhoff, "The Current State of Social Mobility Research," *Sociological Quarterly* 25 (1984): 139–53; William Miller, "American Historians and the American Business Elite in the 1870s," in *Men in Business*, ed., William Miller (1952); C. Wright Mills, "The American Business Elite: A Collective Portrait," *Journal of Eonomic History* (December 1945): 20–44.

did in the past. Ambition no longer seeks a "competence." "Moving up," as Berry says, appears to be the only prize worth pursuing. "One does not think to improve oneself by becoming better at what one is doing or by assuming some measure of public responsibility in order to improve local conditions; one thinks to improve oneself . . . by 'moving up' to a 'place of higher consideration.' "

Berry takes this last phrase from a memoir written by Justin Smith Morrill in 1874, in which Morrill explained the purposes behind the 1862 legislation bearing his name, legislation establishing a system of land-grant colleges for teaching "agriculture and the mechanic arts." The Morrill Act, as Berry sees it, can be seen both as the fulfillment of the Jeffersonian tradition and the beginning of its undoing. On the one hand, it was designed to discourage "short occupancy and a speedy search for new homes," practices associated with an exploitive, wasteful pattern of farming and with the "rapid deterioration of the soil." In other words, it was designed to discourage mobility, not to promote it. On the other hand, it also appeared to aim at the elevation of agriculture to professional status. Morrill objected to the "monopoly of education" exercised by liberal arts colleges on the grounds that it restricted the "number of those who might be supposed to be qualified to fill places of higher consideration in private or public employments to the limited number of graduates of the literary institutions." As Berry points out, Morrill's intentions were ambiguous. He wished to "exalt the usefulness" of "those who must win their bread by labor," but what he really seemed to exalt was professional status. "Would education exalt their usefulness by raising the quality of their work or by making them eligible for promotion to 'places of higher consideration'?"

Berry's interrogation of Morrill defines the most

important choice a democratic society has to make: whether to raise the general level of competence, energy, and devotion—"virtue," as it was called in an older political tradition—or merely to promote a broader recruitment of elites. Our society has clearly chosen the second course. It has identified opportunity with upward mobility and made upward mobility the overriding goal of social policy. The debate about affirmative action shows how deeply this pathetically restricted notion of opportunity has entered public discourse. A policy designed to recruit minorities into the professional and managerial class is opposed not on the grounds that it strengthens the dominant position of this class but on the grounds that it weakens the principle of meritocracy. Both sides argue on the same grounds. Both see careers open to talent as the be-all and end-all of democracy when in fact, careerism tends to undermine democracy by divorcing knowledge from practical experience, devaluing the kind of knowledge that is gained from experience, and generating social conditions in which ordinary people are not expected to know anything at all. The reign of specialized expertise—the logical result of policies that equate opportunity with open access to "places of higher consideration"—is the antithesis of democracy as it was understood by those who saw this country as the "last, best hope of earth."

Does Democracy Deserve to Survive?

The growing insularity of elites means, among other things, that political ideologies lose touch with the concerns of ordinary citizens. Since political debate is restricted, most of the time, to the "talking classes," as they have been aptly characterized, it becomes increasingly ingrown and formulaic. Ideas circulate and recirculate in the form of buzzwords and conditioned reflex. The old dispute between left and right has exhausted its capacity to clarify issues and to provide a reliable map of reality. In some quarters the very idea of reality has come into question, perhaps because the talking classes inhabit an artificial world in which simulations of reality replace the thing itself.

Both left- and right-wing ideologies, in any case, are now so rigid that new ideas make little impression on their adherents. The faithful, having sealed themselves off from arguments and events that might call their own convictions into question, no longer attempt to engage their adversaries in debate. Their reading consists for the most part of works written from a point of view identical with their own. Instead of engaging unfamiliar arguments, they are content to classify them as either orthodox or heretical. The exposure of ideological deviation, on both sides, absorbs energies that might better be invested in self-criticism, the waning capacity for which is the surest sign of a moribund intellectual tradition.

Ideologues of the right and left, instead of addressing the social and political developments that tend to call conventional pieties into question, prefer to exchange accusations of fascism and socialism—this in spite of the obvious fact that neither fascism nor socialism represents the wave of the future. Their view of the past is just as distorted as their view of things to come. They have studiously ignored the probing social commentary that took shape in the latter half of the nineteenth century, when it became evident that small property was disappearing and people began to ask themselves whether the virtues associated with proprietorship could be preserved, in some other form, under economic conditions that seemed to make proprietorship untenable.

Before the Civil War it was generally agreed, across a broad spectrum of political opinion, that democracy had no future in a nation of hirelings. The emergence of a permanent class of wage earners after the war was a profoundly disturbing development, which troubled commentators on American politics far more widely than we have realized. The agrarian movements that came to a climax in the People's party were not alone in their attempt to preserve small-scale production through cooperative buying and selling. Liberals like E. L. Godkin, influential editor of the

Nation and the *New York Evening Post*, also supported cooperative movements, until they discovered that their success
depended on governmental regulation of credit and banking. In the early years of the twentieth century, syndicalists
and guild socialists in Europe proposed bold and imaginative (if ultimately unworkable) solutions to the problem of
wage labor, at a time when social democrats were capitulat-
ing to the "logic of history"—the allegedly inexorable
movement toward centralization and the corresponding
reduction of the citizen to a consumer.

Even in the United States, which never developed a
strong syndicalist movement, the issues raised by syndicalists nevertheless generated a good deal of speculation during the so-called progressive era. Progressive thought was
lively and suggestive precisely because so much of it
resisted the political orthodoxies associated with the idea of
progress. A number of important progressives refused to
accept the division of society into a learned and laboring
class as the price of progress. Nor did they embrace the
welfare state as the only way of protecting workers' interests. They admitted the force of the conservative objection
that welfare programs would promote a "sense of dependence," in Herbert Croly's words, but they rejected the
conservatives' claim that the "wage-earner's only hope is to
become a property owner." Some of the responsibility for
"operating the business mechanism of modern life," Croly
maintained, would have to be transferred to the working
class—or, rather, wrested by the workers from their
employers since their "independence . . . would not
amount to much" if it were "handed down to them by the
state or by employers' associations."

Conventional wisdom, common to left and right alike,
has it that we live in an interdependent society, in which
the virtue of self-reliance has become just as anachronistic

as small-scale production. The populist tradition, as I understand it, took issue with this view. Independence, not interdependence, was the populist watchword. Populists regarded self-reliance (which, of course, does not preclude cooperation in civic and economic life) as the essence of democracy, a virtue that never went out of demand. Their quarrel with large-scale production and political centralization was that they weakened the spirit of self-reliance and discouraged people from taking responsibility for their actions. That these misgivings are more cogent than ever is suggested by the cult of the victim and its prominence in recent campaigns for social reform. It was the strength of the civil rights movement, which can be understood as part of the populist tradition, that it consistently refused to claim a privileged moral position for the victims of oppression. Martin Luther King was a liberal in his social gospel theology but a populist in his insistence that black people had to take responsibility for their lives and in his praise of the petty bourgeois virtues: hard work, sobriety, self-improvement. If the civil rights movement was a triumph for democracy, it was because King's leadership transformed a degraded people into active, self-respecting citizens, who achieved a new dignity in the course of defending their constitutional rights.

King had a more comprehensive understanding of democracy than many democrats, and this broader understanding is also part of the populist legacy. When Walter Lippmann began to argue, in the 1920s, that public opinion is necessarily ill informed and that government is best left to specialists, John Dewey rightly took issue with this view. For Lippmann, democracy meant nothing more than universal access to the good things of life. For Dewey, it had to rest on the "assumption of responsibility" by ordinary men and women, on a "stable and balanced development of

mind and character." What he failed to explain was just
how responsibility could thrive in a world dominated by
giant organizations and mass communications. Classical
theorists of democracy doubted whether self-government
could work very effectively beyond the local level—which
is why they favored as much localism as possible. Dewey
himself hoped for a "return movement . . . into the local
homes of mankind," but he could not tell his readers how
such a return was to come about, since he took the inevitability of centralization for granted, together with the "disin-
tegration of the family, church, and neighborhood."

Dewey's exchange with Lippmann raises the disturbing
question of whether democracy implies high standards of
personal conduct. Unlike many contemporary liberals,
Dewey clearly thought it did. In *The Public and Its Problems*
he noted with alarm that "the loyalties which once held
individuals, which gave them support, direction, and unity
of outlook on life, have well-nigh disappeared." The problem to which his title referred was how to reconstitute
them. Like other progressive thinkers, notably Charles H.
Cooley, Dewey was bent on refuting critics of democracy
who claimed that it fostered mediocrity, self-indulgence, an
excessive love of comfort, sloppy workmanship, and a timid
conformity to prevailing opinion. The idea that democracy
is incompatible with excellence, that high standards are
inherently elitist (or, as we would say today, sexist, racist,
and so on) has always been the best argument against it.
Unfortunately many democrats secretly (or not so secretly)
share this belief and are therefore unable to answer it.
Instead they fall back on the claim that democratic men and
women make up in tolerance what they lack in the way
of character.

The latest variation on this familiar theme, its *reductio ad
absurdum*, is that a respect for cultural diversity forbids us

to impose the standards of privileged groups on the victims of oppression. This is so clearly a recipe for universal incompetence (or at least for a disastrous split between the competent classes and the incompetent) that it is rapidly losing whatever credibility it may have had when our society (because of its abundance of land and other natural resources, combined with its chronic shortage of labor) offered a more generous margin for incompetence. The mounting evidence of widespread inefficiency and corruption, the decline of American productivity, the pursuit of speculative profits at the expense of manufacturing, the deterioration of our country's material infrastructure, the squalid conditions in our crime-ridden cities, the alarming and disgraceful growth of poverty, and the widening disparity between poverty and wealth, which is morally obscene and politically explosive as well—these developments, the ominous import of which can no longer be ignored or concealed, have reopened the historic debate about democracy. At the moment of its dazzling triumph over communism, democracy is coming under heavy fire at home, and criticism is bound to increase if things continue to fall apart at the present rate. Formally democratic institutions do not guarantee a workable social order, as we know from the example of India and Latin America. As conditions in American cities begin to approach those of the Third World, democracy will have to prove itself all over again.

Liberals have always taken the position that democracy can dispense with civic virtue. According to this way of thinking, it is liberal institutions, not the character of citizens, that make democracy work. Democracy is a legal system that makes it possible for people to live with their differences. The impending crisis of competence and civic trust, however, casts a heavy pall of doubt over the agreeable assumption that institutions, as opposed to character, provide all the virtue democracy needs. The crisis of competence suggests the need for a revisionist interpretation of American history, one that stresses the degree to which liberal democracy has lived off the borrowed capital of moral and religious traditions antedating the rise of liberalism. A second element in this revisionism is a heightened respect for hitherto neglected traditions of thought, deriving from classical republicanism and early Protestant theology, that never had any illusions about the unimportance of civic virtue. The more we come to appreciate the loyalties that once gave individuals "support, direction, and unity of outlook on life," the more we will need to look for guidance to thinkers—Emerson, Whitman, Brownson, Hawthorne, Josiah Royce, Cooley, Dewey, Randolph Bourne—who understood that democracy has to stand for something more demanding than enlightened self-interest, "openness," and toleration.

I T I S N'T S I M P L Y a question of whether democracy can survive. That alone is enough to give new urgency to the issues we have always been so eager to avoid. But the deeper question, of course, is whether democracy deserves to survive. For all its intrinsic attractions, democracy is not an end in itself. It has to be judged by its success in producing superior goods, superior works of art and learning, a superior type of character. "Democracy can never prove itself beyond cavil," Walt Whitman wrote in *Democratic Vistas*, "until it founds and luxuriously grows its own forms of art," its own "religious and moral character," the "perfect personalities" that will make "our western world a nationality superior to any hither known." The test of democracy, Whitman thought, was whether it could produce an "aggregate of heroes, characters, exploits, sufferings, prosperity or misfortune, glory or disgrace, common to all, typical of all."

For those who cherish the ideal of the open mind (even if it turns out to be an empty mind), this talk of heroes, exploits, glory, and disgrace is automatically suspect—frightening, in fact. The call for models of heroism "common to all" seems to threaten the pluralism of ethical commitments that democracy is obliged to protect. In the absence of common standards, however, tolerance becomes indifference, and cultural pluralism degenerates into an aesthetic spectacle in which the curious folkways of our neighbors are savored with the relish of the connoisseur. However, our neighbors themselves, as individuals, are never held up to any kind of judgment. The suspension of ethical judgment, in the conception or misconception of pluralism now current, makes it inappropriate to speak of "ethical commitments" at all. Aesthetic appreciation is all that can be achieved under current definitions of cultural diversity. The questions that allegedly divide us beyond hope of compromise turn out to be lifestyle questions, in the jargon of the day. How should I dress? What should I eat? Whom should I marry? Whom should I take as my friends? In this context the question that really matters—How should I live?—also becomes a matter of taste, of idiosyncratic personal preference, at best of religious or ethnic identification. But this deeper and more difficult question, rightly understood, requires us to speak of impersonal virtues like fortitude, workmanship, moral courage, honesty, and respect for adversaries. If we believe in these things, moreover, we must be prepared to recommend them to everyone, as the moral preconditions of a good life. To refer everything to a "plurality of ethical commitments" means that we make no demands on anyone and acknowledge no one's right to make any demands on ourselves. The suspension of judgment logically condemns us to solitude. Unless we are prepared to make demands on one another, we can enjoy only the most rudimentary kind of common life.

Even if we can't agree on the definition of a good life—and it could be argued that we have not yet seriously made the effort—we can surely agree on minimal standards of workmanship, literacy, and general competence. Without these, we have no basis on which either to demand respect or to grant it. Common standards are absolutely indispensable to a democratic society. Societies organized around a hierarchy of privilege can afford multiple standards, but a democracy cannot. Double standards mean second-class citizenship.

The recognition of equal rights is a necessary but insufficient condition of democratic citizenship. Unless everyone has equal access to the means of competence (as we might speak of them), equal rights will not confer self-respect. That is why it is a mistake to base the defense of democracy on the sentimental fiction that people are all alike. In fact, people are not alike in their capacities (this, of course, does not prevent us from imaginatively entering the lives of others). As Hannah Arendt has pointed out, the Enlightenment got it backward. It is citizenship that confers equality, not equality that creates a right to citizenship. Sameness is not equality, and "political equality, therefore, is the very opposite of the equality before death," Arendt says, ". . . or of equality before God." Political equality—citizenship—equalizes people who are otherwise unequal in their capacities, and the universalization of citizenship therefore has to be accompanied not only by formal training in the civic arts but by measures designed to assure the broadest distribution of economic and political responsibility, the exercise of which is even more important than formal training in teaching good judgment, clear and cogent speech, the capacity for decision, and the willingness to accept the consequences of our actions. It is in this sense that universal citizenship implies a whole world of heroes. Democracy requires such a world if citizenship is not to become an empty formality.

Democracy also requires a more invigorating ethic than tolerance. Tolerance is a fine thing, but it is only the beginning of democracy, not its destination. In our time democracy is more seriously threatened by indifference than by intolerance or superstition. We have become too proficient in making excuses for ourselves—worse, in making excuses for the "disadvantaged." We are so busy defending our rights (rights conferred, for the most part, by judicial decree) that we give little thought to our responsibilities. We seldom say what we think, for fear of giving offense. We are determined to respect everyone, but we have forgotten that respect has to be earned. Respect is not another word for tolerance or the appreciation of "alternative lifestyles and communities." This is a tourist's approach to morality. Respect is what we experience in the presence of admirable achievements, admirably formed characters, natural gifts put to good use. It entails the exercise of discriminating judgment, not indiscriminate acceptance.

Our society labors in the grip of two great, paralyzing fears: fanaticism and racial warfare. Having belatedly discovered the contingency of all belief systems and ideologies, we are obsessed with the terrors that arise when partial truths are taken as universal. In a century dominated by fascism and communism, this fear is understandable, but by this time it is surely possible to argue, without being accused of complacency, that the totalitarian menace is receding. Nor is Islamic fundamentalism an equivalent danger, as we are so often told. Those who worry overmuch about ideological fanaticism often fall into a complacency of their own, which we see especially in liberal intellectuals. It is as if they alone understood the danger of misplaced universality, the relativity of truth, the need for suspended judgment. They see themselves, these devoutly open-minded intellectuals, as a civilized minority in a sea of fanaticism. Priding themselves on their emancipation from religion, they misunderstand religion as a set of definitive, absolute dogmas resistant to any kind of intelligent appraisal. They miss the discipline against fanaticism in religion itself. The "quest for certainty," as Dewey called it, is nowhere condemned with such relentless passion as in the prophetic tradition common to Judaism and Christianity, which warns again and again against idolatry, the idolatry of the church included. Many intellectuals assume that religion satisfies the need for moral and emotional security—a notion that even a passing knowledge of religion would dispel. There are limits, it seems, even to the openness of the open mind, limits quickly revealed when the conversation turns to religion.

The problem of racial intolerance is closely linked to fanaticism. Here again there is a good deal of complacency and self-righteousness mixed up in the fear of intolerance. The thinking classes seem to labor under the delusion that they alone have overcome racial prejudice. The rest of the country, in their view, remains incorrigibly racist. Their eagerness to drag every conversation back to race is enough in itself to invite the suspicion that their investment in this issue exceeds anything that is justified by the actual state of race relations. Monomania is not a sign of good judgment. But whether it springs from self-righteousness or panic or a mixture of the two, the assumption that most Americans remain racists at heart cannot stand up to close examination. The improvement of racial attitudes is one of the few positive developments of recent decades. Not that racial conflict has subsided, but it is a serious mistake to interpret every conflict as evidence of the retrograde outlook of ordinary Americans, as a revival of the historic intolerance that has played so large a part in our country's history. The new racism is reactive rather than residual, let alone resurgent. It is a response, however inappropriate and offensive, to a double standard of racial justice that strikes most Americans as unreasonable and unfair. Since opposition to an "affirmative" double standard is routinely dismissed as racist, one reaction to this insult, from working- and lower-middle-class people harassed by affirmative action and busing and now from college students harassed by attempts to enforce politically correct language and thought, is to accept "racism" as a badge of honor, to flaunt it, with studied provocation, in the face of those who want to make racism and minority rights the only subject of public discussion.

From the point of view of people who are single-mindedly obsessed with racism and ideological fanaticism, democracy can mean only one thing: the defense of what they call cultural diversity. But there are far more important issues confronting friends of democracy: the crisis of competence; the spread of apathy and a suffocating cynicism; the moral paralysis of those who value "openness" above all. In the 1870s Walt Whitman wrote: "Never was there, perhaps, more hollowness at heart than at present, and here in the United States. Genuine belief seems to have left us." Those words are as timely as ever. When will we be ready to listen to them?

Five

Communitarianism or Populism?

*The Ethic of Compassion and
the Ethic of Respect*

My title is meant to refer to a difference of emphasis, not to an irreconcilable opposition between
two positions having nothing in common. The
populist and communitarian traditions are distinguishable
but historically intertwined; any account of those traditions
and their contemporary significance has to do justice both
to what unites them and to what sets them apart from each
other. Populism is rooted in the defense of small proprietorship, which was widely regarded, in the eighteenth and
early nineteenth centuries, as the necessary basis of civic
virtue. Communitarianism has its intellectual antecedents
in a sociological tradition, initially a conservative tradition,
that found the sources of social cohesion in shared assumptions so deeply ingrained in everyday life that they don't
have to be articulated: in folkways, customs, prejudices,
habits of the heart. Because both traditions shared certain

common reservations about the Enlightenment, however, it has not always been easy to tell them apart. Nor has there seemed to be much point in this exercise. Both fell outside the dominant celebration of progress, and their agreement, on an issue of such importance, has made their differences seem trivial.

If terms like "populism" and "community" figure prominently in political discourse today, it is because the ideology of the Enlightenment, having come under attack from a variety of sources, has lost much of its appeal. The claims of universal reason are universally suspect. Hopes for a system of values that would transcend the particularism of class, nationality, religion, and race no longer carry much conviction. The Enlightenment's reason and morality are increasingly seen as a cover for power, and the prospect that the world can be governed by reason seems more remote than at any time since the eighteenth century. The citizen of the world—the prototype of mankind in the future, according to the Enlightenment philosophers—is not much in evidence. We have a universal market, but it does not carry with it the civilizing effects that were so confidently expected by Hume and Voltaire. Instead of generating a new appreciation of common interests and inclinations—of the essential sameness of human beings everywhere—the global market seems to intensify the awareness of ethnic and national differences. The unification of the market goes hand in hand with the fragmentation of culture.

The waning of the Enlightenment manifests itself politically in the waning of liberalism, in many ways the most attractive product of the Enlightenment and the carrier of its best hopes. Through all the permutations and transformations of liberal ideology, two of its central features have persisted over the years: its commitment to progress and its belief that a liberal state could dispense with civic virtue. The two ideas were linked in a chain of reasoning having as its premise that capitalism had made it reasonable for everyone to aspire to a level of comfort formerly accessible only to the rich. Henceforth men would devote themselves to their private business, reducing the need for government, which could more or less take care of itself. It was the idea of progress that made it possible to believe that societies blessed with material abundance could dispense with the active participation of ordinary citizens in government. In the aftermath of the American Revolution liberals began to argue—in opposition to the older view that "public virtue is the only foundation of republics," in the words of John Adams—that a proper system of constitutional checks and balances would "make it advantageous even for bad men to act for the public good," as James Wilson put it. According to John Taylor, "an avaricious society can form a government able to defend itself against the avarice of its members" by enlisting the "interest of vice . . . on the side of virtue." Virtue lay in the "principles of government," Taylor argued, not in the "evanescent qualities of individuals." The institutions and "principles of a society may be virtuous, though the individuals composing it are vicious."

The paradox of a virtuous society based on vicious individuals, however agreeable in theory, was never adhered to very consistently. Liberals took for granted a good deal more in the way of private virtue than they were willing to acknowledge. Even today liberals who adhere to this minimal view of citizenship smuggle a certain amount of citizenship between the cracks of their free-market ideology. Milton Friedman himself admits that a liberal society requires a "minimum degree of literacy and knowledge," along with a "widespread acceptance of some common set of values." It is not clear that our society can meet even these minimal conditions, as things stand today, but it has always been clear, in any case, that a liberal society needs more virtue than Friedman allows for. A system that relies so heavily on the concept of rights presupposes individuals who respect the rights of others, if only because they expect others to respect their own rights in return. The market itself, the central institution of a liberal society, presupposes, at the very least, sharp-eyed, calculating, and clearheaded individuals—paragons of rational choice. It presupposes not just self-interest but enlightened self-interest. It was for this reason that nineteenth-century liberals attached so much importance to the family. The obligation to support a wife and children, in their view, would discipline possessive individualism and transform the potential gambler, spectator, dandy, or confidence man into a conscientious provider. Having abandoned the old republican ideal of citizenship along with the republican indictment of luxury, liberals lacked any grounds on which to appeal to individuals to subordinate private interest to the public good. But at least they could appeal to the higher selfishness of marriage and parenthood. They could ask, if not for the suspension of self-interest, for its elevation and refinement.

The hope that rising expectations would lead men and women to invest their ambitions in their offspring was destined to be disappointed in the long run. The more closely capitalism came to be identified with immediate gratification and planned obsolescence, the more relentlessly it wore away the moral foundations of family life. The rising divorce rate, already a source of alarm in the last quarter of the nineteenth century, seemed to reflect a growing impatience with the constraints imposed by long-term responsibilities and commitments. The passion to get ahead had begun to imply the right to make a fresh start whenever earlier commitments became unduly burdensome. Material abundance weakened the economic as well as the moral foundations of the "well-ordered family state" admired by nineteenth-century liberals. The family business gave way to the corporation, the family farm (more slowly and painfully) to a collectivized agriculture ultimately controlled by the same banking houses that had engineered the consolidation of industry. The agrarian uprising of the 1870s, 1880s, and 1890s proved to be the first round in a long, losing struggle to save the family farm, enshrined in American mythology, even today, as the *sine qua non* of a good society but subjected in practice to a ruinous cycle of mechanization, indebtedness, and overproduction.

INSTEAD OF SERVING as a counterweight to the market, then, the family was invaded and undermined by the market. The sentimental veneration of motherhood, even at the peak of its influence in the late nineteenth century, could never quite obscure the reality that unpaid labor bears the stigma of social inferiority when money becomes the universal measure of value. In the long run women were forced into the workplace not only because their families needed extra income but because paid labor seemed to represent their only hope of gaining equality with men. In our time it is increasingly clear that children pay the price for this invasion of the family by the market. With both parents in the workplace and grandparents conspicuous by their absence, the family is no longer capable of sheltering children from the market. The television set becomes the principal baby-sitter by default. Its invasive presence deals the final blow to any lingering hope that the family can provide a sheltered space for children to grow up in. Children are now exposed to the outside world from the time they are old enough to be left unattended in front of the tube. They are exposed to it, moreover, in a brutal yet seductive form that reduces the values of the market-place to their simplest terms. Commercial television drama-tizes in the most explicit terms the cynicism that was always implicit in the ideology of the marketplace. The sen-timental convention that the best things in life are free has long since passed into oblivion. Since the best things clearly cost a great deal of money, people seek money, in the world depicted by commercial television, by fair means or foul. The idea that crime doesn't pay—another discarded con-vention—yields to the recognition that law enforcement is a losing battle, that political authorities are helpless in the face of criminal syndicates and often hamper the police in their efforts to bring criminals to book, that all conflicts are settled by violence, and that scruples about violence con-demn the scrupulous to the status of losers.

Throughout the twentieth century liberalism has been pulled in two directions at once: toward the market and (notwithstanding its initial misgivings about government) toward the state. On the one hand, the market appears to be the ideal embodiment of the principle—the cardinal principle of liberalism—that individuals are the best judges of their own interests and that they must therefore be allowed to speak for themselves in matters that concern their happiness and well-being. But individuals cannot learn to speak for themselves at all, much less come to an intelligent understanding of their happiness and well-being, in a world in which there are no values except those of the market. Even liberal individuals require the character-forming discipline of the family, the neighborhood, the school, and the church, all of which (not just the family) have been weakened by the encroachments of the market. The market notoriously tends to universalize itself. It does not easily coexist with institutions that operate according to principles antithetical to itself: schools and universities, newspapers and magazines, charities, families. Sooner or later the market tends to absorb them all. It puts an almost irresistible pressure on every activity to justify itself in the only terms it recognizes: to become a business proposition, to pay its own way, to show black ink on the bottom line. It turns news into entertainment, scholarship into professional careerism, social work into the scientific management of poverty. Inexorably it remodels every institution in its own image.

IN THE ATTEMPT to restrict the scope of the market, liberals have therefore turned to the state. But the remedy often proves to be worse than the disease. The replacement of informal types of association by formal systems of socialization and control weakens social trust, undermines the willingness both to assume responsibility for oneself and to hold others accountable for their actions, destroys respect for authority, and thus turns out to be self-defeating. Consider the fate of neighborhoods, which serve so effectively, at their best, as intermediaries between the family and the larger world. Neighborhoods have been destroyed not only by the market—by crime and drugs or less dramatically by suburban shopping malls—but also by enlightened social engineering. The main thrust of social policy, ever since the first crusades against child labor, has been to transfer the care of children from informal settings to institutions designed specifically for pedagogical and custodial purposes. Today this trend continues in the movement for day care, often justified on the undeniable grounds that working mothers need it but also on the grounds that day care centers can take advantage of the latest innovations in pedagogy and child psychology. This policy of segregating children in age-graded institutions under professional supervision has been a massive failure, for reasons suggested some time ago by Jane Jacobs in *The Death and Life of Great American Cities*, an attack on city planning that applies to social planning in general. "The myth that playgrounds and grass and hired guards or supervisors are innately wholesome for children and that city streets, filled with ordinary people, are innately evil for children, boils down to a deep contempt for ordinary people." In their contempt planners lose sight of the way in which city streets, if they are working as they should, teach children a lesson that cannot be taught by educators or professional caretakers: that "people must take a modicum of public responsibility for each other even if they have no ties to each other." When the corner grocer or the locksmith scolds a child for running into the street, the child learns something that can't be learned simply by formal instruction. What the child learns is that adults unrelated to one another except by the accident of propinquity uphold certain standards and assume responsibility for the neighborhood. With good reason, Jacobs calls this the "first fundamental of successful city life," one that "people hired to look after children cannot teach because the essence of this responsibility is that you do it without being hired."

Neighborhoods encourage "casual public trust," according to Jacobs. In its absence the everyday maintenance of life has to be turned over to professional bureaucrats. The atrophy of informal controls leads irresistibly to the expansion of bureaucratic controls. This development threatens to extinguish the very privacy liberals have always set such store by. It also loads the organizational sector with burdens it cannot support. The crisis of public funding is only one indication of the intrinsic weakness of organizations that can no longer count on informal, every-day mechanisms of social trust and control. The taxpayers' revolt, although itself informed by an ideology of privatism resistant to any kind of civic appeals, at the same time grows out of a well-founded suspicion that tax money merely sustains bureaucratic self-aggrandizement. The state is clearly overburdened, and nobody has much confidence in its ability to solve the problems that need to be solved.

As formal organizations break down, people will have to improvise ways of meeting their immediate needs: patrolling their own neighborhoods, withdrawing their children from public schools in order to educate them at home. The default of the state will thus contribute in its own right to the restoration of informal mechanisms of self-help. But it is hard to see how the foundations of civic life can be restored unless this work becomes an overriding goal of public policy. We have heard a good deal of talk about the repair of our material infrastructure, but our cultural infrastructure needs attention too, and more than just the rhetorical attention of politicians who praise "family values" while pursuing economic policies that undermine them. It is either naïve or cynical to lead the public to think that dismantling the welfare state is enough to ensure a revival of informal cooperation—"a thousand points of light." People who have lost the habit of self-help, who live in cities and suburbs where shopping malls have replaced neighborhoods, and who prefer the company of close friends (or simply the company of television) to the informal sociability of the street, the coffee shop, and the tavern are not likely to reinvent communities just because the state has proved such an unsatisfactory substitute. Market mechanisms will not repair the fabric of public trust. On the contrary, the market's effect on the cultural infrastructure is just as corrosive as that of the state.

WE CAN NOW begin to appreciate the appeal of populism and communitarianism. They reject both the market and the welfare state in pursuit of a third way. This is why they are so difficult to classify on the conventional spectrum of political opinion. Their opposition to free-market ideologies seems to align them with the left, but their criticism of the welfare state (whenever this criticism becomes open and explicit) makes them sound right-wing. In fact, these positions belong to neither the left nor the right, and for that very reason they seem to many people to hold out the best hope of breaking the deadlock of current debate, which has been institutionalized in the two major parties and their divided control of the federal government. At a time when political debate consists largely of ideological slogans endlessly repeated to audiences composed mainly of the party faithful, fresh thinking is desperately needed. It is not likely to emerge, however, from those with a vested interest in the old orthodoxies. We need a "third way of thinking about moral obligation," as Alan Wolfe puts it, one that locates moral obligation neither in the state nor in the market but in "common sense, ordinary emotions, and everyday life." Wolfe's plea for a political program designed to strengthen civil society, which closely resembles the ideas advanced in *The Good Society* by Robert Bellah and his collaborators, should be welcomed by the growing numbers of people who find themselves dissatisfied with the alternatives defined by conventional debate.

These authors illustrate the strengths of the communitarian position along with some of its characteristic weaknesses. They make it clear that both the market and the state presuppose the strength of "noneconomic ties of trust and solidarity," as Wolfe puts it. Yet the expansion of these institutions weakens ties of trust and thus undermines the preconditions for their own success. The market and the "job culture," Bellah writes, are "invading our private lives," eroding our "moral infrastructure" of "social trust." Nor does the welfare state repair the damage. "The example of more successful welfare states . . . suggests that money and bureaucratic assistance alone do not halt the decline of the family" or strengthen any of the other "sustaining institutions that make interdependence morally significant."

Wolfe's recent book *Whose Keeper?* contains a useful analysis of the ideological as well as the social and cultural consequences of the developments that have enhanced the influence of the market and the state at the expense of everyday association. Early admirers of the market—Adam Smith, for example—believed that selfishness was a virtue only if it was confined to the realm of exchange. They did not advocate or even envision conditions in which every phase of life would be organized according to the principles of the market. Now that private life has been largely absorbed by the market, however, a new school of economic thought offers what amounts to a "new moral vision": a society wholly dominated by the market, in which economic relations are "no longer softened by ties of trust and solidarity." In the work of Milton Friedman and other spokesmen for what is misleadingly called neoclassical economic theory, "no area remains outside . . . the market. . . . There is only one compartment in social life: the one defined by self-interested action." The social democratic reply to free-market economics and its extension in the work of philosophers like Robert Nozick is equally unsatisfactory, as Wolfe shows. Like Michael Sandel, Wolfe takes John Rawls as the prime exponent of a social democratic liberalism that conceives of human beings as rootless abstractions wholly absorbed in maximizing their own advantage. Rawls claims that a proper understanding of their own interests leads individuals to appreciate principles of justice that justify a vast expansion of the welfare state, but his view of social relations, as Wolfe explains, is quite similar to the view that elsewhere justifies an expansion of the market. Rawls's theory has no room for trust or conscience, qualities he finds "oppressive." It has no room for affective ties except in their most abstract form. "People in the Rawlsian republic do not love other men and women: they love humankind instead." His theory "teaches people to distrust what will help them most—their personal attachments to those they know—and value what will help them least—abstract principles," which invariably prove a "poor guide to the moral dilemmas of everyday life."

The trouble with the welfare state, as Wolfe sees it, is that it has lost sight of its original purpose, the redistribution of income. Today the welfare state, at least in Scandinavia, is "much more directly involved in the regulation of moral obligations." Wolfe cites the expansion of publicly supported day care as a case in point. "As the state grows and families weaken, it becomes more difficult to remain hopeful that state intervention will not significantly alter the character of the institutions in civil society." This raises a troubling question: "When government is relied on to furnish rules of moral obligation, will it weaken the very social ties that make government possible in the first place?"

Unfortunately Wolfe does not pursue the question very far. He reserves most of his criticism for the market. Whereas he condemns the market, he is merely "ambivalent" about the state. He is aware of the mounting criticism of the welfare state in Sweden, and he acknowledges the force of what is being said—for example, that "individual responsibility" (in the words of Gunnar Heckscher) is undermined by the notion that "society is to blame" for poverty, delinquency, and many other ills. Wolfe quotes portions of the disparaging account of Swedish society written by Hans Magnus Enzensberger in the early 1980s: "The state's power has grown unopposed, creeping into all the cracks of daily life, regulating people's doings in a way without precedent in free societies." Enzensberger's point, Wolfe concedes, "cannot be dismissed." A few pages farther on, however, he insists that Enzensberger is "incorrect" when he claims that "Scandinavians are in danger of losing their moral autonomy to government." In any case, the welfare state in our own country is so pathetically weak that it poses no threat to anyone. It may not be "completely satisfactory," but it is clearly preferable to the market. If we had to choose between the Scandinavian systems and our own, we would have to conclude that "the needs of the future generations would . . . be better served" by the former. Wolfe's book does not live up to its promise. What began as a case for a "third way" ends with a qualified endorsement of the welfare state and a ringing endorsement of sociology—an anticlimax, to say the least.

T H E G O O D S O C I E T Y, like *Whose Keeper?*, is much more an attack on the market than an attack on the welfare state. Communitarianism in this form is difficult to distinguish from social democracy. At one point the authors of the former book explicitly call for a "global New Deal," notwithstanding their reservations about the "administered society." They have a great deal to say about responsibility, but it is "social responsibility," not the responsibility of individuals, that mainly concerns them. In their plea for "responsible attention," I hear overtones of "compassion," the slogan of social democracy, a slogan that has always been used to justify welfare programs, the expansion of the state's custodial and tutelary functions, and the bureaucratic rescue of women, children, and other victims of mistreatment. The ideology of compassion, however agreeable to our ears, is one of the principal influences, in its own right, on the subversion of civic life, which depends not so much on compassion as on mutual respect. A misplaced compassion degrades both the victims, who are reduced to objects of pity, and their would-be benefactors, who find it easier to pity their fellow citizens than to hold them up to impersonal standards, attainment of which would entitle them to respect. We pity those who suffer, and we pity, most of all, those who suffer conspicuously; but we reserve respect for those who refuse to exploit their suffering for the purposes of pity. We respect those who are willing to be held accountable for their actions, who submit to exacting and impersonal standards impartially applied. Today it is widely believed, at least by members of the caring class, that standards are inherently oppressive, that far from being impersonal they discriminate against women, blacks, and minorities in general. Standards, we are told, reflect the cultural hegemony of dead white European males. Compassion compels us to recognize the injustice of imposing them on everybody else.

When the ideology of compassion leads to this kind of absurdity, it is time to call it into question. Compassion has become the human face of contempt. Democracy once implied opposition to every form of double standard. Today we accept double standards—as always, a recipe for second-class citizenship—in the name of humanitarian concern. Having given up the effort to raise the general level of competence—the old meaning of democracy—we are content to institutionalize competence in the caring class, which arrogates to itself the job of looking out for everybody else.

Populism, as I understand it, is unambiguously committed to the principle of respect. It is for this reason, among others, that populism is to be preferred to communitarianism, which is too quick to compromise with the welfare state and to endorse its ideology of compassion. Populism has always rejected both the politics of deference and the politics of pity. It stands for plain manners and plain, straightforward speech. It is unimpressed by titles and other symbols of exalted social rank, but it is equally unimpressed by claims of moral superiority advanced in the name of the oppressed. It rejects a "preferential option for the poor," if that means treating the poor as helpless victims of circumstance, absolving them of accountability, or excusing their derelictions on the grounds that poverty carries with it a presumption of innocence. Populism is the authentic voice of democracy. It assumes that individuals are entitled to respect until they prove themselves unworthy of it, but it insists that they take responsibility for themselves. It is reluctant to make allowances or to withhold judgment on the grounds that "society is to blame." Populism is "judgmental," to invoke a current adjective the pejorative use of which shows how far the capacity for discriminating judgment has been weakened by the moral climate of humanitarian "concern."

Communitarians regret the collapse of social trust but often fail to see that trust, in a democracy, can only be grounded in mutual respect. They properly insist that rights have to be balanced by responsibility, but they seem to be more interested in the responsibility of the community as a whole—its responsibility, say, to its least fortunate members—than in the responsibility of individuals. When the authors of *The Good Society* say that "democracy means paying attention," they seek to recall us to a sense of the common good and to combat the selfish individualism that blinds us to the needs of others. But it is our reluctance to make demands on each other, much more than our reluctance to help those in need, that is sapping the strength of democracy today. We have become far too accommodating and tolerant for our own good. In the name of sympathetic understanding, we tolerate second-rate workmanship, second-rate habits of thought, and second-rate standards of personal conduct. We put up with bad manners and with many kinds of bad language, ranging from the commonplace scatology that is now ubiquitous to elaborate academic evasion. We seldom bother to correct a mistake or to argue with opponents in the hope of changing their minds. Instead we either shout them down or agree to disagree, saying that all of us have a right to our opinions. Democracy in our time is more likely to die of indifference than of intolerance. Tolerance and understanding are important virtues, but they must not become an excuse for apathy.

THE DIFFERENCES BETWEEN populism and communitarianism are differences of emphasis, but they have important political consequences. My strongest objection to the communitarian point of view is that it has too little to say about controversial issues like affirmative action, abortion, and family policy. The authors of *The Good Society* assure their readers that they "do not want to advocate any single form of family life." It is the "quality of family life" that matters, in their view, not its structure. But quality and structure are not so easily separable. Common sense tells us that children need both fathers and mothers, that they are devastated by divorce, and that they do not flourish in day care centers. Without minimizing the difficulty of solving the problems that confront the family, at least we ought to be able to hold up a standard by which to measure the success or failure of our efforts. We need guidelines, not a general statement of good intentions. If communitarians are serious about what Bellah calls a "politics of generativity," they need to address the conditions that are widely believed to make it more difficult than it used to be to raise children. Parents are deeply troubled by the moral climate of permissiveness, by the sex and violence to which children are prematurely exposed, by the moral relativism they encounter in school, and by the devaluation of authority that makes children impatient with any restraints. Much of the opposition to abortion reflects the same kinds of concerns, which cannot be addressed simply by taking the position that abortion, like the structure of the family, ought to be a matter of private choice. The privatization of morality is one more indication of the collapse of the community, and a communitarianism that acquiesces in this development, at the same time calling for a public philosophy, cannot expect to be taken very seriously.

Any attempt to base public policy on a clearly articulated set of moral guidelines, of course, invites the predictable objection that moral perceptions are inherently subjective, that it is impossible to arrive at a general agreement about these matters, and that politics and morality therefore have to be strictly segregated. Any attempt to combine them, according to this reasoning, will result in the imposition of one group's values on everybody else. The most common criticism of communitarianism is that it would lead to the regimentation of opinion, the repression of dissent, and the institutionalization of intolerance, all in the name of morality. Opponents of communitarianism, who include right-wing libertarians as well as left-leaning liberals, cite Calvin's Geneva, Cromwell's Puritan Commonwealth, and the Salem witch trials to show what happens when the state tries to enforce morality. The word "community," in their ears, sounds like a prescription for bigotry and parochialism. It conjures up images of village life out of Sherwood Anderson and Sinclair Lewis: suspicious, gossipy, complacent, ruthless in its suppression of originality and intellectual freedom. From this point of view, communitarianism appears to threaten everything the modern world has achieved in its progress from provincialism to cosmopolitanism, including the respect for "diversity" that has become the hallmark (we are told) of civilized societies.

The best answer to this indictment is that it exaggerates the difficulty of reaching a common understanding about moral issues. Amitai Etzioni, founder of the *Responsive Community*, the leading communitarian journal, argues convincingly that "there is more consensus than at first seems to be the case." The "values we share as a community" include a "commitment to democracy, the Bill of Rights, and mutual respect among the subgroups." Americans believe in fair treatment for all and in the "desirability of treating others with love, respect, and dignity." They believe in the virtues of tolerance and truth telling. They condemn discrimination and violence. It is the breadth and depth of this agreement, Etzioni argues in his recent book *The Spirit of Community* that make it possible to envision a "reasonable intermediate position" between libertarianism and authoritarianism. Unfortunately the inordinate influence wielded by special-interest groups, the media's vested stake in conflict, and the adversarial mode of justice embodied in our legal system promote conflict rather than consensus. We conduct ourselves politically as if we had nothing in common. Some zealots go so far as to urge, in Etzioni's words, that "we forgo the notion of one society and allow it to be replaced by a conglomerate of tribes of various colors." Indeed, they claim that tribalism is the only form of "community" that is likely to take root in a multiracial, multicultural society.

E T Z I O N I   N O T   O N L Y rejects this point of view but is confident that most Americans reject it too, since they share a wide range of basic beliefs. It can still be objected, however, that his description of the "moral infrastructure" consists of vague generalities and that people are bound to disagree about their application to specific issues. There is a good deal of evidence, however—though Etzioni does not avail himself of it—that Americans agree even about concrete issues, the very issues, prominent in recent years as a source of bitter ideological conflict, on which agreement is allegedly impossible. Public opinion polls show that large majorities favor the expansion of economic opportunities for women. A Gallup poll conducted in 1987, moreover, found that 66 percent rejected the proposition that "women should return to their traditional role in society." Yet 68 percent, according to the same poll, believed that "too many children are being raised in day-care centers." Almost 90 percent described themselves as having "old-fashioned values about family and marriage." In 1982 Daniel Yankelovich reported a two-thirds majority simultaneously in favor of women's rights and a "return to more traditional standards of family life and parental responsibility."

E. J. Dionne, who reports these findings in his *Why Americans Hate Politics*, notes that conventional labels do not accurately describe what Americans believe. "In the current era, . . . the concepts of 'left' and 'right' seem less useful than ever." Take the abortion issue, the most divisive issue in American politics, on which compromise is seemingly impossible. When the issue is defined as one of private choice against government interference, prochoice positions win out. But most Americans believe that too many abortions are performed and favor restrictions such as parental consent. The same ambivalence shows up in popular attitudes toward government. Most people agree, in principle, that government is too big and intrusive, but they support Social Security, national health insurance, and full employment. In general, Dionne reports, polls suggest that "Americans believe in helping those who fall on hard times, in fostering equal opportunity and equal rights, in providing broad access to education, housing, health care, and child care." At the same time they believe that "hard work should be rewarded, that people who behave destructively toward others should be punished, that small institutions close to home tend to do better than big institutions run from far away, that private moral choices usually have social consequences." Above all, they believe that families in which mothers and fathers live under the same roof with their children provide the best arrangement for raising the young. This commitment to the "traditional family," Dionne insists, should not be interpreted as opposition to feminism or even to alternative lifestyles. It simply reflects an understanding that "children are usually better off when they live with a mother and a father who have made more than a passing commitment to each other."

As Dionne characterizes them, popular attitudes contain more common sense than the rigid ideologies that dominate public debate. They are often ambivalent but not necessarily contradictory or incoherent. Unfortunately they find no expression in national politics, and it is for this reason, according to Dionne, that Americans take so little interest in politics. The explanations of political apathy and stalemate offered by other commentators, including Bellah and Etzioni, emphasize procedural considerations: sound bites; campaign finance; the overwhelming advantages of incumbency in congressional elections. The real explanation, however, is substantive: The parties no longer represent the opinions and interests of ordinary people. The political process is dominated by rival elites committed to irreconcilable ideologies. If Dionne is to be believed, the politics of ideology has distorted our view of the world and confronted us with a series of false choices: between feminism and the family, social reform and traditional values, racial justice and individual accountability. Ideological rigidity has the effect of obscuring the views Americans have in common, of replacing substantive issues with purely symbolic issues, and of creating a false impression of polarization. It is the prominence of issues that strike most Americans as unreal, Dionne argues, that explains "why Americans hate politics." The issues that give rise to strident professions of faith, on both sides of the ideological divide, seem to have little bearing on the problems most people face in everyday life. Politics has become a matter of ideological gestures, while the real problems remain unsolved. "When Americans say that politics has nothing to do with what really matters, they are largely right."

NONE OF THIS means that a politics that really mattered—a politics rooted in popular common sense instead of the ideologies that appeal to elites—would painlessly resolve all the conflicts that threaten to tear the country apart. Communitarians underestimate the difficulty of finding an approach to family issues, say, that is both profamily and profeminist. That may be what the public wants in theory. In practice, however, it requires a restructuring of the workplace designed to make work schedules far more flexible, career patterns less rigid and predictable, and criteria for advancement less destructive to family and community obligations. Such reforms imply interference with the market and a redefinition of success, neither of which will be achieved without a great deal of controversy.

The problems confronting American society (or any other advanced industrial society, for that matter) can't be solved simply by taking account of "what Americans believe," though that is certainly a step in the right direction. Polls reveal "far more room for agreement" than we might think, as Dionne argues, but they hardly add up to a public philosophy. As Dionne himself admits, the country's ambivalence often shades into schizophrenia. Americans have a "split personality, which by turns emphasizes individual liberty and the importance of community."

These are by no means completely irreconcilable values, but neither can they be neatly balanced simply by splitting the difference. As a guide to sound political practice, schizophrenia is not much better than ideological paranoia. A "coherent notion of the common good"—Dionne's concluding plea—will still have to rest on difficult choices, even if they are not the choices dictated by worn-out ideologies. A public philosophy for the twenty-first century will have to give more weight to the community than to the right of private decision. It will have to emphasize responsibilities rather than rights. It will have to find a better expression of the community than the welfare state. It will have to limit the scope of the market and the power of corporations without replacing them with a centralized state bureaucracy.

An abandonment of the old ideologies will not usher in a golden age of agreement. If we can surmount the false polarizations now generated by the politics of gender and race, we may find that the real divisions are still those of class. "Back to basics" could mean a return to class warfare (since it is precisely the basics that our elites reject as hopelessly outmoded) or at least to a politics in which class became the overriding issue. Needless to say, the elites that set the tone of American politics, even when they disagree about everything else, have a common stake in suppressing a politics of class. Much will depend on whether communitarians continue to acquiesce in this attempt to keep class issues out of politics or whether they will come to see that gross inequalities, as populists have always understood, are incompatible with any form of community that would now be recognized as desirable and that everything depends, therefore, on closing the gap between elites and the rest of the nation.

Part II

Democratic Discourse in Decline

S i x

Conversation and the
Civic Arts

I f elites speak only to themselves, one reason for this is the absence of institutions that promote general conversation across class lines. Civic life requires settings in which people meet as equals, without regard to race, class, or national origins. Thanks to the decay of civic institutions ranging from political parties to public parks and informal meeting places, conversation has become almost as specialized as the production of knowledge. Social classes speak to themselves in a dialect of their own, inaccessible to outsiders; they mingle with each other only on ceremonial occasions and official holidays. Parades and other such spectacles do not make up for the absence of informal gatherings. Even the pub and the coffee shop, which at first appear to have nothing to do with politics or the civic arts, make their contribution to the kind of wide-ranging, free-wheeling conversation on which democracy thrives, and now even they are threatened with extinction as neighborhood hangouts give way to shopping malls, fast-food chains, and takeouts. Our approach to eating and drinking is less and less mixed with ritual and ceremony. It has become strictly functional: We eat and drink on the run. Our fast-paced habits leave neither time nor—more important—places for good talk, even in cities the whole point of which, it might be argued, is to promote it.

Emerson, a writer not usually thought of as an admirer of cities, once called Paris the "social center of the world," adding that its "supreme merit" lay in its being the "city of conversation and cafés." More than most, Emerson appreciated the value of solitude, but he also recognized the "immense benefits" of sociability, "and the one event which never loses its romance," he noted in "Society and Solitude," was the "encounter with superior persons on terms allowing the happiest intercourse."

Jim Sleeper, author of *The Closest of Strangers: Liberalism and the Politics of Race in New York*, refers to city neighborhoods as the "crucibles of the civic culture." Neighborhood adults, Sleeper points out, become models for the young, exemplifying "roles which the urban market rewards only indirectly, if at all: nurturer, defender, uplifter, communicant, teammate, lover, friend." The encounter with superior persons, to use Emerson's phrase, gives us a glimpse of the great world beyond the immediate horizon of family and friends—a glimpse of "romance." If Sleeper is right, it also schools us in the virtues essential to civic life: loyalty, trust, accountability. It tempers romance with responsibility. It encourages us to make something of ourselves, to impose difficult demands on ourselves, and to appreciate the satisfactions conferred by devoted service to an ideal— as opposed to the satisfactions, say, of the marketplace and the street, which offer glitter without substance. Less showy but deeper and more durable satisfactions, according to Sleeper, can be found in many locales and many different kinds of activities, but "to an extent surely underestimated by the more cosmopolitan among us, New Yorkers of all ages find them at least partly in neighborhoods, at the local parish hall or synagogue, and in the nearby tavern, diner, community center or park."

Informal meeting places, which sustain the life of neighborhoods, are also the subject of a lively book by Ray Oldenburg, *The Great Good Place: Cafés, Coffee Shops, Community Centers, Beauty Parlors, General Stores, Bars, Hangouts and How They Get You through the Day*. An important attraction of informal hangouts—"third places," as Oldenburg calls them in order to distinguish them from large, highly structured organizations, on the one hand, and from families and other small groups, on the other—is the fact that "whatever hint of a hierarchy exists is predicated upon human decency" and not on wealth, glamour, aggression, or even intelligence. Reminding us of the Roman proverb that "nothing is more annoying than a low man raised to a high place," Oldenburg contrasts the informal society found in neighborhood hangouts with the hierarchy of the workplace, where Roman wisdom is not much in evidence. In the "great good place," on the other hand, "right prevails." It is an "invariable" rule, in Oldenburg's experience, that "the cream rises." Moreover, it spills over into the neighborhood as a whole; habits of decency acquired in the informal society of their peers are not forgotten when the regulars leave their favorite haunts.

> Promotion of decency in the third place is not limited to it. The regulars are not likely to do any of those things roundly disapproved at the coffee counter. Many items of proper and improper behavior are reviewed in the

countless hours and open agenda of rambling third place conversations. A dim view is taken of people who let their property become an eyesore, of the less-than-human breed who would litter a parking lot with a used paper diaper, of the ethical moron who would look for a pretext to sue somebody in pursuit of unearned and undeserved money, or of someone guilty of not meeting parental duties or responsibilities. One cannot long be a member of the inner circle without having acquired an additional conscience.

The inner voice that asks what the guys would think can serve as a powerful agency of what used to be called social control (when this term referred to self-imposed community sanctions rather than to the authority imposed by experts in behavior modification and other alien specialists). For this reason it is no exaggeration, Oldenburg thinks, to say that informal gathering places promote "more decency without proclaiming it than many organizations that publicly claim to be the embodiment of the virtues."

As these observations ought to suggest, it isn't because they "get you through the day" that third places are valuable but because taverns, coffeehouses, beer gardens, and pubs encourage conversation, the essence of civic life. Conversation is most likely to flourish, according to Oldenburg, in informal gathering places where people can talk without constraint, except for the constraints imposed by the art of conversation itself. Like Emerson, he believes that conversation is the city's raison d'être. Without good talk, cities become places precisely where the main concern is simply to "get through the day."

The home of good talk, then, is the third place—a meeting ground midway between the workplace and the family circle, between the "rat race" and the "womb." This designation calls to mind the familiar realm of voluntary associations, so dear to sociologists and to social critics influenced by the sociological tradition, which allegedly mediate between the individual and the state. As Oldenburg describes it, however, the "third place" sounds more like the poor man's public forum. It isn't exactly a "voluntary association"—that is, an association of those who come together in order to advance some common purpose. Nor is it a "life-style enclave," the term used by Robert Bellah and the other authors of *Habits of the Heart* to refer to informal associations based on shared tastes and personal inclination. You can expect to find a core of regulars at the third place, but you also meet casual acquaintances and complete strangers. Like the larger neighborhood it serves, the third place brings together people involuntarily united by the mere fact of physical proximity. "We may like some selected group better than the company of our neighbors," Mary Parker Follett once wrote, but "the satisfaction and contentment that come with sameness indicate a meager personality." The neighborhood, on the other hand, offers the "bracing effect of many different experiences and ideals." These differences, it might be argued, furnish the materials of lively conversation, as distinguished from mutual admiration and unchallenged agreement.

It is this admixture of involuntary association that gives the third place a quasi-political character. In this milieu, recognition has to be achieved through force of character instead of being conferred by your achievements, let alone by the size of your bank account. As Follett wisely observed in her book *The New State*, published in 1918 but still the best account of the neighborhood's political potential: "My neighbors may not think much of me because I paint pictures, knowing that my back yard is dirty, but my artist friends who like my color do not know or care about my back yard. My neighbors may feel no admiring awe of my scientific researches knowing that I am not the first in the house of a neighbor in trouble." The contrast between voluntary associations and the sociability of neighborhoods helps to explain why decency, as Oldenburg puts it, is more highly regarded in the third place than wealth or brilliant achievement, and decency, we might add, is the preeminent civic or political virtue. These considerations make it appropriate to argue that third-place sociability, in a modest way, encourages virtues more properly associated with political life than with the "civil society" made up of voluntary associations.

It encourages political virtues in other ways as well. It helps people to overcome some of their everyday inhibitions and reserve and to expand a little—to elaborate on the metaphorical implications of Oldenburg's spatial imagery—but it also deflates the balloon of pomposity and pretension. The consumption of alcoholic beverages and other stimulants that accompanies conversation in many third places helps the tongue-tied to find a voice, but conventions that discourage excessive drinking keep verbal exuberance in bounds. Wit and verbal invention are much in demand, as long as they do not slide over into long-winded oratory or histrionics. Conversation is "less inhibited and more eagerly pursued," "more dramatic," and more often attended by laughter or verbal pyrotechnics. Because those who frequent such places "expect more of conversation," however, they have less patience than usual with those who "abuse it, whether by killing a topic with inappropriate remarks or by talking more than their share of the time."

It is easy to see why third places, historically, have been the natural haunts of pamphleteers, agitators, politicos, newspapermen, revolutionaries, and other verbal types. Before the rise of modern journalism, taverns and coffeehouses (often located on turnpikes or major crossroads) also served as media in their own right, places where news was gathered and circulated. In totalitarian countries they have retained this function to the present day. This history makes it doubly appropriate to emphasize the protopolitical character of the third place and to speculate—even if Oldenburg doesn't—that the decline of participatory democracy may be directly related to the disappearance of third places. As neighborhood hangouts give way to suburban shopping malls, or, on the other hand, to private cocktail parties, the essentially political art of conversation is replaced by shoptalk or personal gossip. Increasingly, conversation literally has no place in American society. In its absence, how—or, better, *where*—can political habits be acquired and polished?

The third place, Oldenburg argues, re-creates some of the best features of small-town life in the big city. Taking issue with those who see the small town as hopelessly insular, he praises its ability to amuse itself, its gregarious habits, and its capacity to provide a window on the wider world. He quotes from a letter written to him by a woman who grew up in a small Ohio town during the Depression and who credits "all those conversations overheard at the drugstore" with supplying her a growing awareness that "the world was much wider than Barkerton, Ohio." She suspects that eavesdropping as a child gave her a "lifetime interest in politics, economics, and philosophy (none of which were part of the world of home), but which were the core" of small-town sociability.

If the small town and its urban extension, the neighborhood, nurture an "interest in people and their infinite capacity to amuse and enlighten one another," as Oldenburg puts it, the same thing cannot plausibly be said of the shopping mall, even though it is often touted as a new

version of Main Street. Those who claim that malls promote a new sense of community "skate freely on the brink
of total nonsense," Oldenburg insists. Malls are populated
by transients and serve corporations, not the community.
A local Chamber of Commerce makes no bones about the
mall's purpose: It "welcomes shoppers, not loafers." Bars
and restaurants are designed for high volume and rapid
turnover. A paucity of benches discourages loitering. Background music takes the place of conversation. Oldenburg
calls comparisons with Main Street "ridiculous"; Main
Street offers a "cast of characters," the shopping mall a
"drifting amalgam of nonpersons."

The case for the suburban way of life as opposed to the
small town or the old-style city neighborhood cannot very
well rest on the claim that it promotes a sense of community. It has to rest on a *critique* of community—on the claim
that small towns and city neighborhoods are narrow, ethno-
centric, suspicious of outsiders, and intolerant of "difference" (the supposed celebration of which has become the
hallmark of academic "postmodernism"). Mary Parker Follett reported that when she tried to extol the advantages of
neighborhoods, those who disagreed would "at once
become violent on the subject."

I have never understood why it inflames them more easily than other topics. They immediately take it for
granted that I am proposing to shut them up tight in their
neighborhoods and seal them hermetically; they assume
that I mean to substitute the neighborhood for every
other contact. They tell me of the pettiness of neighborhood life, and I have to listen to stories of neighborhood
iniquities ranging from small gossip to determined boy-
cotting. Intolerance and narrowness thrive in the neighborhood group, they say; in the wider group they do not.

The strongest objection to the neighborhood, these days, is that it oppresses women. Oldenburg's third place turns out to be an all-male institution, for the most part, and this fact alone is enough to condemn it in the eyes of those who regard any form of sexual segregation (except, of course, for the self-segregation of emancipated women) as incompatible with sexual equality. Oldenburg does not flinch from this objection. He concedes "men's dominance of the third place tradition," but he argues that women used to have other meeting places of their own and that sexual segregation, moreover, served useful purposes. For one thing, it prevented men and women from investing all their emotional expectations in marriage. Oldenburg argues that it was a new and "basically flawed" ideal of marital intimacy, not the women's movement, that undermined single-sex sociability. Like the shopping mall, marital "togetherness" was an essentially suburban invention, which led people to seek all their emotional satisfactions in private, leaving the public square to the single-minded pursuit of profitable exchange. Although Oldenburg minimizes women's long-standing opposition to all-male sociability, I think he is right in linking this opposition to an ideal of intimacy that loaded marriage (as many other observers have noted) with more emotional weight than it could bear.

He is also right in his contention that the decline of sexual segregation has coincided with the rise of a more insidious form of segregation by age. The tavern, he points out, used to be an "important agency linking the generations and encouraging a young man to set aside the lesser habits of adolescence." The corner drugstore, as his Ohio correspondent reminds us, could serve young people in the same way. In general, young people used to be more actively involved in the adult world than they are now. They had more opportunities to observe adults in unguarded moments. Today it is the young who are professionally observed by an army of well-meaning adults, in settings deliberately set aside for pedagogical purposes. As a result, children and adolescents have less opportunity to improvise a social life of their own and to appropriate adult territory for their own use.* Oldenburg points out that the suburban environment (which now includes the city as well, except for the deteriorating areas at its core) is not susceptible to "user modification" by the young, who spend much of their time, accordingly, in supervised activities confined to places designated for the exclusive use of young people. The organization of childhood by adults has to be seen as another chapter in the decline of the third place and the corresponding rise of "that powerful dissolving agent known as the American way of life."

The most characteristic feature of this way of life, if we consider it from the point of view of changing patterns of sociability, is the substitution of choice and personal preference for involuntary and therefore somewhat haphazard, promiscuous, and unpredictable types of informal association. This is the common element in the breakdown of sexual segregation and the increase in age-group segregation. The networks formed by adults who share the same interests and tastes include both men and women, but they necessarily exclude the young. Networks, as Oldenburg points out, "are . . . anti-child." They are also "elitist," since most of them presuppose plenty of money and education, not to mention private transportation. They are designed, more-

---

*Boys used to learn the rudiments of baseball on the city streets, in vacant lots, or in country meadows far from the presence of adults. They organized their own games on the spur of the moment. Sticks and bottle caps served in the absence of more refined equipment. Today the Little League has organized everything down to the last detail.

over, to shield people from the "neighbors fate has put next door and across the way."

The attraction of personal networks, which depends on the equation of freedom with personal choice, remains today what it was in the time of Mary Parker Follett. Oldenburg's capsule description of the ideal embodied in the "American way of life" sounds just like her friends' sophisticated objections to neighborhoods.

> Each of us has his or her own personal community [as Oldenburg summarizes the "American" ideal], and its apologists make the network sound like an advanced form of society rather than an artifact of atomization. Those who have networks, we are told, are cosmopolitan. Their interests and relationships transcend the local neighborhood. The "networker" is "liberated" from local gossip and prejudice and is "free" to choose his or her friends on more rational and more personal bases than that of mere geographical proximity.

In 1994, as in 1918, the contention that the neighborhood is more truly cosmopolitan than the superficial cosmopolitanism of the like-minded falls on deaf ears.

The point Oldenburg wants to make about third places can be made most simply by setting them beside an antithetical institution, the private club. Clubs, as he reminds us, are exclusive, snobbish, and zealous in their guardianship of social privilege. They are "polar opposites" of neighborhood gathering places, and it tells us something about the social and political implications of "post-modernist bourgeois liberalism," as Richard Rorty calls it in his well-known essay of that name, that it takes the club, not the third place, as its model of sociability. A "civil society of the bourgeois democratic sort," which Rorty defends as the best hope for a new "world order," resembles a "bazaar surrounded by lots and lots of exclusive private clubs." A world in which ethnic and racial isolation is breaking down, in which diverse nationalities are thrown together in conglomerations that are unavoidably multicultural and multiracial, cannot be held together by common culture, according to Rorty; but a well-ordered bazaar presupposes nothing, after all, in the way of common beliefs or shared values. It presupposes nothing more than acceptance of a few procedural rules. Conflicting values and beliefs do not prevent those who do business there from "haggling profitably away." If they yearn for the company of people who share their own outlook on life, they can "retreat" to their clubs "after a hard day's haggling."

Rorty's ideal world comes close to describing the world as it actually exists, at least in the United States, and many Americans are ready to accept it, I suppose, as the best that can be hoped for. Oldenburg's book helps to identify what is missing from such a world: urban amenities, conviviality, conversation, politics—almost everything, in short, that makes life worth living. When the market preempts all the public space, and sociability has to "retreat" into private clubs, people are in danger of losing the capacity to amuse and even to govern themselves. As long as they recognize the danger, however, it is still possible to hope that they will find a way to reverse the suburban trend of our civilization and to restore the civic arts to their rightful place at the center of things.

Seven

Racial Politics in New York

The Attack on Common Standards

The glory of New York, according to Jim Sleeper, lies in its "integration of proletarian strength with professional excellence and high cultural achievement"—precisely the integration that is breaking down, as we have seen, in city after city and will break down in New York as well, if current trends continue unabated. It is because he has come to know and love the city so well, as a reporter and columnist successively for the *Brooklyn Phoenix*, the *North Brooklyn Mercury*, *New York Newsday*, and the *New York Daily News*, that Sleeper's unsparing account of its decline, *The Closest of Strangers: Liberalism and the Politics of Race in New York*, carries so much conviction. It did not take him long to discover, when he moved to New York from his native Boston in 1977, that New York, like other great cities of the world, is a city of "walkers" and "readers." Its array of civic institutions—public transit, schools (including a city-wide university system), hospitals, libraries, parks, museums—makes "intellectual development possible without the sums of money usually needed to cross the threshold of higher education." Such institutions provide larger numbers of New Yorkers with "more than a leg up the ladder of personal advancement." They link "the poor city-dweller's personal upward mobility to a broader cosmopolitan purpose."* Unlike those neoconservatives who preach self-help to minorities, Sleeper wants us to see that opportunity is dependent on a vigorous public sector and that public institutions, moreover, can shape the very structure of ambition. New York's cultural institutions

---

*Many of the city's cultural institutions were designed, in the nineteenth century, with just this result in mind. Henry Tappan, among others, advocated the establishment of a metropolitan university that would incorporate the Astor Library, the Cooper Union, and other scientific and literary societies "into a harmonious whole," in his words. His object, he said, was to educate the public in general, not to encourage professional specialization. Professors would be "required to give popular courses to the public" in addition to lectures in their special field. "The libraries, cabinets, laboratories, and lecture rooms of the University would become the resort of students of every grade; it would thus become the great centre of intellectual activity" in the city. Alexander Dallas Bache advanced a similar conception of a "great university of the arts and sciences, in which the practical man may meet on equal terms with the scholar." Bache's university would bring together "men of progress, scholars, practical men, mechanics, artists."

By the end of the nineteenth century, as Thomas Bender explains, these ambitious designs for a civic culture had given way to a new model of learning organized around specialized disciplines and professionalism. The original vision did not altogether disappear, however; something of it survived in a different form and in the very different institutional context of the little magazines—*Seven Arts*, the *Nation*, the *New Republic*, *Menorah Journal*, *Commentary*, *Partisan Review*, *Politics*, *Dissent*—that made New York the nation's cultural capital throughout the first half of the twentieth century.

direct ambition not to the conventional goals of money and suburban exile but to the kind of intelligent awareness of their surroundings that is the hallmark (or used to be) of native New Yorkers—a knowledgeable, fast-talking, contentious lot.

Civic institutions link neighborhoods, based on ethnic and familial ties and highly parochial as a result, to the impersonal culture of the larger world. To say that neighborhoods play an invaluable part in forming civic virtue does not imply glorification of neighborhood life as an end in itself. Neighborhoods provide shelter from the anonymity of the market, but they also prepare young people for participation in a civic culture that reaches far beyond the neighborhood. A stable neighborhood where the priest, the teacher, the basketball coach, the corner grocer, and the policeman are clearly visible as models of adult authority can teach lessons that will prove invaluable in the larger world beyond the neighborhood. Sleeper's summary of these lessons stresses personal responsibility and respect for others—the qualities essential to civic life, in other words, not necessarily the qualities that bring commercial success and professional advancement: "Don't drop out of school unless you've got a steady job; don't parent offspring until you can support them; treat other people and their property with respect."

Insularity and cosmopolitanism: the tension between them is the story of urban life. Irving Howe, Alfred Kazin, and many other autobiographers have evoked both the rich background of New York's insular communities and the break with the old neighborhood, at once painful and exhilarating, that enabled ambitious young people to make themselves at home in the international republic of letters. To reduce this complex narrative to the conventional saga of upward mobility, as Norman Podhoretz has in *Making*

It, is to simplify it almost beyond recognition. The break is not irrevocable unless the object is conceived simply as success in the crudest sense of the term. Finding the world implies, above all, finding oneself through an imaginative return to one's roots, not losing oneself in the struggle to succeed or to acquire the cultural distinctions that go with material success. It is a common mistake to think that exposure to the world's culture necessarily leads to the loss or renunciation of one's particular subculture. Except for those whose only aim is complete assimilation—the ostentatious display of all the cultural trappings of one's power and status—moving beyond one's parochial identity leads to a more complex, even to a painfully divided identity. The creative tension between the neighborhood and the city, in the case of New York between the subcultures peculiar to its many nationalities and the world culture embodied in its civic institutions, has always been the source of the vitality peculiar to urban life.

In the past efforts to relax this tension—which can easily become almost unbearable for individuals torn between two cultures and which, in any case, is easier to grasp in its negative than in its positive dimension—have usually taken one of two forms. Condemnation of particularism, in the name of "Americanism" or some other form of cultural conformity, invited an embattled defense of particularism that verged on racial and ethnic separatism. In the black community the long-standing conflict between nationalist and integrationist strategies obscured the way in which both strategies worked to resist a more complex understanding of black identity. Nationalists held that black people would never be accepted as Americans and should think of themselves as African exiles, while integrationists envisioned assimilation into the mainstream as the logical consequence of political equality. Neither program captured the "twoness" of Afro-American experience, as W. E. B. Du Bois called it: the divided loyalty that was painful, unavoidable, yet promising as well, if it contributed to a new definition of Americanism that reflected particularism without denying the need for a common American culture.

Neither black nationalism nor integration retains much of a following today. These positions may have been one-sided, but at least they had a certain consistency and coherence. Each addressed one side of a complex reality. Integration rested on the understanding that the color of one's skin is irrelevant to a whole range of human pursuits—to building bridges, say, or to running a business or discharging the obligations of citizenship. Black nationalism, on the other hand, took account of the dense historical background that made it impossible simply to discount the importance of race. As long as these positions confronted each other in a clearly defined opposition, it was possible to see why each was incomplete and to hope for a synthesis that would do justice to both sides of the black experience. The civil rights movement of the fifties and early sixties, unfairly dismissed by nationalist critics as purely integrationist, in fact anticipated the elements of such a synthesis.

THE COLLAPSE OF the civil rights movement has left a confused and more deeply discouraging situation in which the merits of black nationalism and integration alike have disappeared in clouds of racial rhetoric. On the one hand, champions of "cultural diversity" have carried the nationalist argument to the extreme of denying any universal or transracial values at all. It is no longer a matter of asserting (in the manner, say, of Marcus Garvey or Malcolm X) that blacks have nothing to gain from integration into a corrupt society, a society that refuses to practice what it preaches.

Now it is Western culture as a whole, Western rationalism as such, the very notion of a common tradition or a common civic language or a set of common standards, that is said to be necessarily and unavoidably racist. On the other hand, this extreme form of rhetorical particularism, which has come to dominate discussions of the race question, has grown up side by side with a relentless assault on neighborhoods, which deprives cultural particularism of the only material conditions in which it can be expected to flourish. The "new tribalism," which finds favor not only among postmodernist academics but in the media, in the world of commercial entertainment, and in the cultural boutiques and salons frequented by yuppies, appears on the scene at the very moment when tribalism has ceased to have any substantive content. "Tribalism" is the latest fashion thrown up by a consumerist capitalism that is rapidly replacing neighborhoods with shopping malls, thereby undermining the very particularism it eagerly packages as a commodity.

"Some New Yorkers," Sleeper notes, "seem not to want neighborhoods at all." The business and professional classes, for the most part, make up a restless, transient population that has a home—if it can be said to have a home at all—in national and international organizations based on esoteric expertise and dominated by the ethic of competitive achievement. From the professional and managerial point of view, neighborhoods are places in which the unenterprising are left behind—backwaters of failure and cultural stagnation.

Political battles over open housing and school desegregation have exposed neighborhoods to additional criticism on the grounds that they breed racial exclusiveness and intolerance. From the mid-sixties on, the racial policies favored by liberals have sought to break up the black ghetto, another kind of undesirable neighborhood, at the expense of other ethnic "enclaves" that allegedly perpetuate racial prejudice. The goal of liberal policy, in effect, is to remake the city in the image of the affluent, mobile elites that see it as a place merely to work and play, not as a place to put down roots, to raise children, to live and die.

Racial integration might have been conceived as a policy designed to give everyone equal access to a common civic culture. Instead it has come to be conceived largely as a strategy for assuring educational mobility. Integrated schools, as the Supreme Court explained in the *Brown* decision, would overcome the psychological damage inflicted by segregation and make it possible for black people to compete for careers open to talent. The misplaced emphasis on professional careers, as opposed to jobs and participation in a common culture, helps to explain the curious coexistence, in the postsixties politics of race, of a virulent form of cultural particularism (according to which, for example, black children should read only black writers and thus escape exposure to "cultural imperialism") with strategies having the practical effect of undermining particularism in its concrete expression in neighborhoods.

In the forties and fifties, according to Sleeper, liberals took for granted a "social order cohesive and self-confident enough to admit blacks" on its own terms. There was a great deal of racial tension and injustice, but there was also a considerable reservoir of goodwill on both sides. White ethnics, Sleeper thinks, were still "up for grabs." Uneasy about black migration into their neighborhoods, they were nevertheless committed to principles of fair play. (Even today, Sleeper observes, "the city's beleaguered white ethnics know that . . . it isn't really minorities they're losing out to; there are the eternal rich and a new managerial elite that, in an exquisite irony, includes radicals who tormented them in the sixties and then cleaned themselves up in the eighties to claim their class prerogatives.") Those who feared or resented black people found themselves disarmed by the moral heroism, self-discipline, and patriotism of the civil rights movement. Participants in the movement, by their willingness to go to jail when they broke the law, proved the depth of their loyalty to the country whose racial etiquette they refused to accept. The movement validated black people's claim to be better Americans than those who defended segregation as the American way. By demanding that the nation live up to its promise, they appealed to a common standard of justice and to a basic sense of decency that transcended racial lines.

The social engineering initiated in the mid-sixties, on the other hand, led to a rapid deterioration of race relations. Busing, affirmative action, and open housing threatened the ethnic solidarity of neighborhoods and drove lower-middle-class whites into opposition. In the face of their resistance, liberals "reacted with self-righteous indignation," in Sleeper's words. Black militants encouraged racial polarization and demanded a new politics of "collective grievance and entitlement." They insisted that black people, as victims of "white racism," could not be held to the same educational or civic standards as whites. Such standards were themselves racist, having no other purpose than to keep blacks in their place. The white left, which romanticized Afro-American culture as an expressive, sexually liberated way of life free of bourgeois inhibitions, collaborated in this attack on common standards. The civil rights movement originated as an attack on the injustice of double standards; now the idea of a single standard was itself attacked as the crowning example of "institutional racism."

Just how far professional black militants, together with their liberal and left admirers, have retreated from any con-

ception of common standards—even from any residual conception of truth—is illustrated by the Brawley fiasco. When
the "rape" of Tawana Brawley, proclaimed by Al Sharpton
and Alton Maddox as a typical case of white oppression,
was exposed as a hoax, the anthropologist Stanley Diamond
argued in the *Nation* that "it doesn't matter whether the
crime occurred or not." Even if the incident was staged by
"black actors," it was staged with "skill and controlled hys-
teria" and described what "actually happens to too many
black women." William Kunstler took the same predictable
line: "It makes no difference anymore whether the attack
on Tawana really happened. . . . [It] doesn't disguise the
fact that a lot of young black women are treated the way she
said she was treated." It was to the credit of black militants,
Kunstler added, that they "now have an issue with which
they can grab the headlines and launch a vigorous attack on
the criminal justice system."

It is (or ought to be) a sobering experience to contemplate
the effects of a campaign against "racism" that turns
increasingly on attempts to manipulate the media—politics
as racial theater. While Sharpton and Maddox "grab the
headlines," living conditions for most of the black people in
New York continue to decline. Affirmative action gives
black elites access to the municipal bureaucracy and the
media but leaves the masses worse off than ever. It is bad
enough, Sleeper points out, that "one's surname or skin
color becomes by itself a means of advancement"—a policy
that "undermines the classic liberal American ideal in
which individuals are held significantly responsible for
their fates and rewarded according to their performance."
What is even worse is that most blacks do not advance at all
and that they are held back by the very militance that is
supposed to set them free. Black-culture strategies reinforce
the defensive solidarity of black students against academic

overachievers, accused of "acting white." They excuse academic failure on the grounds that black students should not have to master a "Eurocentric" curriculum. They use victimization as an excuse for every kind of failure and thereby perpetuate one of the deepest sources of failure: the victim's difficulty in gaining self-respect.

It is not surprising, under these circumstances, that young people in the black ghetto, young men in particular, are obsessed with respect or that an affront to one's honor— "dissing," the open display of contempt or "disrespect"—is thought to justify violent retaliation. When self-respect is hard to come by, it is tempting to confuse it with the capacity to inspire fear. The criminal subculture of the ghetto serves not only as a substitute for social mobility, easy money (even with all its attendant risks) providing an attractive alternative to dead-end jobs, but also as a proving ground on which to win the respect that is so difficult to achieve by legal means. The retrospective canonization of Malcolm X can be understood as a politicized version of this misplaced preoccupation with violence, intimidation, and self-respect. Thanks to Spike Lee, Malcolm is now seen as a leader who promised, in effect, to restore his people's self-respect "by any means necessary"—that is, by means of racial intimidation. Martin Luther King, on the other hand, is condemned by ghetto youth as an Uncle Tom; his insistence that the civil rights movement needed precisely to allay white fears, not to intensify them, has become utterly incomprehensible—for eminently comprehensible reasons—to those who can no longer distinguish between fear and respect.

MEANWHILE, THE URBAN economy continues to deteriorate. The flight of industry creates a vacuum that is only partially filled by finance, communications, tourism, and entertainment. The new industries do not provide jobs for the unemployed. New York needs a tax base and full employment; instead it gets words and symbols and lots of restaurants. The new industries encourage a self-absorbed, hedonistic way of life, one deeply at odds with the way of life promoted by family-centered neighborhoods. Real estate speculation—an industry, as Sleeper points out, that "is to New York City what big oil has been to Houston"— is equally subversive of an older way of life, since neighborhood turnover is more profitable than neighborhood stability. Speculators let buildings run down and then collect insurance when they go up in flames. The real estate industry spreads the word that a given neighborhood is on the rise or going down, thus "creating self-fulfilling prophecies of neighborhood improvement or decay."

Sleeper, to his credit, is simply not interested in parceling out praise and blame. As long as debate remains stuck at that level, it can only go around in circles. He is interested in understanding what makes a city work and how a city can fall apart. When he insists that a city as complicated as New York cannot be neatly divided into two camps, "oppressed people of color and unthinking white oppressors," his intention is not to deny the reality of white oppression but to show that it cannot be corrected by breast-beating, radical posturing, and political theatrics. When he advocates a "transracial" politics, he does not speak as a supporter of the socioeconomic status quo. On the contrary, the question raised by David Dinkins's election as mayor, according to Sleeper, is precisely whether a transracial politics can avoid the pitfall of establishment politics. (In Dinkins's case, the answer seems to have been that it can't.)

What New York needs, Sleeper argues, is a politics that

will emphasize class divisions instead of racial ones, addressing the "real problem, which is poverty, and the real need, which is jobs." Working people have a common stake in liberating the city from the parasitic interests and industries that now control it. To be sure, they also have a common stake in "upholding standards of personal accountability, public honesty, and trust." A commitment to common standards is a necessary ingredient in any interracial coalition. But a populist coalition of the kind Sleeper has in mind has to include a commitment to egalitarian economic reforms, to a frontal assault on corporate power and privilege. Instead of a politics of radical gestures, Sleeper offers a substantive radicalism that would lead to real and not merely rhetorical changes—always an unwelcome prospect for those (including many self-styled radicals and cultural revolutionaries) with a heavy investment in the existing arrangements.

Eight

The Common Schools

*Horace Mann and
the Assault on Imagination*

I f we cast a cold eye over the wreckage of the school
system in America, we may find it hard to avoid the
impression that something went radically wrong at
some point, and it is not surprising, therefore, that so many
critics of the system have turned to the past in the hope of
explaining just when things went wrong and how they
might be set to rights.* The critics of the fifties traced the

---

* All the quotations in this chapter, except the ones from Adam Smith
and Orestes Brownson, come from the long reports Mann submitted to
the Massachusetts legislature as secretary of the Board of Education. The
page references cited in the text are from the *Annual Report of the Board of
Education, together with the Annual Report of the Secretary of the Board* (Boston: Dutton and Wentworth, 1838–1848), in twelve volumes. Smith's
reflections on the demoralizing effects of commerce appear in *The Wealth
of Nations*, Book V, chapter 1 ("incapable either of defending or of revenging himself"), and *The Theory of Moral Sentiments*, ed. D. D. Raphael

and A. L. Macfie (Oxford: Clarendon Press, 1976), pp. 146 ("great school of self-command"), 152–53 ("war and faction"), 205 ("general security and happiness"). Brownson's attack on Mann appeared in the *Boston Quarterly Review* 2 (1839): 394 ("educated in the streets"), 404 ("a faith, which embraces generalities only"; "much in general, nothing in particular"), 411 ("respect and preserve what is"; "licentiousness of the people"; "love of liberty"), 434 ("free action of mind on mind").

Jonathan Messerli, *Horace Mann* (New York: Alfred A. Knopf, 1972) is the standard biography. Discussions of Mann's educational ideas and program appear in Merle Curti, *The Social Ideas of American Educators* (New York: Scribner's, 1935); Rush Welter, *Popular Education and Democratic Thought in America* (New York: Columbia University Press, 1962); David Tyack and Elizabeth Hansot, *Managers of Virtue: Public School Leadership in America, 1820–1980* (New York: Basic Books, 1982); Maxine Green, *The Public School and the Private Vision* (New York: Random House, 1965); Carl F. Kaestle, *Pillars of the Republic: Common Schools and American Society, 1780–1860* (New York: Hill and Wang, 1983); R. Freeman Butts, *Public Education in the United States* (New York: Holt, Rinehart, and Winston, 1978); and many other books on American education. See also Maris A. Vinovskis, "Horace Mann on the Economic Productivity of Education," *New England Quarterly* 43 (1970): 550–71; Barbara Finkelstein, "Perfecting Childhood: Horace Mann and the Origins of Public Education in the United States," *Biography* 13/1 (1990): 6–20; and Lawrence Cremin's introduction to his collection of Mann's writings, *The Republic and the School: Horace Mann on the Education of Free Men* (New York: Teachers College Press, 1959). The historical scholarship of the fifties, which deplored the influence of progressive dogma on American education, is best exemplified by Arthur Bestor, *The Restoration of Learning* (New York: Alfred A. Knopf, 1955). Revisionist works of the sixties and seventies, which saw the school system essentially as an agency for the imposition of industrial work discipline, middle-class morals, and political conformity, include Raymond E. Callahan, *Education and the Cult of Efficiency* (Chicago: University of Chicago Press, 1962); Michael J. Katz, *The Irony of Early School Reform* (Cambridge: Harvard University Press, 1968), and *Class, Bureaucracy, and Schools* (New York: Praeger, 1971); Robert H. Wiebe, "The Social Functions of Public Education," *American Quarterly* 21 (1969): 147–64; Raymond A. Mohl, "Education as Social Control in New York City, 1784–1825," *New York History* 51 (1970): 219–37; Ivan Illich, *Deschooling Society* (New York: Harper & Row, trouble to progressive ideologies, which allegedly made things too easy for the child and drained the curriculum of its intellectual rigor. In the sixties a wave of revisionist historians insisted that the school system had come to serve as a "sorting machine," in Joel Spring's phrase, a device for allocating social privileges that reinforced class divisions while ostensibly promoting equality. Some of these revisionists went so far as to argue that the common school system was distorted from the outset by the requirements of the emerging industrial order, which made it almost inevitable that the schools would be used not to train an alert, politically active body of citizens but to inculcate habits of punctuality and obedience.

There is a good deal to be learned from the debates that took place in the formative period of the school system, the 1830s and 1840s, but an analysis of those debates will not

---

1971); Joel H. Spring, *Education and the Rise of the Corporate State* (Boston: Beacon Press, 1972), and *The Sorting Machine* (New York: David McKay, 1976); Colin Greer, *The Great School Legend* (New York: Basic Books, 1972); and Clarence J. Karier, *The Individual, Society, and Education* (Urbana: University of Illinois Press, 1986). Not all these studies deal specifically with Mann, and those that do by no means refuse to credit him with any good intentions at all. Taken together, however, they leave the impression that school reform, like other reform movements, owed less to humanitarian or democratic considerations than to a pervasive, almost obsessive concern with social order and industrial productivity. The usual reply to this kind of interpretation—that humanitarian considerations were more important after all—does nothing to challenge the existing terms of debate. For this type of argument, see Lawrence Frederick Kohl, "The Concept of Social Control and the History of Jacksonian America," *Journal of the Early Republic* 5 (1985): 21–34; David Rothman, "Social Control: The Uses and Abuses of the Concept in the History of Incarceration," *Rice University Studies* 67 (1981): 9–20; and Thomas L. Haskell, "Capitalism and the Origins of the Humanitarian Sensibility," *American Historical Review* 90 (1985): 339–61, 547–66.

support any such one-dimensional interpretation of the school's function as an agency of "social control." I do not see how anyone who reads the writings of Horace Mann, which did so much to justify a system of common schools and to persuade Americans to pay for it, can miss the moral fervor and democratic idealism that informed Mann's program. It is true that Mann resorted to a variety of arguments in favor of common schools, including the argument that they would teach steady habits of work. But he insisted that steady habits would benefit workers as well as employers, citing in favor of this contention the higher wages earned by those who enjoyed the advantages of a good education. He was careful to point out, moreover, that a positive assessment of the effects of schooling on men's "worldly fortunes or estates" was far from the "highest" argument in favor of education. Indeed, it might "justly be regarded as the lowest" (V:81). More important arguments for education, in Mann's view, were the "diffusion of useful knowledge," the promotion of tolerance, the equalization of opportunity, the "augmentation of national resources," the eradication of poverty, the overcoming of "mental imbecility and torpor," the encouragement of light and learning in place of "superstition and ignorance," and the substitution of peaceful methods of governance for coercion and warfare (IV:10; V:68, 81, 101, 109; VII:187). If Mann pretty clearly preferred the high ground of moral principle to the lower ground of industrial expediency, he could still appeal to prudential motives with a good conscience, since he did not perceive a contradiction between them. Comforts and conveniences were good things in themselves, even if there were loftier goods to aim at. His vision of "improvement" was broad enough to embrace material as well as moral progress; it was precisely their compatibility, indeed their inseparability, that distinguished Mann's version of the idea of progress from those that merely celebrated the wonders of modern science and technology.

As a child of the Enlightenment, Mann yielded to no one in his admiration for science and technology, but he was also a product of New England Puritanism, even though he came to reject Puritan theology. He was too keenly aware of the moral burden Americans inherited from their seventeenth-century ancestors to see a higher standard of living as an end in itself or to join those who equated the promise of American life with the opportunity to get rich quick. He did not look kindly on the project of getting enormously rich even in the long run. He deplored extremes of wealth and poverty—the "European theory" of social organization, as he called it—and upheld the "Massachusetts theory," which stressed "equality of condition" and "human welfare" (XII:55). It was to escape "extremes of high and low," Mann believed, that Americans had "fled" Europe in the first place, and the reemergence of those extremes, in nineteenth-century New England, should have been a source of deepest shame to his countrymen (VII:188, 191). When Mann dwelled on the accomplishments of his ancestors, it was with the intention of holding Americans to a higher standard of civic obligation than the standard prevailing in other countries. His frequent appeals to the "heroic period of our country's history" did not issue from a "boastful or vain-glorious spirit," he said. An appreciation of America's mission brought "more humiliation than pride" (VII:195). America should have "stood as a shining mark and exemplar before the world," instead of which it was lapsing into materialism and moral indifference (VII:196).

It is quite pointless to ask whether reformers like Horace Mann were more interested in humanitarianism than in work discipline and "social control." A good deal of fruitless debate among historians has been devoted to this question. Mann was not a radical, and he was undeniably interested in social order, but that does not make him any less a humanitarian. He was genuinely moved by the spectacle of poverty and suffering, though he also feared that poverty and suffering would breed "agrarianism," as he and his contemporaries called it—the "revenge of poverty against wealth" (XII:60). When he preached the duty to "bring forward those unfortunate classes of the people, who, in the march of civilization, have been left in the rear," there is no reason to think that he was concerned only with the danger of social revolution (XII:135). He defended property rights, to be sure, but he denied that property rights were "absolute and unqualified" (X:115). The earth was given to mankind "for the subsistence and benefit of the whole race," and the "rights of successive owners" were "limited by the rights of those who are entitled to the subsequent possession and use" (X:114–15). Every generation had an obligation to improve its inheritance and to pass it on to the next. "The successive generations of men, taken collectively, constitute one great commonwealth" (X:127). The doctrine of absolute property rights, which denied the solidarity of mankind, was a morality for "hermits" (X:120). In Mann's view, the "successive holders" of property were "trustees, bound to the faithful execution of their trust, by the most sacred obligations" (X:127). If they defaulted on those obligations, they could expect "terrible retributions" in the form of "poverty and destitution," "violence and misrule," "licentiousness and debauchery," "political profligacy and legalized perfidy" (X:126). Here Mann was truly prophetic, in the strict sense of the term. He called his people to account, pointing out that they had inherited a demanding set of obligations to live up to and foretelling the "certain vengeance of Heaven" if they failed (X:126). He was a prophet in the vulgar sense as well: His predictions have come true—his predictions, that is, of the specific evils that would follow from a failure to provide a system of education assuring "knowledge and virtue," the necessary foundations of a republican form of government (XII:142). Who can look at America today without recognizing the accuracy of Mann's cautionary rhetoric, right down to the "legalized perfidy" of our political leaders? The only thing Mann failed to foresee was the drug epidemic, though that could be included, I suppose, under the heading of "licentiousness and debauchery."

Yet Mann's efforts on behalf of the common schools bore spectacular success, if we consider the long-term goals (and even the immediate goals) he was attempting to promote. His countrymen heeded his exhortations after all. They built a system of common schools attended by all classes of society. They rejected the European model, which provided a liberal education for the children of privilege and vocational training for the masses. They abolished child labor and made school attendance compulsory, as Mann had urged. They enforced a strict separation between church and state, protecting the schools from sectarian influences. They recognized the need for professional training of teachers, and they set up a system of normal schools to bring about this result. They followed Mann's advice to provide instruction not only in academic subjects but in the "laws of health," vocal music, and other character-forming disciplines (VI:61, 66). They even followed his advice to staff the schools largely with women, sharing his belief that women were more likely than men to govern their pupils by the gentle art of persuasion. They honored Mann himself, even during his lifetime, as the founding father of their schools. If Mann was a prophet in some respects, he was hardly a prophet without honor in his own country. He succeeded beyond the wildest dreams of most reformers, yet the result was the same as if he had failed.

Here is our puzzle, then: Why did the success of Mann's program leave us with the social and political disasters he predicted, with uncanny accuracy, in the event of his failure? To put the question this way suggests that there was something inherently deficient in Mann's educational vision, that his program contained some fatal flaw in its very conception. The flaw did not lie in Mann's enthusiasm for "social control" or his halfhearted humanitarianism. The history of reform—with its high sense of mission, its devotion to progress and improvement, its enthusiasm for economic growth and equal opportunity, its humanitarianism, its love of peace and its hatred of war, its confidence in the welfare state, and, above all, its zeal for education— is the history of liberalism, not conservatism, and if the reform movement gave us a society that bears little resemblance to what was promised, we have to ask not whether the reform movement was insufficiently liberal and humanitarian but whether liberal humanitarianism provides the best recipe for a democratic society.

We get a little insight into Mann's limitations by considering his powerful aversion to war—superficially one of the more attractive elements of his outlook. Deeply committed to the proposition that a renunciation of war and warlike habits provided an infallible index of social progress, of the victory of civilization over barbarism, Mann complained that school and town libraries were full of history books glorifying war.

> How little do these books contain, which is suitable for children! . . . Descriptions of battles, sackings of cities, and the captivity of nations, follow each other with the quickest movement, and in an endless succession. Almost the only glimpses, which we catch of the educa-

tion of youth, present them, as engaged in martial sports, and the mimic feats of arms, preparatory to the grand tragedies of battle;—exercises and exhibitions, which, both in the performer and the spectator, cultivate all the dissocial emotions, and turn the whole current of the mental forces into the channel of destructiveness [III:58].

Mann called himself a republican (in order to signify his opposition to monarchy), but he had no appreciation of the connection between martial virtue and citizenship, which had received so much attention in the republican tradition. Even Adam Smith, whose liberal economics dealt that tradition a crippling blow, regretted the loss of armed civic virtue. "A man, incapable either of defending or of revenging himself, evidently wants one of the most essential parts of the character of a man." It was a matter for regret, in Smith's view, that the "general security and happiness which prevail in ages of civility and politeness" gave so "little exercise to the contempt of danger, to patience in enduring labor, hunger, and pain." Given the growth of commerce, things could not be otherwise, according to Smith, but the disappearance of qualities so essential to manhood and therefore to citizenship was nevertheless a disturbing development. Politics and war, not commerce, served as the "great school of self-command." If commerce was now displacing "war and faction" as the chief business of mankind (to the point where the very term "business" soon became a synonym for commerce), the educational system would have to take up the slack, sustaining values that could no longer be acquired through participation in public events.

Horace Mann, like Smith, believed that formal education could take the place of other character-forming experiences, but he had a very different conception of the kind of character he wanted to form. He shared none of Smith's enthusiasm for war and none of his reservations about a society composed of peace-loving men and women going about their business and largely indifferent to public affairs. As we shall see, Mann's opinion of politics was no higher than his opinion of war. His educational program did not attempt to supply the courage, patience, and fortitude formerly supplied by "war and faction." It therefore did not occur to him that historical narratives, with their stirring accounts of exploits carried out in the line of military or political duty, might fire the imagination of the young and help to frame their own aspirations. Perhaps it would be more accurate to say that he distrusted *any* sort of appeal to the imagination. His educational philosophy was hostile to imagination as such. He preferred fact to fiction, science to mythology. He complained that young people were given a "mass of fictions," when they needed "true stories" and "real examples of real men" (III:90–91). But his conception of the truths that could safely be entrusted to children turned out to be very limited indeed. History, he thought, "should be rewritten" so as to enable children to compare "the right with the wrong" and to give them "some option of admiring and emulating the former" (III:59–60). Mann's objections to the kind of history children were conventionally exposed to was not only that it acclaimed military exploits but that right and wrong were confusingly mixed up together—as they are always mixed up, of course, in the real world. It was just this element of moral ambiguity that Mann wanted to eliminate. "As much of History now stands, the examples of right and wrong . . . are . . . brought and shuffled together" (III:60). Educators had a duty to sort them out and to make it unambiguously clear to children which was which.

Mann's plea for historical realism betrayed not only an

impoverished conception of reality but a distrust of peda-gogically unmediated experience—attitudes that have con-tinued to characterize educational thinking ever since. Like many other educators, Mann wanted children to receive their impressions of the world from those who were profes-sionally qualified to decide what it was proper for them to know, instead of picking up impressions haphazardly from narratives (both written and oral) not expressly designed for children. Anyone who has spent much time with children knows that they acquire much of their understanding of the adult world by listening to what adults do not necessarily want them to hear—by eavesdropping, in effect, and just by keeping their eyes and ears open. Information acquired in this way is more vivid and compelling than any other since it enables children to put themselves imaginatively in the place of adults instead of being treated simply as objects of adult solicitude and didacticism. It was precisely this imaginative experience of the adult world, however—this unsupervised play of young imaginations—that Mann hoped to replace with formal instruction. Thus he objected to "novels and all that class of books," which offered "mere *amusement*, as contradistinguished from instruction in the practical concerns of life." His objection, to be sure, was directed mainly against "light reading," which allegedly distracted people from "reflection upon the great realities of experience"; but he did not specifically exempt more seri-ous works of fiction, nor is there any indication, in the vast body of his educational writings, that he recognized the possibility that the "great realities of existence" are treated more fully in fiction and poetry than in any other kind of writing (III:60).

The great weakness in Mann's educational philosophy was the assumption that education takes place only in schools. Perhaps it is unfair to say that Mann bequeathed this fatal assumption to subsequent generations of educators, as part of his intellectual legacy. An inability to see beyond the school after all—a tendency to speak as if schooling and education were synonymous terms—should probably be regarded as an occupational hazard of professional educators, a form of blindness that is built into the job. Still, Mann was one of the first to give it official sanction. His thinking on this point was more striking in what it omitted than in what it said in so many words. It simply did not occur to him that activities like politics, war, and love—the staple themes of the books he deplored—were educative in their own right. He believed that partisan politics, in particular, was the bane of American life. In his Twelfth Report he described the excitement surrounding the presidential election of 1848 in language that unmistakably conveyed the importance of politics as a form of popular education, only to condemn the campaign (in which he himself had won election to the House of Representatives) as a distraction from his more important work as an educator.

> Agitation pervaded the country. There was no stagnant mind; there was no stagnant atmosphere. . . . Wit, argument, eloquence, were in such demand, that they were sent for at the distance of a thousand miles—from one side of the Union to the other. The excitement reached the humblest walks of life. The mechanic in his shop made his hammer chime to the music of political rhymes; and the farmer, as he gathered in his harvest, watched the aspects of the political, more vigilantly than of the natural, sky. Meetings were every where held. . . . The press showered its sheets over the land, thick as snowflakes in a wintry storm. Public and private histories

were ransacked, to find proofs of honor or proofs of dis-honor; political economy was invoked; the sacred names of patriotism, philanthropy, duty to God, and duty to man, were on every tongue.

The campaign of 1848, as Mann described it, elicited an intensity of popular response that would be the envy of our own times, yet Mann could find in all this only "violence" and "din"—a "Saturnalia of license, evil speaking, and falsehood." He wished that the energy devoted to politics could be devoted instead to "getting children into the schools" (XII:25–26). Elsewhere in the same report he lik-ened politics to a conflagration, a fire raging out of control, or again to a plague, an "infection" or "poison" (XII:87).

Reading these passages, one begins to see that Mann wanted to keep politics out of the school not only because he was afraid that his system would be torn apart by those who wished to use it for partisan purposes but because he distrusted political activity as such. It produced an "inflammation of the passions" (XII:26). It generated con-troversy—a necessary part of education, it might be argued, but in Mann's eyes, a waste of time and energy. It divided men instead of bringing them together. For these reasons Mann sought not only to insulate the school from political pressures but to keep political history out of the curriculum. The subject could not be ignored entirely; oth-erwise children would gain only "such knowledge as they may pick up from angry political discussions, or from party newspapers." But instruction in the "nature of a republican government" was to be conducted so as to emphasize only "those articles in the creed of republicanism, which are accepted by all, believed in by all, and which form the com-mon basis of our political faith." Anything controversial was to be passed over in silence or, at best, with the admonition that "the schoolroom is neither the tribunal to adjudicate, nor the forum to discuss it" (XII:89).

Although it is somewhat tangential to my main point, it is worth pausing to see what Mann considered to be the common articles in the republican creed, the "elementary ideas" on which everyone could agree (XII:89). The most important of these points, it appears, were the duty of citizens to appeal to the courts, if wronged, instead of taking the law into their own hands, and the duty to change the laws "by an appeal to the ballot, and not by rebellion" (XII:85). Mann did not see that these "elementary ideas" were highly controversial in themselves or that others might quarrel with his underlying assumption that the main purpose of government was to keep order. But the substance of his political views is less germane to my purpose than his attempt to palm them off as universal principles. It is bad enough that he disguised the principles of the Whig party as principles common to all Americans and thus protected them from reasonable criticism. What is even worse is the way in which his bland tutelage deprived children of anything that might have appealed to the imagination or—to use his own term—the "passions." Political history, taught along the lines recommended by Mann, would be drained of controversy, sanitized, bowdlerized, and therefore drained of excitement. It would become mild, innocuous, and profoundly boring, trivialized by a suffocating didacticism. Mann's idea of political education was of a piece with his idea of moral education, on which he laid such heavy-handed emphasis in his opposition to merely intellectual training. Moral education, as he conceived it, consisted of inoculation against "social vices and crimes": "gaming, intemperance, dissoluteness, falsehood, dishonesty, violence, and their kindred offenses" (XII:97). In the

republican tradition—compared with which Mann's republicanism was no more than a distant echo—the concept of
virtue referred to honor, ardor, superabundant energy, and
the fullest use of one's powers. For Mann, virtue was only
the pallid opposite of "vice." Virtue was "sobriety, frugal-
ity, probity"—qualities not likely to seize the imagination
of the young (XII:97).

The subject of morality brings us by a short step to religion, where we see Mann's limitations in their clearest
form. Here again I want to call into question the very
aspects of Mann's thought that have usually been singled
out for the highest praise. Even his detractors—those who
see his philanthropy as a cover for social control—congratu-
late Mann on his foresight in protecting the schools from
sectarian pressures. He was quite firm on the need to banish religious instruction based on the tenets of any particular denomination. In his lifetime he was unfairly accused
of banishing religious instruction altogether and thus
undermining public morals. To these "grave charges" he
replied, plausibly enough, that sectarianism could not be
tolerated in schools that everyone was expected to attend—
compelled to attend, if he were to have his way (XII:103).
But he also made it clear that a "rival system of 'Parochial'
or 'Sectarian' schools" was not to be tolerated either
(XII:104). His program envisioned the public school system
as a monopoly, in practice, if not in law. It implied the
marginalization, if not the outright elimination, of institutions that might compete with the common schools.

His opposition to religious sectarianism did not stop with
its exclusion from the public sector of education. He was
against sectarianism as such, for the same reasons that made
him take such a dim view of politics. Sectarianism, in his
view, breathed the spirit of fanaticism and persecution. It
gave rise to religious controversy, which was no more

acceptable to Mann than political controversy. He spoke of both in images of fire. If the theological "heats and animosities engendered in families, and among neighbors, burst forth in a devouring fire" into school meetings, the "inflammable materials" would grow so intense that no one could "quench the flames," until the "zealots" themselves were "consumed in the conflagration they have kindled" (XII:129). It was not enough to keep the churches out of the public schools; it was necessary to keep them out of public life altogether, lest the "discordant" sounds of religious debate drown out the "one, indivisible, all-glorious system of Christianity" and bring about the "return of Babel" (XII:130). The perfect world, as it existed in Mann's head, was a world in which everyone agreed, a heavenly city where the angels sang in unison. He sadly admitted that "we can hardly conceive of a state of society upon earth so perfect as to exclude all differences of opinion," but at least it was possible to relegate disagreements "about rights" and other important matters to the sidelines of social life, to bar them from the schools and, by implication, from the public sphere as a whole (XII:96).

None of this meant that the schools should not teach religion; it meant only that they should teach the religion that was common to all, or at least to all Christians. The Bible should be read in school, on the assumption that it could "speak for itself," without commentaries that might give rise to disagreement (XII:117). Here again Mann's program invites a type of criticism that misses the point. His nondenominational instruction is open to the objection that it still excluded Jews, Muhammadans, Buddhists, and atheists. Ostensibly tolerant, it was actually repressive in equating religion narrowly with Christianity. This is a trivial objection. At the time Mann was writing, it still made sense to speak of the United States as a Christian nation, but the reasoning on which he justified a nondenominational form of Christianity could easily be extended to include other religions as well. The real objection is that the resulting mixture is so bland that it puts children to sleep instead of awakening feelings of awe and wonder. Orestes Brownson, the most perceptive of Mann's contemporary critics, pointed out in 1839 that Mann's system, by suppressing everything divisive in religion, would leave only an innocuous residue. "A faith, which embraces generalities only, is little better than no faith at all." Children brought up in a mild and nondenominational "Christianity ending in nothingness," in schools where "much will be taught in general, but nothing in particular," would be deprived of their birthright, as Brownson saw it. They would be taught "to respect and preserve what is"; they would be cautioned against the "licentiousness of the people, the turbulence and brutality of the mob," but they would never learn a "love of liberty" under such a system.

Although Brownson did not share Mann's horror of dissension, he too deplored the widening gap between wealth and poverty and saw popular education as a means of overcoming these divisions. Unlike Mann, however, he understood that the real work of education did not take place in the schools at all. Anticipating John Dewey, Brownson pointed out that

> our children are educated in the streets, by the influence of their associates, in the fields and on the hill sides, by the influences of surrounding scenery and overshadowing skies, in the bosom of the family, by the love and gentleness, or wrath and fretfulness of parents, by the passions or affections they see manifested, the conversations to which they listen, and above all by the general pursuits, habits, and moral tone of the community.

These considerations, together with Brownson's extensive discussion of the press and the lyceum, seemed to point to the conclusion that people were most likely to develop a love of liberty through exposure to wide-ranging public controversy, the "free action of mind on mind."

Wide-ranging public controversy, as we have seen, was just what Mann wanted to avoid. Nothing of educational value, in his view, could issue from the clash of opinions, the noise and heat of political and religious debate. Education could take place only in institutions deliberately contrived for that purpose, in which children were exposed exclusively to knowledge professional educators considered appropriate. Some such assumption, I think, has been the guiding principle of American education ever since. Mann's reputation as the founding father of the public school is well deserved. His energy, his missionary enthusiasm, his powers of persuasion, and the strategic position he enjoyed as secretary of the Massachusetts Board of Education made it possible for him to leave a lasting mark on the educational enterprise. One might go so far as to say that the enterprise has never recovered from the mistakes and misconceptions built into it at the very outset.

Not that Horace Mann would be pleased with our educational system as it exists today. On the contrary, he would be horrified. Nevertheless, the horrors are at least indirectly a consequence of his own ideas, unleavened by the moral idealism with which they were once associated. We have incorporated into our schools the worst of Mann and somehow managed to lose sight of the best. We have professionalized teaching by setting up elaborate requirements for certification, but we have not succeeded in institutionalizing Mann's appreciation of teaching as an honorable calling. We have set up a far-ranging educational bureaucracy without raising academic standards or improving the quality of teaching. The bureaucratization of education has the opposite effect, undermining the teacher's autonomy, substituting the judgment of administrators for that of the teacher, and incidentally discouraging people with a gift for teaching from entering the profession at all. We have followed Mann's advice to de-emphasize purely academic subjects, but the resulting loss of intellectual rigor has not been balanced by an improvement in the school's capacity to nourish the character traits Mann considered so important: self-reliance, courteousness, and the capacity for deferred gratification. The periodic rediscovery that intellectual training has been sacrificed to "social skills" has led to a misplaced emphasis on the purely cognitive dimension of education, which lacks even Mann's redeeming awareness of its moral dimension. We share Mann's distrust of the imagination and his narrow conception of truth, insisting that the schools should stay away from myths and stories and legends and stick to sober facts, but the range of permissible facts is even more pathetically limited today than it was in Mann's day.

History has given way to an infantilized version of sociology, in obedience to the misconceived principle that the quickest way to engage children's attention is to dwell on what is closest to home: their families; their neighborhoods; the local industries; the technologies on which they depend. A more sensible assumption would be that children need to learn about faraway places and olden times before they can make sense of their immediate surroundings. Since most children have no opportunity for extended travel, and since travel in our world is not very broadening anyway, the school can provide a substitute—but not if it clings to the notion that the only way to "motivate" them is to expose them to nothing not already familiar, nothing not immediately applicable to themselves.

Like Mann, we believe that schooling is a cure-all for everything that ails us. Mann and his contemporaries held that good schools could eradicate crime and juvenile delinquency, do away with poverty, make useful citizens out of "abandoned and outcast children," and serve as the "great equalizer" between rich and poor (XII:42, 59). They would have done better to start out with a more modest set of expectations. If there is one lesson we might have been expected to learn in the 150 years since Horace Mann took charge of the schools of Massachusetts, it is that the schools can't save society. Crime and poverty are still with us, and the gap between rich and poor continues to widen. Meanwhile, our children, even as young adults, don't know how to read and write. Maybe the time has come—if it hasn't already passed—to start all over again.

Nine

The Lost Art of Argument

For many years now we have been regaled with the promise of the information age. The social effects of the communications revolution, we are told, will include an insatiable demand for trained personnel, an upgrading of the skills required for employment, and an enlightened public capable of following the issues of the day and of making informed judgments about civic affairs. Instead we find college graduates working at jobs for which they are vastly overqualified. The demand for menial labor outstrips the demand for skilled specialists. The postindustrial economy, it appears, promotes an interchangeability of personnel, a rapid movement from one type of work to another, and a growing concentration of the labor force in technically backward, labor-intensive, nonunion sectors of the economy. Recent experience does not bear out the expectation that technological innovations, improvements in communications in particular, will create an abundance of skilled jobs, eliminate disagreeable jobs, and make life easy for everyone. Their most important effect, on the contrary, is to widen the gap between the knowledge class and the rest of the population, between those who find themselves at home in the new global economy and who "relish the thought that the information flows to them can become bigger" all the time (in the words of Arno Penzias of AT&T Bell Laboratories) and those who, having little use for cellular phones, fax machines, or on-line information services, still live in what Penzias contemptuously refers to as the Age of Paper Work.

As for the claim that the information revolution would raise the level of public intelligence, it is no secret that the public knows less about public affairs than it used to know. Millions of Americans cannot begin to tell you what is in the Bill of Rights, what Congress does, what the Constitution says about the powers of the presidency, how the party system emerged or how it operates. A sizable majority, according to a recent survey, believe that Israel is an Arab nation. Instead of blaming the schools for this disheartening ignorance of public affairs, as is the custom, we should look elsewhere for a fuller explanation, bearing in mind that people readily acquire such knowledge as they can put to good use. Since the public no longer participates in debates on national issues, it has no reason to inform itself about civic affairs. It is the decay of public debate, not the school system (bad as it is), that makes the public ill informed, notwithstanding the wonders of the age of information. When debate becomes a lost art, information, even though it may be readily available, makes no impression.

What democracy requires is vigorous public debate, not information. Of course, it needs information too, but the kind of information it needs can be generated only by debate. We do not know what we need to know until we ask the right questions, and we can identify the right questions only by subjecting our own ideas about the world to the test of public controversy. Information, usually seen as the precondition of debate, is better understood as its by-product. When we get into arguments that focus and fully engage our attention, we become avid seekers of relevant information. Otherwise we take in information passively—if we take it in at all.

POLITICAL DEBATE BEGAN to decline around the turn of the century, curiously enough at a time when the press was becoming more "responsible," more professional, more conscious of its civic obligations. In the early nineteenth century the press was fiercely partisan. Until the middle of the century papers were often financed by political parties. Even when they became more independent of parties, they did not embrace the ideal of objectivity or neutrality. In 1841 Horace Greeley launched his *New York Tribune* with the announcement that it would be a "journal removed alike from servile partisanship on the one hand and from gagged, mincing neutrality on the other." Strong-minded editors like Greeley, James Gordon Bennett, E. L. Godkin, and Samuel Bowles objected to the way in which the demands of party loyalty infringed upon editorial independence, making the editor merely a mouthpiece for a party or faction, but they did not attempt to conceal their own views or to impose a strict separation of news and editorial content. Their papers were journals of opinion in which the reader expected to find a definite point of view, together with unrelenting criticism of opposing points of view.

It is no accident that journalism of this kind flourished

during the period from 1830 to 1900, when popular participation in politics was at its height. Of the eligible voters, 80 percent typically went to the polls in presidential elections. After 1900 the percentage declined sharply (to 65 percent in 1904 and 59 percent in 1912), and it has continued to decline more or less steadily throughout the twentieth century. Torchlight parades, mass rallies, and gladiatorial contents of oratory made nineteenth-century politics an object of consuming popular interest, in which journalism served as an extension of the town meeting. The nineteenth-century press created a public forum in which issues were hotly debated. Newspapers not only reported political controversies but participated in them, drawing in their readers as well. Print culture rested on the remnants of an oral tradition. Print was not yet the exclusive medium of communication, nor had it severed its connection with spoken language. The printed language was still shaped by the rhythms and requirements of the spoken word, in particular by the conventions of verbal argumentation. Print served to create a larger forum for the spoken word, not yet to displace or reshape it.

The Lincoln-Douglas debates exemplified the oral tradition at its best. By current standards, Lincoln and Douglas broke every rule of political discourse. They subjected their audiences (which were as large as fifteen thousand on one occasion) to a painstaking analysis of complex issues. They spoke with considerably more candor, in a pungent, colloquial, sometimes racy style, than politicians think prudent today. They took clear positions from which it was difficult to retreat. They conducted themselves as if political leadership carried with it an obligation to clarify issues instead of merely getting elected.

The contrast between these justly famous debates and present-day presidential debates, in which the media define the issues and draw up the ground rules, is unmistakable and highly unflattering to ourselves. Journalistic interrogation of political candidates—which is what debate has come to—tends to magnify the importance of journalists and to diminish that of the candidates. Journalists ask questions—prosaic, predictable questions for the most part—and press the candidates for prompt, specific answers, reserving the right to interrupt and to cut the candidates short whenever they appear to stray from the prescribed topic. To prepare for this ordeal, candidates rely on their advisers to stuff them full of facts and figures, quotable slogans, and anything else that will convey the impression of wide-ranging, unflappable competence. Faced not only with a battery of journalists ready to pounce on the slightest misstep but with the cold, relentless scrutiny of the camera, politicians know that everything depends on the management of visual impressions. They must radiate confidence and decisiveness and never appear to be at a loss for words. The nature of the occasion requires them to exaggerate the reach and effectiveness of public policy, to give the impression that the right programs and the right leadership can meet every challenge.

The format requires all candidates to look the same: confident, untroubled, and therefore unreal. But it also imposes on them the obligation to explain what makes them different from the others. Once the question has to be asked, it answers itself. Indeed, the question is inherently belittling and degrading, a good example of TV's effect of lowering the object of estimation, of looking through every disguise, deflating every pretension. Bluntly stated with the necessary undertone of all-pervasive skepticism that is inescapably part of the language of TV, the question turns out to be highly rhetorical. What makes *you* so special? Nothing.

This is the quintessential question raised by TV, because it is in the medium's nature to teach us, with relentless insistence, that no one is special, contrary claims notwithstanding. At this point in our history the best qualification for high office may well be a refusal to cooperate with the media's program of self-aggrandizement. A candidate with the courage to abstain from "debates" organized by the media would automatically distinguish himself from the others and command a good deal of public respect. Candidates should insist on directly debating each other instead of responding to questions put to them by commentators and pundits. Their passivity and subservience lower them in the eyes of the voters. They need to recover their self-respect by challenging the media's status as arbiters of public discussion. A refusal to play by the media's rules would make people aware of the vast, illegitimate influence the mass media have come to exercise in American politics. It would also provide the one index of character that voters could recognize and applaud.

W HAT HAPPENED TO the tradition exemplified by the Lincoln-Douglas debates? The scandals of the Gilded Age gave party politics a bad name. They confirmed the misgivings entertained by the "best men" ever since the rise of Jacksonian democracy. By the 1870s and 1880s a bad opinion of politics had come to be widely shared by the educated classes. Genteel reformers—"mugwumps" to their enemies—demanded a professionalization of politics, designed to free the civil service from party control and to replace political appointees with trained experts. Even those who rejected the invitation to declare their independence from the party system, like Theodore Roosevelt (whose refusal to desert the Republican party infuriated the "independents"), shared the enthusiasm for civil service reform. The "best men" ought to challenge the spoilsmen on their own turf, according to Roosevelt, instead of retreating to the sidelines of political life.

The drive to clean up politics gained momentum in the progressive era. Under the leadership of Roosevelt, Woodrow Wilson, Robert La Follette, and William Jennings Bryan, the progressives preached "efficiency," "good government," "bipartisanship," and the "scientific management" of public affairs and declared war on "bossism." They attacked the seniority system in Congress, limited the powers of the Speaker of the House, replaced mayors with city managers, and delegated important governmental functions to appointive commissions staffed with trained administrators. Recognizing that political machines were welfare agencies of a rudimentary type, which dispensed jobs and other benefits to their constituents and thereby won their loyalty, the progressives set out to create a welfare state as a way of competing with the machines. They launched comprehensive investigations of crime, vice, poverty, and other "social problems." They took the position that government was a science, not an art. They forged links between government and the university so as to assure a steady supply of experts and expert knowledge. But they had little use for public debate. Most political questions were too complex, in their view, to be submitted to popular judgment. They liked to contrast the scientific expert with the orator, the latter a useless windbag whose rantings only confused the public mind.

Professionalism in politics meant professionalism in journalism. The connection between them was spelled out by Walter Lippmann in a notable series of books: *Liberty and the News* (1920), *Public Opinion* (1922), and *The Phantom Public* (1925). These provided a founding charter for modern journalism, the most elaborate rationale for a journalism guided by the new ideal of professional objectivity. Lippmann held up standards by which the press is still judged—usually with the result that it is found wanting.

What concerns us here, however, is not whether the press has lived up to Lippmann's standards but how he arrived at those standards in the first place. In 1920 Lippmann and Charles Merz published a long essay in the *New Republic* examining press coverage of the Russian Revolution. This study, now forgotten, showed that American papers gave their readers an account of the Revolution distorted by anti-Bolshevik prejudices, wishful thinking, and sheer ignorance. *Liberty and the News* was also prompted by the collapse of journalistic objectivity during the war, when the newspapers had appointed themselves "defenders of the faith." The result, according to Lippmann, was a "breakdown of the means of public knowledge." The difficulty went beyond war or revolution, the "supreme destroyers of realistic thinking." The traffic in sex, violence, and "human interest"—staples of modern mass journalism—raised grave questions about the future of democracy. "All that the sharpest critics of democracy have alleged is true if there is no steady supply of trustworthy and relevant news."

In *Public Opinion* and *The Phantom Public*, Lippmann answered the critics, in effect, by redefining democracy. Democracy did not require that the people literally govern themselves. The public's stake in government was strictly procedural. The public interest did not extend to the substance of decision making: "The public is interested in law, not in the laws; in the method of law, not in the substance." Questions of substance should be decided by knowledgeable administrators whose access to reliable information immunized them against the emotional "symbols" and "stereotypes" that dominated public debate. The public was incompetent to govern itself and did not even care to do so, in Lippmann's view. But as long as rules of fair play were enforced, the public would be content to leave government to experts—provided, of course, that the experts delivered the goods, the ever-increasing abundance of comforts and conveniences so closely identified with the American way of life.

Lippmann acknowledged the conflict between his recommendations and the received theory of democracy, according to which citizens ought to participate in discussions of public policy and to have a hand, if only indirectly, in decision making. Democratic theory, he argued, had roots in social conditions that no longer obtained. It presupposed an "omnicompetent citizen," a "jack of all trades" who could be found only in a "simple self-contained community." In the "wide and unpredictable environment" of the modern world, the old ideal of citizenship was obsolete. A complex industrial society required a government carried on by officials who would necessarily be guided—since any form of direct democracy was now impossible—either by public opinion or by expert knowledge. Public opinion was unreliable because it could be united only by an appeal to slogans and "symbolic pictures." Lippmann's distrust of public opinion rested on the epistemological distinction between truth and mere opinion. Truth, as he conceived it, grew out of disinterested scientific inquiry; everything else was ideology. The scope of public debate accordingly had to be severely restricted. At best public debate was a disagreeable necessity—not the very essence of democracy but its "primary defect," which arose only because "exact knowledge," unfortunately, was in limited supply. Ideally public debate would not take place at all; decisions would be based on scientific "standards of measurement" alone. Science cut through "entangling stereotypes and slogans," the "threads of memory and emotion" that kept the "responsible administrator" tied up in knots.

THE ROLE OF the press, as Lippmann saw it, was to circulate information, not to encourage argument. The relationship between information and argument was antagonistic, not complementary. He did not take the position that reliable information was a necessary precondition of argument; on the contrary, his point was that information precluded argument, made argument unnecessary. Arguments were what took place in the absence of reliable information. Lippmann had forgotten what he learned (or should have learned) from William James and John Dewey: that our search for reliable information is itself guided by the questions that arise during arguments about a given course of action. It is only by subjecting our preferences and projects to the test of debate that we come to understand what we know and what we still need to learn. Until we have to defend our opinions in public, they remain opinions in Lippmann's pejorative sense—half-formed convictions based on random impressions and unexamined assumptions. It is the act of articulating and defending our views that lifts them out of the category of "opinions," gives them shape and definition, and makes it possible for others to recognize them as a description of their own experience as well. In short, we come to know our own minds only by explaining ourselves to others.

The attempt to bring others around to our own point of view carries the risk, of course, that we may adopt their point of view instead. We have to enter imaginatively into our opponents' arguments, if only for the purpose of refuting them, and we may end up being persuaded by those we sought to persuade. Argument is risky and unpredictable, therefore educational. Most of us tend to think of it (as Lippmann thought of it) as a clash of rival dogmas, a shouting match in which neither side gives any ground. But arguments are not won by shouting down opponents. They are won by changing opponents' minds—something that can happen only if we give opposing arguments a respectful hearing and still persuade their advocates that there is something wrong with those arguments. In the course of this activity we may well decide that there is something wrong with our own.

I F W E I N S I S T on argument as the essence of education, we will defend democracy not as the most efficient but as the most educational form of government, one that extends the circle of debate as widely as possible and thus forces all citizens to articulate their views, to put their views at risk, and to cultivate the virtues of eloquence, clarity of thought and expression, and sound judgment. As Lippmann noted, small communities are the classic locus of democracy—not because they are "self-contained," however, but simply because they allow everyone to take part in public debates. Instead of dismissing direct democracy as irrelevant to modern conditions, we need to re-create it on a large scale. From this point of view the press serves as the equivalent of the town meeting.

This is what Dewey argued, in effect—though not, unfortunately, very clearly—in *The Public and Its Problems* (1927), a book written in reply to Lippmann's disparaging studies of public opinion. Lippmann's distinction between truth and information rested on a "spectator theory of knowledge," as James W. Carey explains in his *Communication as Culture*. As Lippmann understood these matters, knowledge is what we get when an observer, preferably a scientifically trained observer, provides us with a copy of reality that we can all recognize. Dewey, on the other hand, knew that even scientists argue among themselves. "Systematic inquiry," he contended, was only the beginning of knowledge, not its final form. The knowledge needed by any community—whether it was a community of scientific inquirers or a political community—emerged only from "dialogue" and "direct give and take."

It is significant, as Carey points out, that Dewey's analysis of communication stressed the ear rather than the eye. "Conversation," Dewey wrote, "has a vital import lacking in the fixed and frozen words of written speech. . . . The connections of the ear with vital and outgoing thought and emotion are immensely closer and more varied than those of the eye. Vision is a spectator; hearing is a participator."

The press extends the scope of debate by supplementing the spoken word with the written word. If the press needs to apologize for anything, it is not that the written word is a poor substitute for the pure language of mathematics. What matters, in this connection, is that the written word is a poor substitute for the spoken word. It is an acceptable substitute, however, as long as written speech takes spoken speech and not mathematics as its model. According to Lippmann, the press was unreliable because it could never give us accurate representations of reality, only "symbolic pictures" and stereotypes. Dewey's analysis implied a more penetrating line of criticism. As Carey puts it, "The press, by seeing its role as that of informing the public, abandons its role as an agency for carrying on the conversation of our culture." Having embraced Lippmann's ideal of objectivity, the press no longer serves to cultivate "certain vital habits" in the community: "the ability to follow an argument, grasp the point of view of another, expand the boundaries of understanding, debate the alternative purposes that might be pursued."

THE RISE OF the advertising and public relations industries, side by side, helps to explain why the press abdicated its most important function—enlarging the public forum—at the same time that it became more "responsible." A responsible press, as opposed to a partisan or opinionated one, attracted the kind of readers advertisers were eager to reach: well-heeled readers, most of whom probably thought of themselves as independent voters. These readers wanted to be assured that they were reading all the news that was fit to print, not an editor's idiosyncratic and no doubt biased view of things. Responsibility came to be equated with the avoidance of controversy because advertisers were willing to pay for it. Some advertisers were also willing to pay for sensationalism, though on the whole they preferred a respectable readership to sheer numbers. What they clearly did not prefer was "opinion"— not because they were impressed with Lippmann's philosophical arguments but because opinionated reporting did not guarantee the right audience. No doubt they also hoped that an aura of objectivity, the hallmark of responsible journalism, would also rub off on the advertisements that surrounded increasingly slender columns of print.

In a curious historical twist, advertising, publicity, and other forms of commercial persuasion themselves came to be disguised as information. Advertising and publicity substituted for open debate. "Hidden persuaders" (as Vance Packard called them) replaced the old-time editors, essayists, and orators who made no secret of their partisanship. Information and publicity became increasingly indistinguishable. Most of the "news" in our newspapers—40 percent, according to the conservative estimate of Professor Scott Cutlip of the University of Georgia—consists of items churned out by press agencies and public relations bureaus and then regurgitated intact by the "objective" organs of journalism. We have grown accustomed to the idea that most of the space in newspapers, so called, is devoted to advertising—at least two-thirds in most newspapers. But if we consider public relations as another form of advertising, which is hardly farfetched since private, commercially inspired enterprises fuel both, we now have to get used to the idea that much of the "news" consists of advertising too.

THE DECLINE OF the partisan press and the rise of a new type of journalism professing rigorous standards of objectivity do not assure a steady supply of usable information. Unless information is generated by sustained public debate, most of it will be irrelevant at best, misleading and manipulative at worst. Increasingly information is generated by those who wish to promote something or someone—a product, a cause, a political candidate or officeholder—without arguing their case on its merits or explicitly advertising it as self-interested material either. Much of the press, in its eagerness to inform the public, has become a conduit for the equivalent of junk mail. Like the post office—another institution that once served to extend the sphere of face-to-face discussion and to create "committees of correspondence"—it now delivers an abundance of useless, indigestible information that nobody wants, most of which ends up as unread waste. The most important effect of this obsession with information, aside from the destruction of trees for paper and the mounting burden of "waste management," is to undermine the authority of the word. When words are used merely as instruments of publicity or propaganda, they lose their power to persuade. Soon they cease to mean anything at all. People lose the capacity to use language precisely and expressively or even to distinguish one word from another. The spoken word models itself on the written word instead of the other way around, and ordinary speech begins to sound like the clotted jargon we see in print. Ordinary speech begins to sound like "information"—a disaster from which the English language may never recover.

Ten

Academic Pseudo-radicalism

The Charade of "Subversion"

ebates about higher education, as they are
reported in the national media, strengthen the
impression that the new elites live in a little world
of their own, far removed from the everyday concerns of
ordinary men and women. The noisy battles over the
"canon," which have convulsed faculties at a handful of
leading universities, are completely irrelevant to the plight
of higher education as a whole. Four-year state colleges and
two-year community colleges, after all, enroll far more students than renowned universities like Harvard or Stanford,
which receive a disproportionate share of attention. By
1990 more than half the nation's freshmen attended community colleges. Thanks to inflated tuitions, moreover, the
middle class has been forced out of the glamorous schools
at the top of the educational system. Increased enrollment
of lower-income groups, notably black and Hispanic, has

obscured a more important development, the gentrification of the leading colleges and universities, both public and private. According to Russell Jacoby, whose *Dogmatic Wisdom: How the Culture Wars Have Misled America* provides a salutary corrective to the usual emphasis on elite institutions, more than 60 percent of the freshmen entering UCLA in 1991 came from families with incomes over sixty thousand dollars, 40 percent from families with incomes over a hundred thousand dollars. Observers applaud ethnic diversity but fail to notice the "affluent homogeneity," in Jacoby's words, that "renders false the claims of vast cultural differences among students."

Economic stratification means that a liberal education (such as it is) has become the prerogative of the rich, together with a small number of students recruited from select minorities. The great majority of college students, relegated to institutions that have given up even the pretense of a liberal education, study business, accounting, physical education, public relations, and other practical subjects. They get little training in writing (unless "Commercial English" is an acceptable substitute), seldom read a book, and graduate without exposure to history, philosophy, or literature. Their only acquaintance with the world's culture comes through required courses like "Introduction to Sociology" and "General Biology." Most of them hold part-time jobs, in any case, that leave little time for reading and reflection. While liberals and conservatives debate the revision of an allegedly "Eurocentric" curriculum, policies designed to promote racial diversity and "sensitivity," and the theoretical implications of poststructuralism, the fundamental issue goes unnoticed: the abandonment of the historic mission of American education, the democratization of liberal culture.

The academic left, which claims to speak for the common people, might be expected to resist a restructuring of higher education that effectively leaves them to their own fate. But academic radicals, these days, are more interested in the defense of their professional privileges against criticism from outside. Joan Scott of Princeton's Institute for Advanced Study dismisses this criticism as the work of "disaffected scholars" and "marginal intellectuals." Left-wing academics cannot be bothered to argue with opponents or to enter into their point of view. They speak, with irritating complacency, as members of a professional establishment that has given up the attempt to communicate with a broader audience, either as teachers or as writers. They defend their incomprehensible jargon as the language of "subversion," plain speech having been dismissed as an instrument of oppression. "The language of 'clarity,' " they maintain, "plays . . . a dominant [role in a] culture that cleverly and powerfully uses 'clear' and 'simplistic' language to systematically undermine . . . complex and critical thinking." It follows that fellow specialists alone are qualified to speak about the condition of the humanities. Jacoby quotes Michael Berube, an English professor, who discounts journalistic criticism of the academy on the grounds that "reception theory," the "new historicism," and other such mysteries are accessible only to the initiated. The "academy bashers," according to another radical professor, have "failed to learn the new critical languages" and can therefore be ignored. Fredric Jameson, a leading practitioner of "cultural studies," finds it surprising that laymen expect to find his work intelligible—"laid out with all the leisurely elegance of a coffee-table magazine"—when they would never make the same demand of "nuclear physics, linguistics, symbolic logic," and other bodies of professional expertise. One of Jameson's admirers, David Kaufmann, insists that his "technical prose" shows that cultural theory now stands on the same level as the hard sciences.

This kind of talk helps to bolster the humanities' self-image and to sustain morale in the face of criticism, but it does not play very well outside the academy. The general public listens to conservatives like William Bennett, Allan Bloom, and Lynne Cheney because they address the widespread perception that the educational system is falling apart and seem to have important things to say about the resulting crisis. People on the left, on the other hand—with notable exceptions like Jacoby—refuse to take the issue seriously. No crisis exists, in their view. The only trouble with the educational system is that it is still too resistant to the currents of cultural change. The changes that are taking place—usually summarized as a trend toward cultural "pluralism"—will have beneficial effects if they are allowed to continue. They will introduce new voices and new points of view into a system too long dominated by white males. They will correct the canon of acknowledged masterpieces or else destroy the "elitist" idea of a canon altogether. Cultural pluralism will break down the exaggerated respect for great art and high culture that has served only to exclude oppressed minorities. It will encourage critical habits of thought and make it clear that nothing is sacred, nothing exempt from criticism.

These goals may or may not be desirable, but they do not address the issue that troubles critics of education. Talk of pluralism and diversity provides no comfort when young people can't seem to learn how to read or write, when they graduate with no more than a smattering of culture, when their stock of general knowledge grows more meager every day, when they can't recognize allusions to Shakespeare or the classics or the Bible or their own country's history, when SAT scores keep falling, when American workmanship and productivity are no longer the envy of the world, and when superior education is widely cited as the reason for the economic success of countries like Japan and the former West Germany. These are the developments that trouble ordinary people, and any serious talk about education has to speak to those developments.

It also has to speak to the perception of moral breakdown, the belief that our children are growing up without proper values. Critics of moral relativism and "secular humanism" may simplify the issue, but their concerns should not be dismissed out of hand. Many young people are morally at sea. They resent the ethical demands of "society" as infringements of their personal freedom. They believe that their rights as individuals include the right to "create their own values," but they cannot explain what that means, aside from the right to do as they please. They cannot seem to grasp the idea that "values" imply some principle of moral obligation. They insist that they owe nothing to "society"—an abstraction that dominates their attempts to think about social and moral issues. If they conform to social expectations, it is only because conformity offers the line of least resistance.

D E B A T E S   A B O U T   E D U C A T I O N resemble debates about the family, a closely related issue. The right talks about breakdown and crisis, the left about pluralism and diversity. The right does not offer a convincing explanation of the problem, let alone a convincing solution, but at least it acknowledges the problem's existence: the frequency of divorce; the increase in female-headed households; the instability of personal relations; the shattering effects of this instability on children. For the left these things are healthy signs of change, a movement away from the male-dominated nuclear family to a pluralistic family structure in which people will be able to choose from a whole range of living arrangements. That any one arrangement should be socially sanctioned strikes progressive people as no less objectionable than a common culture or a common curriculum. The transition from uniformity to pluralism, they argue, may give rise to confusion, but confusion is a small price to pay for freedom of choice.

To those who cannot take such a rosy view of things, these arguments merely disguise the collapse of the family as progress. From their point of view, the same objection applies to those who defend recent trends in the humanities on the grounds that "precisely those things now identified as failings in the humanities actually indicate enlivening transformations."*

---

*These reassuring words appear in a 1989 report, *Speaking for the Humanities*, published by the American Council of Learned Societies, edited by George Levine, and written jointly by Peter Brooks, Jonathan Culler, Marjorie Garber, E. Ann Kaplan, and Catharine R. Stimpson. A number of other scholars are listed as having "endorsed its position"—among them Jules Chametzsky, Murray Krieger, Dominick LaCapra, Richard L. McCormick, Hillis Miller, and Richard Vann, all leading lights in their respective disciplines.

Where critics of the humanities see confusion and disarray, these authors see "intellectual ferment," searching debate, and fearless innovation. They are undaunted in their resolute optimism by declining enrollments, overspecialization, incomprehensible jargon, or the subordination of teaching to research. "Cross-disciplinary activity," they think, will furnish a corrective to specialization. Declining enrollments reflect "economic pressure," not "intellectual and pedagogical failure." Jargon is bad but generally recognized as such—"certainly by the writers of this report." Teaching and research complement each other, and so on. These authors say nothing about the most important criticism of all: that students graduate from college in a condition of profound ignorance about the world. The possibility that this criticism might contain a good deal of truth seems not to have occurred to them. Perhaps it does not trouble them.

It is easy to show that conservative perceptions of cultural crisis, whether they are prompted by the condition of the family or by the state of higher education, are often exaggerated and ill informed. The claim that Marxism has come to dominate academic life cannot stand up even to casual investigation. If Marxism is no longer automatically suspect, that is because it no longer provides the main source of radical ideas. Marxism has "tacitly ceded its claim to a dominant status in radical discourse," as Martin Jay observes. But that does not settle the question of whether or not "radical discourse" sets the tone of academic life, at least in the humanities. Jay himself notes that the "new shibboleth 'race-gender-class' " is "now invoked with numbing predictability in certain academic discussions." If that is the case, we need to pay attention to what conservative critics are saying about this new form of "radical discourse." Nor can we ignore those who attack this pseudoradicalism from a position on the left. With what might be called numbing predictability, Jay dismisses Jacoby's critique of academic radicalism *The Last Intellectuals* as a "nostalgic lamentation" for the decline of "*soi-disant* universal intellectuals able to speak to and for the whole of society." Whether social criticism really requires any such assumption of universality is an important question to which I shall return, but the question left unanswered by Jay's casual dismissal of Jacoby is whether social criticism of any kind can flourish when the "radical discourse" increasingly ascendant in the humanities makes so little contact with the world outside the academy.

Roger Kimball is not particularly interested in the fate of social criticism, but his attack on academic radicalism, *Tenured Radicals*, can be read with a good deal of profit by anyone who is. Kimball is managing editor of Hilton Kramer's *New Criterion*, now one of the last bastions of modernism and high culture. That in itself is enough to discredit him in the eyes of those whose reading consists chiefly of *Yale French Studies*, *New German Critique*, *Critical Inquiry*, *Social Text*, and *October*. In the age of the "postmodern," the "posthumanist," the "poststructural," and the "postcontemporary," the *New Criterion*'s defense of literary modernism—a defense formerly left largely to avant-garde intellectuals identified with the left—puts it unmistakably in the reactionary camp. But anyone who reads Kimball's book with an open mind will recognize the accuracy of many of his observations. By translating the "overcharged verbiage" of deconstruction into plain English, he deflates its pretensions and shows "just how far" it "can intrude on the reader's credulity without making concessions to common sense." He shows, for example, how Michael Fried can torture Courbet's painting *The Quarry* into a metaphorical representation of castration, of the violence inflicted by the artist on nature; how certain theorists of architecture "can pretend that architecture is really about 'interrogating form,' subverting 'the logic of the wall,' etc., not about building appropriate, serviceable, perhaps even beautiful buildings"; and how apologists for Paul de Man, confronted with his wartime articles in support of the Nazis, can reduce the whole controversy about de Man to a debate about language.

Kimball exposes the careerism that underlies all this "airy intellectualizing" about the indeterminacy of language and the problematical status of truth and selfhood. Seemingly indifferent to the workaday world in their insistence that language, art, and even architecture refer only to themselves, the new humanists become worldly enough when it comes to their own advancement up the academic ladder. Literary studies have become self-referential in a sense not alluded to by those who dwell on the inescapably self-referential quality of language: Their main function is to make academic reputations, to fill the pages of academic journals, and to sustain the enterprise of literary studies. The contempt for the general public, so unmistakable in the work of the new literary theorists, reflects an unwarranted conviction of their intellectual superiority, but it also reflects their understanding that no one gets tenure by writing for the general public.

Since the new humanistic establishment claims to stand against all establishments, on the side of oppressed minorities excluded from the academic "canon," it is important to recognize the condescension with which it views not only the public outside the academy but the minorities on behalf of which it pretends to speak. As Kimball argues, the assertion that writings produced by "white Western males before 1900"—now a standard term of reproach—are inaccessible to women, blacks, and Hispanics shows little respect for these groups' intelligence or their powers of imaginative identification. This kind of thinking "implies that the highest achievements of civilization are somehow off-limits or inaccessible to certain groups," in Kimball's words. The "emancipation rhetoric" of the academic turns out to be "deeply exclusionary—one might even say racist and sexist" in its underlying assumptions. Ordinary people, it appears—especially if they belong to the wrong ethnic group or race—cannot read the classics with any comprehension, if indeed they can read anything at all. Hence the curriculum has to be redesigned to emphasize film, photography, and books that make no particular demands on the reader—all in the name of democratizing culture.

THE STUDY OF popular culture, according to the authors of *Speaking for the Humanities*, a recent manifesto of the academic left, "provides students with a framework in which to criticize the materials they consume daily and unthinkingly." It may or may not have that happy effect, but one suspects that it commends itself to many teachers simply because it is more accessible to students than books full of unrecognizable allusions to cultural traditions and historical events beyond their immediate experience. Those who celebrate the "vigor and pertinence of contemporary discussion in the humanities" argue, quite rightly, that "instruction in otherness" is "one of the major roles of humanistic study." But their reforms often have the opposite effect. In the name of pluralism, students are deprived of access to experience beyond their immediate horizon and encouraged, moreover, to dismiss much of this experience—often preserved in works of classic stature—as the culture of "Western white males." At best, exposure to "otherness" turns out to be a one-way street. The children of privilege are urged—even required—to learn something about "marginalized, suppressed interests, situations, traditions," but blacks, Hispanics, and other minorities are exempted from exposure to "otherness" in the work of "Western white males." An insidious double standard, masking as tolerance, denies those minorities the fruits of the victory they struggled so long to achieve: access to the world's culture. The underlying message that they are incapable of appreciating or entering into that culture comes through just as clearly in the new academic "pluralism" as in the old intolerance and exclusion; more clearly, indeed, since exclusion rested on fear more than contempt. Thus slaveowners feared that access to the best of Euro-American culture would encourage a taste for freedom.

The case of Frederick Douglass (or of W. E. B. Du Bois, Langston Hughes, Richard Wright, Ralph Ellison, Harold Cruse, and other black intellectuals) shows that such fears were not misplaced. Douglass recalled in his autobiography that he began to study the art of rhetoric after reading of a slave who argued the case for freedom so eloquently that he converted his master. Douglass accordingly immersed himself in the acknowledged eighteenth-century masters of British oratory—Pitt, Sheridan, Burke, and Fox. "The reading of these speeches," he says, "added much to my limited stock of language, and enabled me to give tongue to many interesting thoughts, which had recently flashed through my soul, and died away for want of utterance." Today these same speeches would be disparaged as inappropriate objects of study for black people, part of a hateful canon of oppression (though in fact, they disappeared from the canon a long time ago), the perpetuation of which serves only to shore up the cultural imperialism of white males. But Douglass did not stop to ask himself—poor, benighted fellow that he was—whether a black man's mind would be deformed by exposure to the oppressor's culture or whether the case for freedom might better be argued in the idiom of his own people (or settled not by arguments at all but by force), and the eloquence of the Augustan Age, however stilted by twentieth-century standards, gave him a voice of his own and made it possible for him to enter into the public debate about slavery that was raging in his own time. His studies did not diminish his commitment to freedom or his identification with his own people, but they enabled him to speak on their behalf, and not only to speak but to order "interesting thoughts" that would otherwise have remained confused, incoherent, baffled, and abortive. The power of speech—acquired through the equivalent of a classical education—gave him access both to the inner world of his own thoughts and to the public world in which the fate of his people would be decided for better or worse.

Most of the shortcomings of our educational system can

be traced, in one way or another, to the growing inability to believe in the reality either of the inner world or of the public world, either in a stable core of personal identity or in a politics that rises above the level of platitudes and propaganda.

THE SIMPLIFICATION OF the humanities curriculum, in our time, has not led to increased enrollments in the humanities. Students understand all too clearly that courses in the humanities seldom offer much beyond "ideological posturing, pop culture, and hermetic word games," in Kimball's words. No doubt he underestimates the pressure on students to study subjects that will lead more directly to gainful employment, but it is nevertheless true, in my experience, that students—the better ones, anyway—reject a starvation diet of popular culture and literary theory, which tells them that "texts" refer only to themselves and to other texts and therefore cannot be expected to change the way we live. I think students are also put off by the prevailing mode of cultural criticism, which easily degenerates into a "species of cynicism," as Kimball says, "for which nothing is properly understood until it is exposed as corrupt, duplicitous, or hypocritical."

According to Kimball, the linguistic theories now so influential in the humanities, in their fascination with the ambiguity and imprecision of language, overlook the "middle ground between nihilistic skepticism and naive belief." Partisans of these theories hold up a false standard of disinterested objectivity, a "super-Cartesian" view of language as a "perfectly transparent medium that renders our thoughts about the world without loss or ambiguity," and then conclude that since language cannot possibly meet such a standard, it can never make any truth claims at all.

That is a telling criticism of the cynicism that refuses to distinguish between ideas and propaganda, argumentation and ideological warfare. But Kimball throws it around indiscriminately. He does not stop with an indictment of nihilists who insist that arguments are invariably political in the crudest sense and that the winners in any argument are those who have the power to impose their views on others. His indictment extends to anyone who questions the need for epistemological foundations. "Foundationalism," he notes with disapproval, "has emerged as a prime whipping boy for many contemporary academic humanists." It is more than a whipping boy, however; it is a serious issue that cannot be settled by citing the excesses and absurdities of those who seize on the slogan of antifoundationalism without understanding what the debate is about.

The attack on foundationalism is not just another academic fashion, even though it has become fashionable in some quarters. It grows out of the very same consideration that troubles Kimball himself: the fear that the "quest for certainty," as John Dewey called it, collapses into skepticism as soon as intellectual certainty is revealed as an illusion. The hope of grounding our knowledge of the world in propositions unassailable by doubt—the hope that inspired the Cartesian revolution in philosophy, the seventeenth-century scientific revolution, and much of the Enlightenment—has collapsed, and the attempt to weigh the consequences of this collapse is the subject of twentieth-century philosophy. Some philosophers have tried to rescue the old epistemology by narrowing the range of philosophical discourse to technical, formal questions on which it is supposedly possible to speak with mathematical precision. Others insist that nothing remains but complete skepticism. A third school, which includes the many varieties of twentieth-century pragmatism, holds that the impossibility of certainty does not preclude the possibility of reasoned discourse—of assertions that command provisional assent even though they lack unimpeachable foundations and are therefore subject to revision.

Inevitably, philosophical debates about foundationalism have influenced work in the humanities—for example, by prompting a more positive view of ideology than the views we were brought up with. Thus Clifford Geertz has argued that the postwar disparagement of ideology by social scientists like Raymond Aron, Edward Shils, Daniel Bell, and Talcott Parsons had the effect of proscribing not only politically self-serving statements but all claims not subject to scientific verification. (This was before Thomas Kuhn cast doubt on the idea of scientific verification itself.) The critique of ideology had the effect, in other words, of banning from political discussion and serious study a whole range of allusive, symbolic, metaphorical, and emotionally charged strategies of communication. The twentieth-century attack on ideology echoed the Enlightenment's attack on religion, compromising the analysis of political thought (by reducing it to lies, distortions, and rationalizations) in the same way that analysis of religious thought is compromised by reducing it to superstition.*

---

*"This analogy," Geertz insists, "is not farfetched. In Raymond Aron's *The Opium of the Intellectuals*, for example, not only the title—ironically echoic of Marx's bitter iconoclasm—but the entire rhetoric of the argument ('political myths,' 'the idolatry of history,' 'churchmen and faithful,' 'secular clericalism,' and so forth) reminds one of nothing so much as the literature of militant atheism. Shils's tack of invoking the extreme pathologies of ideological thought—Nazism, Bolshevism, or whatever—as its paradigmatic forms is reminiscent of the tradition in which the Inquisition, the personal depravity of the Renaissance popes, the savagery of Reformation wars, or the primitiveness of Bible-belt fundamentalism is offered as an archetype of religious belief and behavior. And Parsons's view that ideology is defined by its cognitive insufficien-

If Geertz is right, the cynicism that makes no distinction between power and persuasion was already implicit in the neo-positivist critique of ideology, the rhetoric of which was so unmistakably reminiscent of the rhetoric of militant atheism. Those who looked forward to the end of ideology hoped that political discussion could be confined to technical questions on which experts could agree. When the end of ideology failed to materialize, it was easy to conclude, with Foucault and Derrida, that knowledge of any kind is purely a function of power or, as Stanley Fish puts it, that "might makes right" if that means that "in the absence of a perspective independent of interpretation some interpretive perspective will always rule by having won out over its competitors." Geertz argues, on the other hand, that a given ideology prevails in the struggle with other ideologies not because its advocates have the power to silence opposition but because it provides a better "map" of reality, a more reliable guide to action. His rehabilitation of ideology—and, by extension, the critique of foundationalism, at least in some of its forms—serves to reopen the possibility of subjecting moral and political issues to serious discussion and of refuting those who deny the possibility of intelligently defending any moral or political position.

I N R E P L Y T O right-wing criticism of the humanities, the authors of *Speaking for the Humanities* summarize the skeptical position when they write: "We have learned to ask whether universalist claims do not in fact promote as a

---

cies vis-à-vis science is perhaps not so distant as it might appear from the Comtean view that religion is characterized by an uncritically figurative conception of reality, which a sober sociology, purged of metaphor, will soon render obsolete: we may wait as long for the 'end of ideology' as the positivists have waited for the end of religion."

norm the concerns of a particular group and set aside as partial or limited those of other groups." But "universalist claims" cannot be dismissed so easily. As Gramsci taught us a long time ago, no ideology could ever achieve "hegemony" if it served merely to legitimate the interests of a particular class and to "set aside" those of others. It is their capacity to speak to enduring human needs and desires that makes ideologies compelling, even though their view of the world is necessarily blind to their own limitations. To the extent to which ideologies express universal aspirations, their critics have to argue on the same grounds, not just to dismiss them as self-serving rationalizations. The need to argue on this common ground—not universal agreement on epistemological foundations—is what creates the possibility of a common culture.

Kimball rightly emphasizes the need for a common culture, but his rigid distinction between "objective" and "impartial judgment" and *"partis pris* lobbying"—between "dispassionate description and partisan propaganda," "truth" and "persuasion," "reason" and "rhetoric"—leaves little room for the important work of intellectual debate. Description is never "dispassionate" unless it addresses trivial or unimportant issues; judgment is never completely "impartial." Kimball's indiscriminate attack on the "antifoundationalist creed" implies that a common culture has to command universal assent and that instruction in the humanities therefore has to center on a canon of undisputed classics. But canons are always in dispute, always in the process of revision. Think how the canon of American literature looked a hundred years ago: lots of Longfellow and Whittier, no Whitman or Melville or Thoreau. The trouble with the humanities today is not that people want to revise the canon but that too many of them can't be bothered to argue for the exclusion or inclusion of particular works.

They engage not in argument but in blanket dismissal, often on the grounds that aesthetic judgments are irretrievably arbitrary and subjective. The practical effect of this kind of criticism is to install parallel curricula—one for women, one for blacks, one for Hispanics, one for white males—or to patch up the old curriculum (as at Stanford) on the principle of equal time. In either case, argumentation goes by the board, but it also goes by the board if we take the position that "politics" has to be kept out of education. It isn't "politics" that has "corrupted our higher education" (as Kimball announces in his subtitle) but the assumption that politics is another name for warfare. If politics is nothing more than "ideological posturing," as Kimball puts it, obviously it can have nothing to do with "reason," "impartial judgment," or "truth." Here again the academic left turns out to be in fundamental agreement with the right. Both hold the same debased view of politics as the rule of the strongest, a shouting match that drowns out the voice of reason.

The right and the left share another important assumption: that academic radicalism is genuinely "subversive." Kimball takes the radical claims of the academic left at face value. He does not object to the "tenured radicals" because they are more interested in tenure than in radicalism. He objects to them because in his view, they use the security of their academic position to attack the foundations of social order. "When the children of the sixties received their professorships and deanships they did not abandon the dream of radical cultural transformation; they set out to implement it. Now, . . . instead of attempting to destroy our educational institutions physically, they are subverting them from within." No doubt they would like to think so, but their activities do not seriously threaten corporate control of the universities, and it is corporate control, not academic radicalism, that has "corrupted our higher education." It is corporate control that has diverted social resources from the humanities into military and technological research, fostered an obsession with quantification that has destroyed the social sciences, replaced the English language with bureaucratic jargon, and created a top-heavy administrative apparatus whose educational vision begins and ends with the bottom line. One of the effects of corporate and bureaucratic control is to drive critical thinkers out of the social sciences into the humanities, where they can indulge a taste for "theory" without the rigorous discipline of empirical social observation. "Theory" is no substitute for social criticism, the one form of intellectual activity that would seriously threaten the status quo and the one form that has no academic cachet at all. Social criticism that addressed the real issue in higher education today—the university's assimilation into the corporate order and the emergence of a knowledge class whose "subversive" activities do not seriously threaten any vested interest—would be a welcome addition to contemporary discourse. For obvious reasons, however, this kind of discourse is unlikely to get much encouragement either from the academic left or from its critics on the right.

Part III

The Dark Night of the Soul

Eleven

The Abolition of Shame

Those who write about shame like to begin by deploring the shameful neglect of the subject by their predecessors. If they happen to be psychiatrists, they insist that shame has been not just neglected but actively suppressed. The time has come, they say, to lift the curtain of censorship and "bring shame out of the closet," in the words of Michael P. Nichols. Their self-conception requires the imagery of bold exploration, of the conquest of forbidden territory. Even when they reject everything else in Freud's work—and the current vogue of shame coincides with a growing reaction against Freud—the current generation of psychotherapists finds his iconoclasm irresistible: his air of defying accepted canons of modesty and reticence, his insistence on speaking the unspeakable.

Freud had good reason to see himself as a lonely intruder bravely risking his professional life in pursuit of knowledge everyone else preferred to conceal. The new archaeologists of shame, on the other hand, enter a field already mined by anthropologists, by the postwar generation of psychoanalysts (many of them refugees from Nazi Germany and well acquainted with the social repercussions of shame), and for that matter by Dale Carnegie and Norman Vincent Peale, who discovered the importance of self-esteem long before psychiatrists and developmental psychologists agreed to define shame as the absence of self-esteem and began to prescribe appropriate remedies. Shame, the latest site of intensive excavation by theorists and clinicians in search of buried treasure, is no longer a neglected, let alone a forbidden, subject. Donald L. Nathanson admits that it has become more than a little "trendy."

Anyway, the charge of concealment looks implausible on its face. Is there anything our culture still attempts to conceal—anything, that is, that can be exploited for its shock value? Nothing can shock us anymore, least of all intimate revelations about personal life. The mass media do not hesitate to parade the most outlandish perversions, the most degraded appetites. Moralists advise us that words like "outlandish," "perverse," and "degraded" belong to a discredited, excessively "judgmental" vocabulary of hierarchy and discrimination. The only thing forbidden in our culture of exposure is the inclination to forbid—to set limits on disclosure.

Instead of asking how we can lift the conspiracy of silence supposedly surrounding shame, we should ask why it gets so much attention in a shameless society. Perhaps the best answer is provided by Leon Wurmser in *The Mask of Shame*, the best of the psychoanalytic studies of shame and quite possibly the last, given the probable collapse of the whole psychoanalytic enterprise. By 1981, when it appeared, the reaction against psychoanalysis was in full swing: A chorus of critics denounced Freud's ideas as unscientific, elitist, patriarchal, and therapeutically useless. Within psychoanalysis, Heinz Kohut and his followers had shifted the emphasis from intrapsychic conflict to the "whole self" and its relations with others. The need to counter these tendencies led Wurmser to undertake a much deeper analysis of the inner conflicts leading to shame than anything offered by his predecessors.

Earlier studies had made much of the distinction between shame and guilt. In technical terms, guilt took its cue from the punishing aspect of the superego, shame from the loving and beloved aspect (the ego ideal). Guilt issued from defiance of the father, shame from the failure to live up to his internalized example. Although Wurmser himself built on this tradition, he cautioned against too much emphasis on the ego ideal. "A mere falling short of ego standards or even of the postulates of the ego ideal does not evoke shame." No less than guilt, shame had to be seen as a form of self-punishment, a fierce condemnation of the self that is rooted, in the case of shame, in the "absolute sense of unlovability." If this element of self-torture was missing, it was appropriate to speak only of a "loss of self-esteem." Wurmser's refusal to confuse this with shame made intelligible much that otherwise remained obscure.

Psychoanalysis, as Wurmser understood it, was, above all, the interpretation of inner psychic conflict and the inner defenses against it. His insistence on the "centrality of conflict," in the face of an "incessant pull away" from conflict that was making the psychoanalytic method increasingly superficial, had the added and unexpected advantage of restoring some of the moral and religious associations that once clustered around the concept of shame. Wurmser asked himself, in effect, how the same word could refer both to the impulse to pry and to the impulse to conceal.

Mindful of Freud's dictum that opposites share an underlying affinity, he found that his patients were simultaneously obsessed with seeing and with being seen.

One of them, a woman suffering from anxiety, depression, and a consuming suspiciousness, told him: "I want to find out the hidden, forbidden truth about who creates and who does not create"—a statement worthy of Faust or Prometheus. But she was also consumed with the fear that her own secrets would be revealed. Penetrating other people's secrets (those of her parents in particular) became a way of preserving her own. Her fear of defilement and dishonor made her wish to defile others—a striking illustration of the connection between shameful disgrace and the shameless act of exposure. Another patient wished to hide her face from the world—the characteristic stance of shame—but also had a compulsion to exhibit herself. It was as if she were saying, "I want to show the world how magnificently I can hide." Here the rage for exposure was redirected to the self, in the form of an exhibitionism that "knew no shame," as we used to say.

On the one hand, these patients wanted to see everything, as if they hoped to merge with the world through the medium of the eye. On the other hand, they wanted to dominate the world by making themselves objects of universal fascination. Fearing exposure, they wore the frozen, expressionless faces Wurmser came to recognize as the mask of shame: "the immovable, inscrutable, enigmatic expression of a sphinx." Yet this forbidding countenance served, in their fantasies, not only to hide their own secrets but to fascinate and dominate others, to punish others, as well, for attempting to penetrate their facades. The self-protective mask of shame was also the magically aggressive face of Medusa, which turns onlookers to stone.

Beneath the contradictory wish to hide and to spy, to

see and be seen, Wurmser detected a deeper set of paired opposites: the "polarity" between the "yearning for boundless union" and a "murderous contempt." Both arose out of an underlying fear of abandonment. According to a well-developed tradition of psychoanalytic speculation, attempts to restore a primal sense of omnipotence can take either of two forms. In the first the subject seeks to merge symbiotically with the world; in the other, to become absolutely self-sufficient. Wurmser's study of shame stood (somewhat uneasily, since he distrusted its Kleinian overtones) in this same tradition. The most intense experience of shame, he noted, grew out of the "conflict of union vs. separateness." The "archaic conflicts" that were "basic to severe psychopathology" originated, at the deepest level, in a "denial of everything that is not absolute"—everything, that is, "that is not total union and merger or its opposite, total isolation and destruction." Here again we see the baneful effects of the search for certainty.

What Wurmser's patients experience as shameful is the contingency and finitude of human life, nothing less. They cannot reconcile themselves to the intractability of limits. The record of their suffering makes us see why shame is so closely associated with the body, which resists efforts to control it and therefore reminds us, vividly and painfully, of our inescapable limitations, the inescapability of death above everything. It is man's bondage to nature, as Erich Heller once said, that makes him ashamed. "Anything that is nature about him, . . . anything that shows him to be enslaved by laws and necessities impervious to his will," becomes a source of unbearable humiliation, which can express itself in seemingly incompatible ways: in the effort to hide from the world but also in the effort to penetrate its secrets. What these opposite reactions share is a kind of outrage in the face of whatever is mysterious and therefore resistant to human control. "Shame," wrote Nietzsche, "exists everywhere where there is a 'mystery.' "

WHEN PSYCHOANALYSTS REJECT the temptation to dismiss shame as the vestigial remnant of an outmoded prudery, they have much to tell us about its moral and existential implications. Wurmser's study owes its power and its clarity not only to his sensitive reporting of case histories but also to his insistence on the philosophical dimension of psychoanalysis. He conceives his work as a "dialogue with the best minds that still speak directly to us across the abyss of death and time." It disturbs him that "the vast symbolic fields of the humanities no longer form the shared matrix in which psychoanalytic work is organically embedded." The newer studies of shame and self-esteem—only a few of which will be considered here, a small selection from a huge outpouring—owe very little to the best psychoanalytic tradition and suffer accordingly.

The decline in quality is immediately evident. The value of Donald Nathanson's *Shame and Pride*, the most ambitious of these studies, is inversely proportional to its pretensions. Nathanson wants to show that shame performs certain functions that contribute to psychic equilibrium, but his system often seems to yield little more than banalities. "Shame will occur whenever desire outruns fulfillment." "Shame affect is triggered any time interest or enjoyment is impeded." "Life is full of impediments to positive affect." "It seems that nearly everybody needs an inferior."

Nathanson thanks Wurmser for unstinting "support and assistance," but his approach exemplifies precisely the behaviorism that Wurmser cautions against. It treats "shame affect" as a "unique biological mechanism." It aims to "return psychology entirely to biological science" and to banish "mysticism." It rests on a mechanistic model of the psyche as a computer, a system for processing information. Evidently struggling for scientific precision, Nathanson writes much of the time in a barbarous jargon in which "startle" becomes a noun and "dissmell" refers to the recoil from unpleasant odors. He is deaf to the conversation of the ages, and perhaps to his patients as well, since he reports no case histories. As for his therapy, it seems to consist largely of drugs. "We stopped the medication, and the symptom disappeared." "All of these symptoms vanished when he began to take the drug *fluoxetine*." "She was astonished to see these feelings of shame disappear when she resumed her medication."

In place of the interpretation of intrapsychic conflict, Nathanson offers a mechanistic theory, derived from the work of Silvan Tomkins, in which affect acts as an "amplifier," informing the organism of unruly appetites in need of intelligent management. Shame, an essential component in our "basic wiring pattern," protects the organism "from its growing avidity for positive affect." By forcing us to "know and remember our failures," it acts as a "teacher." Just what it teaches remains a little unclear: To modify our expectations? To pursue more realistic goals? Whenever his prose veers too close to clarity, Nathanson interjects an explanation that defies explanation: "It [shame] is a biological system by which the organism controls its affective output so that it will not remain interested or content when it may not be safe to do so, or so that it will not remain in affective resonance with an organism that fails to match patterns stored in memory." In plain English, shame keeps us from taking ourselves too seriously; this seems to be the gist of it.

Whereas Wurmser pleads for the "heroic transcendence of shame" through love and work, Nathanson recommends a kind of inoculation against shame—a healthy dose of

shame in manageable amounts, such as we find in the therapeutic comedy of Buddy Hackett, that keeps it from
becoming lethal. What he finds appealing, I take it, is the
lowering effect of Hackett's bathroom humor. The
reminder that no one escapes "the call of nature," as our
grandmothers used to put it so delicately, serves both to
deflate self-importance and to mock false modesty—all the
more effectively, Nathanson seems to think, when it is
couched in coarse, uninhibited language.

Hackett's "comedy of acceptance" reconciles us to our
limitations, according to Nathanson. I think it merely
encourages us to lower our sights. There is a crucial difference between the acceptance of limitations and the impulse
to reduce everything exalted to its lowest common denomi-
nator. "Acceptance" becomes shameless, cynical surrender
when it can no longer distinguish between nobility and
pomposity, refinement of taste and social snobbery, modesty and prudery. Cynicism confuses delusions of grandeur, which call for moral and therapeutic correction, with
grandeur itself.

Cynicism, of course, is the last thing Nathanson intends
to promote. He wants only to replace shame with what he
calls pride—a sense of accomplishment based on acceptance
of our limitations. But his vaccine is worse than the disease.
By recommending the deflation of ideals as the prescription
for mental health, he proposes, in effect, to cure shame
with shamelessness. This is itself a well-known defense
(and, as such, hardly a cure), the strategy cogently identified by Wurmser as the "lifelong reversal" of the "'shameless' cynic," the transvaluation of values by means of which
"narcissistic grandiosity and contemptuousness defend
against a fatal brittleness and woundedness." As Wurmser
points out, this defense, shameless cynicism, now sets the
tone of our culture as a whole.

Everywhere there is an unrestrained exposure of one's emotions and of one's body, a parading of secrets, a wanton intrusion of curiosity. . . . It has . . . become hard to express tender feelings, feelings of respect, of awe, of idealization, of reverence. It almost belongs to the "good tone" to be irreverent. It is no accident that in German and Greek, words for shame are also words of reverence. . . . The culture of shamelessness is also the culture of irreverence, of debunking and devaluing ideals.

Trust in life carries the risk of disappointment, so we inoculate ourselves with irreverence.*

Even the most obtuse students of shame understand, in principle, that shamelessness is a strategy, not a solution. In *No Place to Hide*, Michael Nichols warns that "shamelessness is a reaction formation against shame, a defiant, counterphobic attempt to deny and overcome a profound inner fear of weakness." But Nichols and his like recognize the affinity between shamelessness and shame only in its most blatant form. They can see shamelessness in "defiance" but not in their own ideology of "acceptance." The deflation of "extravagant expectations"—Nichols's favorite remedy for the oppressive sense of failure—amounts to a milder version of Nathanson's strategy of existential distrust. Thus he warns against religion, which purveys "oversimplified messages about right and wrong" and holds up impossible standards—"a vision of righteousness that remains forever out of reach." The old religions preached the sinfulness of sex and divorce, discouraged "understanding and acceptance." Fortunately "today's enlightened min-

---

*The devaluation of ideals and the compulsion to drag everything down to the lowest level are central themes in the work of Philip Rieff, which is discussed in chapter 12.

isters and rabbis are preaching a humanistic acceptance of the self and the body." Indeed, they are "more attuned to humanistic concerns than most psychiatrists"—surely a backhanded compliment, though Nichols intends it as high praise.

"The story of Adam and Eve," in Nichols's retelling, "reflects the general awareness that children of nature don't know shame; they have to be taught." From this Panglossian point of view, we can rid the world of shame and many other evils simply by treating children with "empathy," engineering settings in which they can "feel good about themselves," and "validating their right to think and feel whatever they wish."

There is some value in the advice to "let them be themselves" if it helps to discourage overmanagement of children by adults. We do children a terrible disservice, however, by showering them with undeserved approval. The kind of reassurance they need comes only with a growing ability to meet impersonal standards of competence. Children need to risk failure and disappointment, to overcome obstacles, to face down the terrors that surround them. Self-respect cannot be conferred; it has to be earned. Current therapeutic and pedagogical practice, all "empathy" and "understanding," hopes to manufacture self-respect without risk. Not even witch doctors could perform a medical miracle on that order.

THE EARLY FREUDIANS warned against "prophylactic" misapplications of psychoanalysis, as Anna Freud called them. They knew that a superficial reading of Freud encouraged the notion that enlightened methods of child rearing could do away with suffering and neurosis. They countered this foolish optimism with the reminder that growing up is never easy, that children will never achieve maturity unless they work things out for themselves. But the helping professions paid no attention to this realism. In order to justify the expansion of therapeutic authority over the family, the school, and large areas of public policy, they made extravagant claims for their expertise. They set themselves up as doctors not only to sick patients but to a sick society.

By 1937 Karen Horney, one of the first of the Freudian revisionists, was already insisting that "neurosis and culture" were problems "not only for psychiatrists but for social workers and teachers," for "anthropologists and sociologists," and for all those professionals, indeed, who had become "aware of the significance of psychic factors" in social life. Therapy was no longer the business of psychiatrists alone, nor could it be confined to individuals. In an influential essay published in the same year, the sociologist Lawrence Frank took the position that society itself was the patient.

This has remained the dominant view, right down to the present day. It has come to be widely shared even by "religious and ethical groups," singled out (along with lawyers) by Frank as bastions of the old ethic of individual accountability. As Nichols says, the contemporary church is just as "enlightened" as the helping professions. "Pastors . . . speak out about healthy self-esteem. . . . You wouldn't have heard this twenty years ago." His description of pastoral speech is accurate enough, but his memory is too short. The clergy began to see the light a long time ago. The social gospel, an important influence in American Protestantism since the turn of the century, had prepared them for the idea that society is the patient. Henry J. Cadbury, a critic of the social gospel, observed in 1937 that it had become the "staple diet of American liberals," who "affirm with one voice that society, not individuals merely, is the subject of redemption." Thirty years later the Harvard theologian Harvey Cox argued in *The Secular City* that "the achievement of health in place of neurosis on the individual level cannot be separated from the restoration of wholeness to the entire society." Freud "concentrated on the sick individual in his therapy," Cox complained, but the sick individual could no longer be treated apart from the "sick society."

Low self-esteem is merely the latest form of social pathology commending itself to specialists in the cure of souls. It should not surprise us when the new pathologists of shame announce that a "more articulated theory" of shame, in the words of Michael Lewis, has "applicability to the social as well as to the individual level." Lewis readily embraces the cliché that blacks and women are "shamed by the culture in which they live," in need of "understanding rather than humiliation." Raising their self-esteem, he thinks, would "eliminate many social problems." "The solution I propose," he writes, "is a cognitive-affective program designed to reduce shame."

GLORIA STEINEM, LIKE Lewis, dwells at length on the social implications of low self-esteem, especially in women. Feminists have criticized her new book *Revolution from Within* as a retreat from political involvements, but it is better understood as another plea to the effect that politics and therapy are indistinguishable. It is completely consistent with the dominant brand of liberalism, a liberalism obsessed with the rights of women and minorities, with gay rights and unlimited abortion rights, with the allegedly epidemic spread of child abuse and sexual harassment, with the need for regulations against offensive speech, and with curricular reforms designed to end the cultural hegemony of "dead white European males." "Social justice," as liberals have come to define it, now refers to political therapies intended to undo the unwholesome effects of "authoritarian," "patriarchal" attitudes and to prevent anyone from "blaming the victim." The therapeutic discovery of shame finds its political expression in remedial programs administered by caretakers professing to speak on behalf of the downtrodden but concerned, above all, to expand their professional jurisdiction. Steinem's "revolution from within" does not signal a flight from politics, only a continuation of politics by other means.

Her therapeutic assault on shame requires political action for its completion. As a salutary example, she recommends California's Statewide Task Force to Promote Self-Esteem. She maintains that although journalists and politicians have ridiculed this noble experiment, it showed that almost every social problem can be traced to a failure of self-esteem. Self-contempt, the task force discovered, was a "primary causal factor" in "crime and violence, alcohol abuse, drug abuse, teenage pregnancy, child and spousal abuse, chronic welfare dependency, and failure to achieve in school"—the "very problems," Steinem adds, that "Americans fear most."

She does not bother to explain how the California task force arrived at this finding—that is, by ignoring the reservations that were advanced by the experts on whose testimony its report was based. Papers prepared for the task force repeatedly spoke of the "paucity of good research" linking low self-esteem to social pathology, but the chairman of the body, John Vasconcellos, dismissed these reservations on the grounds that they came from "those who only live in their heads, in the intellectual." The importance of self-esteem, he said, was confirmed by our "intuitive knowledge."

Steinem says nothing about the controversy surrounding the Vasconcellos report. It is enough for her that California's dubious example has been imitated by other states and by California's fifty-eight counties, almost every one of which now has its own task force on self-esteem. She too prefers to rely on "intuitive knowledge." Her book overflows with it. Children, she explains, should "feel loved and valued from the beginning." Most of us, however, were ignored or abused as children, and since we all "continue to treat ourselves the way we were treated as children," we therefore abuse ourselves as adults. But a "unique and true self resides in each one of us," the discovery of which will set us free. "The moment we find the true reason for some feeling that has an irrationally powerful hold over us, . . . the spell is broken."

It is hard to see how anyone could take such stuff seriously, but it commands automatic assent in many quarters and provides much of the rationale for the expansion of the welfare state. That liberal "activists," as Steinem refers to them admiringly, now find themselves reduced to such slogans may indicate that welfare liberalism is suffering from terminal fatigue. Is it really necessary to point out, at this late date, that public policies based on a therapeutic model of the state have failed miserably over and over again? Far from promoting self-respect, they have created a nation of dependents. They have given rise to a cult of the victim in which entitlements are based on the display of accumulated injuries inflicted by an uncaring society. The professionalization of compassion has not made us a kinder, gentler nation. Instead it institutionalizes inequality, under the pretense that everyone is "special" in his own way. Since the pretense is transparent, the attempt to make people feel good about themselves only makes them cynical instead. "Caring" is no substitute for candor.

If psychotherapy has failed as politics, most recently as the politics of self-esteem, it has also failed as a replacement for religion. The founder of psychoanalysis believed that men and women would outgrow the need for religion as they came to depend on their own resources. He was wrong about that, as it turned out. Still, his kind of therapy encouraged introspection and aimed at moral insight, and it was not entirely unreasonable, therefore, to suppose that psychiatry could take over the healing functions performed by priests and confessors—performed very clumsily at that, according to Freud.

For some time now, however, the psychiatric profession has been moving toward therapies aimed more at behavior modification than insight. Whatever it has gained in the management of symptoms, often with the help of drugs, has been achieved at the expense of introspection. This trend may be regrettable, but it is easy to see why psychoanalytic therapies, in their classic form, no longer have much of a following in the profession as a whole. They cost too much, last too long, and demand too much intellectual sophistication from the patient. Even the most enthusiastic admirers of the psychoanalytic method might be disconcerted to read that one of Wurmser's patients "abruptly" broke off analysis "in the 1,172nd session." Another patient of Wurmser's remained in analysis for eleven years. Still another "eventually killed herself by jumping off a bridge." When psychoanalytic treatment threatens to become interminable and often ends in failure, sometimes after years of intensive self-exploration, both doctors and patients understandably turn to methods promising fast relief, even at the price of deep understanding.

At its best psychoanalytic theory exposes the moral and existential dimension of mental conflict, but even then it cannot compete with religion. Wurmser's book on shame, a work in the grand tradition of psychoanalytic speculation, reminds us that psychoanalytically informed interpretation can reclaim ageless moral wisdom and deepen our understanding of it. Reading Wurmser, we see why shame and curiosity have always been so closely linked in people's minds, why shame ought to evoke feelings of awe and reverence, and why it refers, above all, to the irreducible element of mystery in human affairs.

But this very depth of moral understanding, so compelling at the level of moral theory, can also render psychoanalysis useless not only for therapeutic purposes but also as a guide to the conduct of life. The more it infringes on the territory once occupied by religion, the more it invites unflattering comparisons with its rival. Can psychoanalysis really do anything for people who suffer from an inner conviction of "absolute unlovability"? Maybe religion is the answer after all. It is not at all clear, at any rate, that religion could do much worse.

Twelve

Philip Rieff and the Religion of Culture

Violence, crime, and general disorder almost invariably strike foreign visitors as the most salient features of American life. First impressions, in this case, do not yield much to further acquaintance. A closer look reveals only less dramatic signs of the impending collapse of social order. American workers, it is said, are less efficient than their counterparts in Europe and Japan. American managers are no better than those who work for them. Their obsession with short-term profits allegedly makes them indifferent to the long run. A lust for immediate gratification pervades American society from top to bottom. There is a universal concern with the self—with "self-fulfillment" and more recently with "self-esteem," slogans of a society incapable of generating a sense of civic obligation. For native as well as foreign observers, the disinclination to subordinate self-interest to the general will comes

■ 213

uncomfortably close to capturing the essence of Americanism as the twentieth century approaches its end.

The picture may be overdrawn, but it contains enough
truth to raise the disturbing but inescapable question of
whether a democratic society can flourish, or even survive,
in the absence of the internal constraints that formerly supported the work ethic and discouraged self-indulgence.
Police and prisons are clearly inadequate to deal with the
lawlessness that is rapidly approaching critical dimensions.
The relentless increase of crime overwhelms the criminal
justice system, itself corrupted by cynical plea bargaining,
by the persistence of a racial double standard, and, on the
other hand, by misguided attempts to replace a punitive
with a therapeutic regime. Thanks to a misplaced clem-
ency, hard-core criminals gain premature release from
prison and resume their depredations seemingly undeterred
by the prospect of reincarceration.

In some ways the most disturbing symptom of all is the
recruitment of children into the culture of crime. With
nothing to look forward to in the way of a future, they are
deaf to the claims of prudence, let alone conscience. They
know what they want, and they want it now. Postpone-
ment of gratification, planning for the future, accumulation
of educational credits mean nothing to these prematurely
hardened children of the street. Since they expect to die
young, they are likewise unimpressed by penal sanctions.
Their way of life is admittedly risky, but at some point
risk becomes its own reward, an alternative to the sheer
hopelessness they would otherwise be left with.

If the collapse of internal constraints were confined to
the criminal classes, it might be possible, by means of a
combination of incentives and stricter enforcement of the
laws, to restore a sense of obligation. But the culture of
shamelessness is not confined to the underclass. In their

desire for immediate gratification, together with their identification of gratification with material acquisition, the
criminal classes merely imitate their betters. We have to
ask ourselves, therefore, what accounts for this wholesale
defection from the standards of personal conduct—civility,
industry, self-restraint—that were once considered indispensable to democracy.

An exhaustive investigation would uncover a great number of influences, but the gradual decay of religion would
stand somewhere near the head of the list. In America, to
be sure, one speaks of the decay of religion with some hesi-
tation. The number of those who profess belief in a personal God, belong to a religious denomination, and attend
services with some regularity remains remarkably high,
compared with other industrial nations. This evidence
might suggest that the United States has somehow managed to escape the secularizing influences that have elsewhere transformed the cultural landscape. The appearance
is deceptive, however. Public life is thoroughly secularized.
The separation of church and state, nowadays interpreted
as prohibiting any public recognition of religion at all, is
more deeply entrenched in America than anywhere else.
Religion has been relegated to the sidelines of public
debate. Among elites it is held in low esteem—something
useful for weddings and funerals but otherwise dispens-
able. A skeptical, iconoclastic state of mind is one of the
distinguishing characteristics of the knowledge classes.
Their commitment to the culture of criticism is understood
to rule out religious commitments. The elites' attitude to
religion ranges from indifference to active hostility. It rests
on a caricature of religious fundamentalism as a reactionary
movement bent on reversing all the progressive measures
achieved over the last three decades.

It is not enough to note that religious enthusiasm has

declined; it is also necessary to ask what has taken its place. The vacuum left by secularization has been filled by a permissive culture that replaces the concept of sin with the concept of sickness. But the therapeutic world view does not stand in relation to religion in unambiguous opposition. In the beginning at least, things were more complicated. The psychoanalytic movement, wellspring of the therapeutic culture, stood in a highly ambiguous relation to religion, at once complementary and competitive. Psychoanalysis too presented itself as a cure of souls, a source of moral insight. Its method, introspection, linked it to a long tradition of speculation in which self-knowledge is seen as the necessary beginning of wisdom. Though many of its practitioners tried to make psychoanalysis a purely technical discipline, with its own jargon and its esoteric procedures, its subject matter drew it irresistibly toward the existential questions that have always defined religious discourse. Melanie Klein, of all Freud's successors the most consistently preoccupied with ethical issues, wrote essays the titles of which unmistakably announced their existential concerns: "Love, Guilt, and Reparation," "Envy and Gratitude," "The Early Development of Conscience in the Child." Freud's own writings, full of allusions to art, religion, and moral philosophy, betrayed his sense of indebtedness to moralizing rather than medical precursors. He spoke of psychoanalysis as a science, but he used the term so broadly at times as to imply that the psychoanalytic practitioner had more in common with a philosopher or a preacher than with a technician in a white coat. He defended lay analysis and resisted the medicalization of psychoanalytic practice. He objected to the "obvious American tendency to turn psychoanalysis into a mere housemaid of psychiatry." Not only did he think that medical training should not be required of analysts, but he went so far as to discourage it.

In his view, analysts ought to be trained in the rudiments of anatomy and physiology but also in mythology, the psychology of religion, and the classics of literature. He insisted that personal experience of suffering, together with the capacity for introspection, represented the indispensable foundation of psychoanalytic understanding.

It was with good reason that Philip Rieff, one of the most astute of Freud's interpreters, entitled one of his studies *Freud: The Mind of the Moralist*. Norman O. Brown nudged psychoanalysis even further in the direction of religion in his *Life against Death*. Carried to its "logical conclusion and transformed into a theory of history," psychoanalysis, Brown observed, "gathers to itself ageless religious aspirations."

Yet psychoanalysis presented itself, at the same time, as the competitor and successor of religion. There was nothing ambiguous in Freud's dismissal of religion as an illusion or in his insistence that this particular illusion had no future. Religious belief, he thought, was a relic of humanity's childhood, when men and women naïvely projected their hopes and fears into the heavens. Now that science had provided human beings with the means by which they could control their own destiny, religion would wither away just as primitive magic had withered under the initial assault of religion itself.

Psychoanalysis and religion were even more deeply at odds than Freud's explicit rejection of religion would imply. In spite of his objections to a psychoanalytic practice that would reduce it to a mere "housemaid of psychiatry," his own discoveries contributed to the emergence of a therapeutic view of the world. Sickness and health replaced guilt, sin, and atonement as the dominant concerns guiding those who struggled to make sense of the buried life of the mind. Psychiatrists found that their practice required a suspension of moral judgment. At the very least they found it necessary to establish a permissive atmosphere in which patients could speak freely without fear of condemnation. What was appropriate in the consulting room, of course, was not necessarily appropriate in the everyday world outside, yet the habit of forbearance, once having established itself as the first principle of psychiatric therapy, soon became a kind of automatic reflex regulating all forms of interpersonal exchange. A "nonjudgmental" habit of mind, easily confused with the liberal virtue of tolerance, came to be regarded as the *sine qua non* of sociability.

It did not take people long to see that a therapeutic point of view could be put to social and political uses. It served to lift the burden of moral failure once associated with poverty and unemployment, to shift the blame from the individual to "society," and to justify policies designed to relieve those who suffered through no fault of their own. During the Great Depression, members of the health, education, and welfare professions were horrified to discover that many Americans, even victims of large-scale unemployment, still clung to the ethic of self-help and refused to acknowledge the individual's right to relief. Partisans of the welfare state had to persuade the public that poverty should not be attributed to lack of enterprise; that the system, not the individual, was at fault; that dependence on public relief was no disgrace; and that self-help, in the era of organization, was a snare and a delusion. "The individual," wrote the sociologist Lawrence Frank in his memorable essay "Society as the Patient," "instead of seeking his own personal salvation and security, must recognize his almost complete dependence upon the group." Frank's statement of the alternatives—individual accountability or "group life"—was profoundly misleading since group life itself presupposes the trust that can prevail only when individuals are held accountable for their actions. But for humanitarians shocked by mass suffering and the passivity with which Americans seemed to accept it, the first step toward recovery was to "absolve the individual from guilt," as Frank put it. The debates touched off by the Depression and the New Deal appeared to confirm the wisdom of therapeutic as opposed to ethical insights into social problems. The "conception of a sick society in need of treatment," according to Frank, was far more illuminating than conceptions stressing "human volition, human autonomy, and individual responsibility." A punitive morality that attributed social ills to "individual wickedness and guilt," on the other hand, had nothing to contribute to an understanding of modern society. Its standard remedies—"more laws, more regulation, and more severe punishment"—had failed over and over again. The time had come for a new departure, at once more scientific and more humane.

Frank's call for a new humanism met with a willing reception. In the second half of the twentieth century therapeutic concepts and jargon have penetrated so deeply into American culture—most recently in the guise of a broad-gauged campaign to raise people's "self-esteem"—that it has become almost impossible to remember how the world appeared to those not yet initiated into the mysteries of mental health. The psychoanalytic profession may have fallen on hard times, but a therapeutic sensibility is diffused even more widely than it was in 1966, when Philip Rieff brought out his second book, aptly entitled *The Triumph of the Therapeutic*. Today the therapeutic has triumphed so completely that Rieff seems to see little hope of challenging it. The prospects of reviving rival models of discourse appear so dim that he now wonders whether there is any point to publishing anything at all. "Why publish?" he asked himself not long ago. "With so many authors, who remains behind to read?" Twenty years have passed since Rieff brought out his last book, *Fellow Teachers;* evidently he meant what he said when he urged authors to file away their best ideas instead of adding to the "babel of criticism" that threatens to deafen us all. Our most eloquent and effective critic of the therapeutic style asks us to consider the possibility, in effect, that the most telling form of criticism, in a culture in which the activity of criticism has itself been assimilated to therapeutic purposes, may turn out to be silence.

A collection of essays written over the course of his career, edited not by Rieff himself but by Jonathan Imber, a former student and now a teacher of sociological theory at Wellesley, shows how insistently he has returned to certain central themes: the displacement of religion by therapy; the conflict between moral attitudes toward experience and aesthetic and therapeutic attitudes; the "hypertrophy of criticism, by which the character disorder of psychologizing intellectuals is best diagnosed." In addition to work on Freud and the emergence of "psychological man," this new collection, *The Feeling Intellect*, contains essays on a great variety of subjects: Disraeli, Orwell, Oscar Wilde, Charles Horton Cooley (Rieff's favorite among American sociologists), the black sociologist Kelly Miller, and the Oppenheimer case, among others. Yet Rieff's central preoccupations seldom recede very far from view. The point of the essay on Oppenheimer (1958) is that both Oppenheimer and his detractors accepted a therapeutic frame of reference: Instead of debating Oppenheimer's record on its political merits, they argued about whether his association with Communists exposed psychological flaws that should disqualify him from public service. The essay on Disraeli (1952) argues that Disraeli (like Freud) refused to disclaim his Jewish heritage and thus escaped the "ultimate risk" (as Rieff says elsewhere in connection with Freud) "of cutting himself off from the devout practice of its creed." Something of the same idea informs the essay on Orwell (1954), another intellectual who lost his religion but managed to keep up the "essential Christian action of brotherliness and compassion." Modernism continues to live off the capital of the creeds it has rejected, and the most admirable among modernist intellectuals, in Rieff's view, have always been aware of this dependence—even when, like Freud, they were urging their readers to outgrow it.

The collapse of religion, its replacement by the remorselessly critical sensibility exemplified by psychoanalysis, and the degeneration of the "analytic attitude" into an all-out assault on ideals of every kind have left our culture in a sorry state. Rieff does not expect immediate improvement, nor does he advance a program of cultural renovation; but neither, on the other hand, does he speak in the voice of doom and despair. Bad as things are, he still thinks it is possible—or was possible, at least, in 1973, when *Fellow Teachers* appeared—to make a modest contribution to the cause of truth and justice. It is possible, for example, to find honorable employment as a teacher, provided that teachers do not give in to the temptation to become "armchair prophets." The university, notwithstanding its present disarray, is a "sacred institution," and teachers can set an example for others if they approach their calling in a spirit of reverence. The office of the devoted teacher is not to deify or even defend a "dying culture" but to resist the "downward identification" that threatens any form of culture at all. Rieff's advice to teachers, which consists largely of negative commandments, reflects his belief that teachers betray their vocation when they become gurus or entertainers. Avoid "idea-mongering," the "marketing of positions." Refuse to join the ranks of "public men." "Abjure prophecy."

IT IS FITTING that Rieff addresses his "fellow teachers" so largely in terms of "what is not to be done." The heart of any culture, as he sees it, lies in its "interdictions." Culture is a set of moral demands—"deeply graven interdicts, etched in superior and trustworthy characters." This is why it makes sense to describe the United States today as a "cultureless society." It is a society in which nothing is sacred and therefore, nothing is forbidden. An anthropologist might object that a cultureless society is a contradiction in terms, but Rieff objects to the way in which social scientists have reduced the concept of culture to a "way of life." According to Rieff, culture is a way of life backed up by the will to condemn and punish those who defy its commandments. A "way of life" is not enough. A people's way of life has to be embedded in "sacred order"—that is, in a conception of the universe, ultimately a religious conception, that tells us "what is not to be done."

Those who regard tolerance as the supreme virtue and confuse love with permissiveness will find these propositions forbidding, if they bother to read Rieff at all; but if they allow themselves to be drawn into his argument, suspending their prejudice against unduly "judgmental" procedures and policies—against the very concept of punishment—they will come to see the justice of his deliberately provocative assertion that "repression is truth." Every culture has to narrow the range of choices in some way, however arbitrary such limitations may seem. To be sure, it also has to see to it that its controls do not reach too far into people's private lives. But if it allows every impulse a public expression—if it boldly declares that "it is forbidden to forbid," in the revolutionary slogan of 1968—then it not only invites anarchy but abolishes the "sacred distances" on which the category of truth finally depends. When every expression is equally permissible, nothing is true. "By the creation of opposing . . . ideals, of militant truths, a seal is fastened upon the terrific capacity of man to express everything."

Rieff's unfashionably "maximal" definition of culture, advanced in opposition to the minimal definition favored by anthropologists and other social scientists, results in a sweeping condemnation of the American way of life, but it also opens a ray of hope. If Rieff is correct in his contention that culture rests on willingness to forbid, a "remissive" culture like our own cannot be expected to survive indefinitely. Sooner or later our remissive elites will have to rediscover the principle of limitation. The modern project may have run its course. The "idea that men need not submit to any power . . . other than their own" is by no means discredited, but it is losing its capacity to inspire heady visions of progress. In the face of accumulating evidence to the contrary, it is more and more difficult to believe that modern men "are becoming gods." The therapeutic movement, moreover, has "not yet penetrated deep down" into the class structure. In *Fellow Teachers* Rieff cites the persistence of old-fashioned moralities among the "less educated" as "another reason to hope." Popular resistance to the "religion of criticism" enables us to "hope for a renascence of guilt."

Optimism about our prospects would be foolish—even more foolish in 1993 than it was in 1963. Modernity may be drawing to an end, as Rieff suggested in 1981, but the postmodern sensibility that claims to replace it is no improvement. Still, Rieff's appeal for patience and hope continues to serve as a useful corrective to apocalyptic discouragement. "We can only have faith and wait; and see."

Rieff's position has remained remarkably consistent over the years. It is the tone and style of his work that have changed. In the fifties and sixties he wrote as a public intellectual, for an audience of general readers who presumably shared a common vocabulary and a common frame of reference. Many of his essays appeared in general magazines like *Commentary*, *Encounter*, and *Partisan Review*. His books were published by houses prominent in the commercial trade, *Freud: The Mind of the Moralist* by Viking (and in a paperback edition by Anchor), *The Triumph of the Therapeutic* by Harper. Even when he wrote for scholarly journals, Rieff's prose exemplified the analytic, critical attitude that he recommended (notwithstanding his awareness of its disintegrating effect on traditional beliefs) as the only attitude available to intellectuals living in a world "spent of sacred forces." His early essays were informed by an ideal of "committed" scholarship, "passionate subjectivity." He praised Anders Nygren's *Agape and Eros*, in 1954, as an "exemplary case of committed history, partial and yet thorough in the exhibition of the other side." He quarreled with Hannah Arendt's *Origins of Totalitarianism* but commended the author's "prophetic intention": "Better a creative error than the uncreative truth." He deplored the "German disease" in scholarship, inveighed against footnotes, and found virtue in unobtrusive erudition. In a 1952 review of John T. McNeill's *History of the Cure of Souls*, he wrote that "McNeill has the final, moral virtue of the historian: . . . he is not neutral."

Between *The Triumph of the Therapeutic* and *Fellow Teachers* there is a significant shift in Rieff's tone. In the later work he warns against "play-acting of the prophetic role" and urges "objectivity." He no longer writes as a public intellectual or addresses himself to the "general readership" he was addressing in 1951. He insists that "it is our duty, as teachers, not to be public men." The public has ceased to exist, for Rieff; there is only a literary market, dominated by the traffic in cultural entertainments (which now include "criticism" and "prophecy"). Communication even with fellow teachers is beset with difficulties. *Fellow Teachers* takes the form of an open letter to Robert Boyers and Robert Orill, editors of *Salmagundi* who had invited Rieff to submit to a public interview at Skidmore College. "Is it possible," Rieff asks, "that my invitation to come to Skidmore . . . was based upon a happy misunderstanding? Did you imagine that I am a herald of the therapeutic?" It is hard to see how anyone could have imagined any such thing, but the remark illustrates Rieff's exaggerated apprehensions about the possibility of clear and open communication between intellectuals. His response was an uncharacteristic assertion of neutrality. "I am neither for nor against [the culture of the therapeutic]. I am a scholar-teacher of sociological theory." The disclaimer was not very convincing; it was symptomatic of a change in the cultural climate, however, that Rieff felt obliged to make it. It was likewise significant that he rejected a public interview, on the grounds that it could not serve to transmit the kind of "privileged knowledge" teachers pass on to their students. Instead of engaging in public exchange, intellectuals who were serious about their calling needed to withdraw into their "academic enclaves" and to encourage the "slower understanding" of the classroom. The forum was a place only for theatrics.

These arguments, which vaguely recall Walter Lippmann's disparaging remarks about public opinion in his debate with Dewey, also anticipated the position taken by Allan Bloom in *The Closing of the American Mind*, a book that upheld the university as a place where scholars could talk to one another and to the best of their students, in a hermetic language deliberately designed to throw outsiders off the track, about enduring philosophical questions that have never been of more than passing interest to the general public. For many intellectuals of integrity, the cultural revolution of the late sixties discredited the idea of committed public scholarship. The concept of the public became indistinguishable from the phenomenon of publicity. Under these circumstances Rieff's decision to write less, to publish with university presses and scholarly journals, and to devote his energies to "strengthening our enclaves" becomes intelligible, if not defensible. The result, however, has been the opposite, at least in Rieff's case, of what might have been expected: an exaggeration of precisely the theatrical and self-dramatizing elements in Rieff's style. His writing has become not more academic but more oracular, more "prophetic" the more it warns against the prophetic role. In his early work Rieff spoke with force and conviction but always in a direct, candid, unaffected tone of voice. Now he prefers to speak, much of the time, in cryptic aphorisms, paradoxes, and double meanings. He himself refers to his characteristic tone as "guarded." He writes too many footnotes—not pedantic bibliographical footnotes, to be sure, but long expository asides that seem to betray an unwillingness to engage the reader more directly. His writing has become, by design, less accessible and at the same time more portentous and apocalyptic even though Rieff is constantly warning himself against those very faults.

NOW THAT THE public arena seems to have been irreversibly corrupted by the aggressive marketing of ideas, the decision to think of oneself as a teacher rather than a public intellectual is one that many others besides Rieff have reluctantly made. In Rieff's case, as in others, it seems to be associated with a new emphasis on the university as a "sacred institution" in which "privileged knowledge" is stored and "guardedly" transmitted. This view of the life of the mind strikes me as inconsistent with Rieff's observation that the worst way to defend culture is by deifying it. It is also inconsistent with his contention that modern intellectuals should not aspire to become successors of the clergy. It tends to make a religion out of culture, something Rieff condemned in his earlier work, particularly in the splendid chapter on religion in *Freud: The Mind of the Moralist*.

Freud's attack on religion, Rieff pointed out in that book, rested on a "misunderstanding of religion itself as social." Like Kant, Freud saw religion as the "solemn air of a sanctity" (in Freud's words) that gave moral duty the status of divine commands and thus perpetuated the "laws of culture." But religion is not culture, and the best interpreters of Christianity, as Rieff noted, have always distinguished "between faith and the institutions and attitudes by which it is transmitted at any given time." Thus Kierkegaard "diagnosed the malaise of the nineteenth century" as the "confusion between religion and culture," Christ and Christendom. Freud, on the other hand, "assumed religion to be conformist," as if its only function were to guarantee social order. For him "Christianity meant always the church, a repressive social institution"—not the prophetic tradition, which exposed the corruption of the church and accused Christians of identifying God's purposes with their own. Freud lost sight of the difference between "prophetic denunciation" and "civic submission," according to Rieff.

In *The Future of an Illusion* Freud posed the question of whether society could get along without religion in the form of an imaginary dialogue. His interlocutor emphasizes the "practical" value of religion in enforcing morality. He concedes that religion is a "hoax" but defends its necessity "for the protection of culture." Freud himself believed that men and women could now dispense with religion, but the important point is that he posed the question in this way. It was the wrong question, according to Rieff. The issue was not whether religion was necessary but whether it was true. Since the publication of *Fellow Teachers*, however, Rieff has begun to sound more and more like Freud's interlocutor, defending religion—the religion of culture at that—as the necessary source of social order.

It takes nothing away from the dignity of the academic calling to remind ourselves that the university is not a sacred institution and that God, not culture, is the only appropriate object of unconditional reverence and wonder. Culture may well depend on religion (Freud's contrary view notwithstanding), but religion has no meaning if it is seen merely as a prop of culture. Unless it rests on a disinterested love of being in general, religious faith serves only to clothe human purposes with a spurious air of sanctity. This is why an honest atheist is always to be preferred to a culture Christian. Freud and Max Weber, Rieff's masters and models, were admirable in their determination to live without this particular form of consolation—the illusion that human purposes coincide with those of God. The very same illusion, however, has always been the principal target of religious prophecy. Indeed, it is their common enmity to the cultural pretensions of pious folk that reveals the kinship between the prophetic tradition and the exemplary tradition of secular intellectuals like Weber and Freud. Rieff belongs to this tradition too, except when he forgets himself and identifies a sense of the sacred too closely with institutions and the "interdictions" they enforce.

We need institutions and interdictions, God knows, but

they are not themselves sacred. Nothing but confusion, as Luther and Calvin pointed out a long time ago—and as Rieff himself has reminded us on many occasions—comes from equating faith with submission to the moral laws mankind makes for its own governance.

T h i r t e e n

The Soul of Man under Secularism

M y title comes from a little book by Oscar Wilde, *The Soul of Man under Socialism*, which was published a little more than a hundred years ago, in February 1891. Wilde's intention, as always, was to dazzle and scandalize his readers, and *his* title served as a typically Wildean affront to respectable opinion. It linked a concept derived from religion, the soul, with an aggressively secular ideology that drew much of its inspiration from Marx's famous condemnation of religion as the opiate of the people.

This was perhaps the only Marxist dictum that Wilde could endorse without reservation. He was hardly an orthodox Socialist. "We are all of us more or less Socialists now-a-days," he told an interviewer in 1894, but his own version of the socialist creed celebrated the artist, not the horny-handed son of toil, and conceived of socialism, moreover, as the best hope for a new kind of individualism—a "new Hellenism," as he referred to it in the closing pages of his non-Communist manifesto. Orthodox Marxists ridiculed his aesthetic brand of socialism, but Wilde had the last laugh. His religion of art has survived the collapse of the Marxist utopia. Of all the secular religions that emerged in the nineteenth century, this one turned out to be the most durable—in its own way the most seductive and insidious as well.

Socialism, as Wilde understood it, was simply another name—in 1891, in the social circles in which Wilde was at home, a deliberately provocative name—for the elimination of drudgery by machines. Wilde had no patience with those who proclaimed the dignity of labor. "There is nothing necessarily dignified about manual labor at all, and most of it is absolutely degrading." In the future it would be done by sophisticated machinery. The progress of science and technology would gradually eliminate poverty, suffering, and injustice. The collectivization of production would liberate the poor from want, but it would also liberate the rich from the burden of managing and defending their property. If manual labor was degrading, property was a "bore," in Wilde's opinion. "Its duties make it unbearable. In the interest of the rich we must get rid of it." No less than manual labor, the administration of property distracted people from the real business of life: the cultivation and enjoyment of "personality." Once the state took over the production of useful objects, individuals could devote themselves to the production of "what is beautiful." The "true personality of man" would come into its own. "It will grow naturally and simply, flowerlike, or as a tree grows. . . . It will never argue or dispute. It will not be always meddling with others, or asking them to be like itself. It will love them because they will be different. . . . The per-

sonality of man will be very wonderful. It will be as wonderful as the personality of a child."

Socialism, in Wilde's conception, would not come about
through the action of the masses. The masses were too stupefied by drudgery to be capable of emancipating themselves. They were "extraordinarily stupid" in their
deference to authority. Indeed, they were "not really conscious" of their own suffering. "They have to be told of it
by other people"—by "agitators," an "absolutely necessary
class without whom "there would be no advance towards
civilization." Agitators were the political equivalent of artists: disturbers of the peace, enemies of conformity, rebels
against custom. They shared with artists a hatred of authority, a contempt for tradition, and a refusal to court popular
favor. Agitators and artists were the supreme embodiment
of individualism, wishing only to please themselves. They
took "no notice whatever of the public." Nor did they pay
the slightest attention to the "sickly cant about doing what
other people want because they want it; or any hideous cant
about self-sacrifice." Artists were accountable only to themselves, and their selfishness, as it might be regarded from
the point of view of conventional morality, was the precondition of any genuine achievement of the imagination. All
the great leaders in history, according to Wilde, had the
artistic temperament. Jesus Christ himself was an artist
with an artist's message to the world. "He said to man, 'You
have a wonderful personality. Develop it. Be yourself.' "

In his *De Profundis*, the long letter to Lord Alfred Douglas written six years later from the depths of his imprison-
ment in Reading Gaol, Wilde amplified this interpretation
of "Christ as the precursor of the romantic movement in
life," the "most supreme of individualists." Having "created
himself" out of "his own imagination," Jesus of Nazareth
preached the power of imagination as the "basis of all spiri-

tual and material life," according to Wilde. He preached imaginative sympathy, not altruism, but his own powers of sympathetic identification made him the "mouthpiece" of the "entire world of the inarticulate, the voiceless world of pain." His life, as recorded in the Gospels, was "just like a work of art." He belonged "with the poets," and "his chief war was against the Philistines"—the "war that every child of light has to wage." Even in the depths of his own public degradation and despair, Wilde saw no reason to modify what he had written in *The Soul of Man under Socialism:* "that he who would lead a Christ-like life must be entirely and absolutely himself." As he put it in the earlier text, "The message of Christ to man was simply 'Be thyself.' That is the message of Christ."

This kind of message, whether or not it came from Christ and whether or not it was cast in a purely secular idiom or in the pseudospiritual idiom of *De Profundis*, appealed to intellectuals in search of a substitute for religious faiths by then widely regarded as offensive to the modern mind. In place of self-denial and self-control, it offered the seductive vision of selfhood unconstrained by civic, familial, or religious obligations. It confirmed artists and intellectuals in their sense of superiority to the common herd. It sanctioned their revolt against convention, against bourgeois solemnity, against stupidity and ugliness. By equating social justice with artistic freedom, the religion of art made socialism palatable to intellectuals who might otherwise have been repelled by its materialism. In the heyday of the socialist movement its attraction for intellectuals cannot be adequately explained without considering the way it overlapped with the bohemian critique of the bourgeoisie. Socialists and aesthetes shared a common enemy, the bourgeois philistine, and the unremitting onslaught against bourgeois culture was far more lasting in its effects, in the

West at least and now probably in the East as well, than the attack on capitalism.

In the 1960s revolutionary students adopted slogans much closer in spirit to Wilde than to Marx: "All power to the imagination"; "It is forbidden to forbid." The continuing appeal of such ideas, thirty years later, should be obvious to anyone who casts an eye over the academic scene and the media. The postmodern mood, so called, is defined on the one hand by a disillusionment with grand historical theories or "metanarratives," including Marxism, and by an ideal of personal freedom, on the other hand, that derives in large part from the aesthetic revolt against middle-class culture. The postmodern sensibility rejects much of modernism as well, but it is rooted in the modernist ideal of individuals emancipated from convention, constructing identities for themselves as they choose, leading their own lives (as Oscar Wilde would have said) as if life itself were a work of art.

The tradition of romantic subjectivity had another advantage over Marxism and other ideologies more firmly rooted in the secularizing soil of the Enlightenment. As the child of the Counter-Enlightenment in Germany and England, the romantic tradition was more keenly aware of the limits of enlightened rationality. Without denying the achievements of the Enlightenment, it recognized the danger that the "disenchantment of the world," in Friedrich von Schiller's phrase, would lead to emotional and spiritual impoverishment. Max Weber seized on this phrase as the key to the historical process of rationalization, the central theme of his own work. Reason enhanced human control over nature, but it deprived humanity of the illusion that its activity had any significance beyond itself. Karl Mannheim, Weber's student and successor, referred to this as the "problem of ecstasy." In his essay "The Democratization of Culture," published in 1932, Mannheim reminded his readers that "a man for whom nothing exists beyond his immediate situation is not fully human." The disenchantment of the world made it "flat, uninspiring, and unhappy." It deprived men and women of the experience of ecstasy—literally the trancelike state of being beside oneself, more broadly a state of overmastering feeling, as of rapture. "There is no Beyond; the existing world is not a symbol for the eternal; immediate reality points to nothing beyond itself."

Mannheim believed that the reduction of "vertical distance," which he associated with democracy, at least created the possibility of authentic, "purely existential human relationships" unmediated by religion or by religiously derived ideologies like romantic love. Weber himself was less sanguine. The famous peroration of his *Protestant Ethic and the Spirit of Capitalism*—"specialists without spirit, sensualists without heart"—offered a chilling view of the human prospect. Like Freud, with whom he had much in common, Weber spurned the consolation of religion and its secular substitutes, insisting on the intellectual's duty to "bear the fate of the times like a man." Freud's tone, likewise, was wistful but firm: Let us put away childish things. Likening religion to a "childhood neurosis," Freud insisted that "men cannot remain children forever." He added that "it is something, at any rate, to know that one is thrown upon one's own resources," and there is a certain heroism in the determination of Freud and Weber to face unflinchingly facts that could not be altered, in their view, and to live without illusions.

Those who were looking for something to believe in could hardly find much comfort in this uncompromising commitment to "intellectual integrity," as Weber called it. They were more likely to be attracted to the aestheticism of Oscar Wilde or to Carl Jung's spiritualized version of psychoanalysis. Freud's version, according to Jung, could not "give modern man what he is looking for." It satisfied only "people who believe they have no spiritual needs or aspirations." Contrary to the Freudians, Jung claimed, spiritual needs were too urgent to be ignored. Treating those needs as if they were analogous to hunger or sexual desire, Jung insisted that they would always find expression in one "outlet" or another. Psychoanalysts accordingly discovered in the course of their practice that they could not escape "problems which, strictly speaking, belong to the theologian."

The beauty of Jung's system, for those threatened with "meaninglessness," as he liked to call it, was that it offered "meaning" without turning its back on modernity. Jung assured his followers, in effect, that they could remain thoroughly modern without sacrificing the emotional solace formerly provided by orthodox religion. His description of the modern condition began with the usual reference to the lost childhood of the race. The medieval world, in which "men were all children of God . . . and knew exactly what they should do and how they should conduct themselves, now lay "as far behind as childhood." Its innocence could not be recaptured; the world could only go forward to a "state of wider and higher consciousness." The fully modern man— "by no means the average man"—had to live without "metaphysical certainties"; he was "thrown back upon himself." But self-dependence contained unprecedented opportunities for self-discovery. Freedom was unnerving but exhilarating. Jung's portrait of modern man was more exuberant than Freud's. According to Freud, the disenchantment of the world had deprived people of the childlike security of dependence but at least given them science, which in his modest assessment had taught them "much since the days of the Deluge" and would gradually "increase their powers still further." In Jung's more enthusiastic formulation of this familiar story of enlightenment, modern man "stands upon a peak, or at the very edge of the world, the abyss of the future before him, above him the heavens, and below him the whole of mankind with a history that disappears in primeval mists." The view from the heights was vertiginous but commanding.

The unexamined premise that history can be compared with the individual's growth from childhood to maturity—the point of reference that Jung shared with Freud and Weber, indeed with most of those who speculate about such issues—made it possible to condemn any form of cultural conservatism, any respect for tradition, as an expression of the natural tendency to resist emotional and intellectual growth, to cling instead to the security of childhood. "Only the man who has outgrown the stages of consciousness belonging to the past . . . can achieve a full consciousness of the present."

It was the gifted individual, the one who accepted the burden of maturity, that Jung addressed in the essays collected in 1933 under the inevitable title *Modern Man in Search of a Soul.* By outgrowing tradition, the fully modern individual gained a wider perspective but unavoidably cut himself off from his more conservative fellows. A "fuller consciousness of the present removes him . . . from submersion in a common consciousness," from the "mass of men who live entirely within the bounds of tradition." This is why the solution of the "modern spiritual problem," as Jung called it, could not possibly lie in a return to "obsolete forms of religion," any more than it could lie in a purely secular world view. Neither the Freudian analyst nor the rabbi or pastor gave modern man "what he is looking for." (As the son of a Protestant minister and the spiritual son of

Freud, Jung presumably knew what he was talking about. He spoke from direct experience of the rival traditions that competed for his allegiance, secular humanism and orthodox religion.) Freud ignored man's unappeasable hunger for some kind of transcendent "meaning," while conventional religion, on the other hand, ignored the creative individual's need "to break with tradition so that he can experiment with his life and determine what value and meanings things have in themselves, apart from traditional presuppositions." If the Freudian analyst backed away from questions of meaning and value, the pastor passed judgment all too quickly. Modern man, having "heard enough about guilt and sin," was rightly suspicious of "fixed ideas as to what is right," suspicious of spiritual counselors who "pretend to know what is right and what is not." Moral judgment, in any case, took "something away from the richness of experience." The old injunction to follow in the footsteps of the Lord had to be translated into a modern idiom. Sounding very much like Oscar Wilde, Jung took the position that imitation of Christ meant not that "we should copy his life" but that "we are to live with our own proper lives as truly as he lived his in all its implications."

Psychoanalysis served the same purpose in Jung's scheme of things that artistic imagination served in Wilde's. Reformulated so as to overcome Freud's unfortunate preoccupation with sex, it became the means by which to liberate the religious imagination from its enslavement to dying creeds. By providing access not only to the unconscious mental life of individuals but to the "collective unconscious" of the human race, Jungian psychoanalysis excavated the permanent structure of religious mythology, the raw material out of which the modern world might construct new forms of religious life appropriate to its needs. Jung invited his patients and readers to range through the whole array of mythologies and spiritual techniques—all of them equally available for inspection, thanks to the expansion of historical consciousness in the modern world—and to experiment with a variety of combinations until they found the one best suited to their individual requirements.

But I am less interested in Jung's remedy for the spiritual malaise of modernity than in his formulation of the problem and especially in the common assumptions Jung shared even with those who rejected his particular solution. The most important of these assumptions was that the inevitable unfolding of consciousness made it impossible, at least for the educated classes, to return to the childlike security of the past. The educated classes, unable to escape the burden of sophistication, might envy the naïve faiths of the past; they might even envy the classes that continued unthinkingly to observe traditional faiths in the twentieth century, not yet having been exposed to the wintry blasts of modern critical thinking. They could not trade places with the unenlightened masses, however, any more than they could return to the past. Once the critical habit of mind had been fully assimilated, no one who understood its implications could find any refuge or resting place in premodern systems of thought and belief. It was this experience of disillusionment, more than anything else, that was held to distinguish the artist and the intellectual from unreflective creatures of convention, who distrusted artists and intellectuals precisely because they could not bear to hear the bad news.

Unenlightened ages past might be forgiven for believing things no educated person could believe in the twentieth century or for taking literally mythologies better understood in a figurative or metaphorical sense; one might even forgive the modern proletarian, excluded from an education by virtue of his unremitting toil, but the bourgeois philistine lived in an enlightened age, with easy access to enlightened culture, yet deliberately chose not to see the light, lest it destroy the illusions essential to his peace of mind. The intellectual alone, in any case, looked straight into the light without blinking.

Disillusioned but undaunted: such is the self-image of modernity, so proud of its intellectual emancipation that it makes no effort to conceal the spiritual price that has to be paid. Again and again commentary on the spiritual condition of modernity—on the soul of man in the modern age, on the "modern temper," as Joseph Wood Krutch referred to it—again and again this commentary returns to its favorite biological analogy as the framing device that defines the problem. Krutch uses it too: *The Modern Temper*, published in 1929 and predictably condemned by the philistines he was eager to offend as an overly pessimistic account of the contemporary plight, begins (no less predictably) with the contrast between childish innocence and experience. Krutch starts right off with Freud: "It is one of Freud's quaint conceits that the child in his mother's womb is the happiest of living creatures." Krutch does not reject this "quaint conceit," as his language might lead one to expect; instead he proceeds, as did Freud himself, to argue that "races as well as individuals have their infancy, their adolescence, and their maturity." As the race matures, "the universe becomes more and more what experience has revealed, less and less what imagination has created." Man reluctantly learns that he must depend on himself alone, not on supernatural powers created in his own image. "Like the child growing into manhood, he passes from a world which is fitted to him into a world for which he must fit himself." At the social level the process was still incomplete since the modern world had not completely outlived its past. Its "predicament" could be compared with that of the "adolescent who has not yet learned to orient himself without reference to the mythology amid which his childhood was passed."

There is a vast body of commentary on the modern spiritual plight, all of which assumes that the experience of doubt, moral relativism, and so on is distinctively modern. I have cited a few representative samples, but a more comprehensive and systematic survey of this literature would only confirm the central importance of imagery that links the history of culture to the life cycle of individuals. Following Krutch, we might call it a quaint conceit, this mental habit of playing off our disillusionment against the innocence of our ancestors, except that it originates in an impulse that is anything but quaint and leads to very serious consequences, not least of which is to prevent an understanding of vitally important matters. It betrays a predisposition to read history either as a tragedy of lost illusions or as the progress of critical reason. I say "either/or," but of course, these two versions of the modernist historical myth are closely related; indeed, they are symbiotically dependent on each other. It is the progress of critical reason that allegedly leads to lost illusions. Disillusionment represents the price of progress. Nostalgia and the idea of progress, as I have argued in *The True and Only Heaven*, go hand in hand. The assumption that our own civilization has achieved a level of unparalleled complexity gives rise to a nostalgic yearning for bygone simplicity. From this point of view, the relation of past to present is defined, above all, by the contrast between simplicity and sophistication.

The barrier that divides the past from the present—an impassable barrier, in the imagination of modernity—is the experience of disillusionment, which makes it impossible to recapture the innocence of earlier days. Disillusionment, we might say, is the characteristic form of modern pride, and this pride is no less evident in the nostalgic myth of the past than in the more aggressively triumphal version of cultural progress that dismisses the past without regrets. Nostalgia is superficially loving in its re-creation of the past, but it evokes the past only to bury it alive. It shares with the belief in progress, to which it is only superficially opposed, an eagerness to proclaim the death of the past and to deny history's hold on the present. Those who mourn the death of the past and those who acclaim it both take for granted that our age has outgrown its childhood. Both find it difficult to believe that history still haunts our enlightened, disillusioned adolescence or maturity or senility (whatever stage of the life cycle we have allegedly reached). Both are governed, in their attitude toward the past, by the prevailing disbelief in ghosts.

Perhaps the most important casualty of this habit of mind is a proper understanding of religion. In the commentary on the modern spiritual predicament, religion is consistently treated as a source of intellectual and emotional security, not as a challenge to complacency and pride. Its ethical teachings are misconstrued as a body of simple commandments leaving no room for ambiguity or doubt. Recall Jung's description of medieval Christians as "children of God [who] knew exactly what they should do and how they should conduct themselves." Krutch says much the same thing. Medieval theology, he thinks, made the conduct of life an "exact science." It offered a "plan of life" that was "delightfully simple." Medieval Christians "accepted the laws of God in a fashion exactly parallel to that in which the contemporary scientist accepts the Laws of Nature," and this unquestioning obedience to an authoritative science of morals, according to Krutch, is the only alternative to "moral nihilism." "As soon as one begins to doubt either the validity of the laws of God considered as the fundamental principles of a science which happens to be called theology, or as soon as one begins to raise a question as to the purpose of life," one begins to slide down the slippery slope to relativism, moral anarchy, and cultural despair.

What has to be questioned here is the assumption that religion ever provided a set of comprehensive and unambiguous answers to ethical questions, answers completely resistant to skepticism, or that it forestalled speculation about the meaning and purpose of life, or that religious people in the past were unacquainted with existential despair. The famous collection of songs written by medieval students preparing for the priesthood *Carmina Burana* would be enough in itself to dispel this notion; these disturbing compositions give voice to an age-old suspicion that the universe is ruled by Fortune, not by Providence, that life has no higher purpose at all, and that the better part of moral wisdom is to enjoy it while you can.

Or consider the varieties of religious experience analyzed by William James in his book of that name, one of the few books about the spiritual crisis of modernity (if that, in fact, is its subject) that has stood the test of time, in part—strange to say—because of its complete indifference to issues of historical chronology. To readers formed by the self-consciously modern tradition I have been referring to, this indifference to chronology might appear to be a weakness of James's book, but that is precisely his point: that the deepest variety of religious faith (the "twice-born type," as he calls it) always, in every age, arises out of a background of despair. Religious faith asserts the goodness of being in the face of suffering and evil. Black despair and alienation—which have their origin not in perceptions exclusively modern but in the bitterness always felt toward a God who allows evil and suffering to flourish—often become the prelude to conversion. An awareness of "radical evil" underlies the spiritual intoxication that finally comes with "yielding" and "self-surrender." The experience of the twice-born, according to James, is more painful but emotionally deeper than that of the "healthy-minded" because it is informed by the "iron of melancholy." Having no awareness of evil, the once-born type of religious experience cannot stand up to adversity. It offers sustenance only so long as it does not encounter "poisonous humiliations." "A little cooling down of animal excitability and instinct, a little loss of animal toughness, will bring the worm at the core of all our usual springs of delight into full view, and turn us into melancholy metaphysicians." When that happens, we need a more rugged form of faith, one that recognizes that "life and its negation are beaten up inextricably together" and that "all natural happiness thus seems infected with a contradiction." If nothing else, the shadow of death hangs over our pleasures and triumphs, calling them into question. "Back of everything is the great spectre of universal death, the all-encompassing blackness."

It needs to be emphasized, once again, that James is contrasting two types of temperament, not two ages of man. The modern world has no monopoly on the fear of death or the alienation from God. Alienation is the normal condition of human existence. Rebellion against God is the natural reaction to the discovery that the world was not made for our personal convenience. The further discovery that suffering is visited on the just and unjust alike is hard to square with a belief in a benign and omnipotent creator, as we know from the Book of Job. But it is the comfortable belief that the purposes of the Almighty coincide with our purely human purposes that religious faith requires us to renounce.

Krutch argues that religion gives man the agreeable illusion that he is the center of the universe, the object of God's loving-kindness and rapt attention. But it is just this illusion that the most radical form of religious faith relentlessly attacks. Thus Jonathan Edwards distinguishes between a "grateful good will"—the root of religious feeling, as he understands it—and the kind of gratitude that depends on being loved and appreciated—the kind of gratitude, in other words, that people might feel toward a creator pre-sumed to have their interests at heart. "True virtue," Edwards wrote, "primarily consists, not in love of any par-ticular Beings . . . nor in gratitude, because they love us, but in a propensity and union of heart to Being simply con-sidered, exciting absolute benevolence . . . to Being in gen-eral." Man has no claim to God's favor, and a "grateful good will" has to be conceived, accordingly, not as an appro-priate acknowledgment of the answer to our prayers, so to speak, but as the acknowledgment of God's life-giving power to order things as he pleases, without "giving any account of his matters," as Edwards puts it.

Edwards's view of God bears no resemblance to the benign father figure conjured up by childlike human beings, according to Freud, out of their unconscious need for dependence. Edwards's God is "absolutely perfect, and infinitely wise, and the fountain of all wisdom," and it is therefore "meet . . . that he should make himself his end, and that he should make nothing but his own wisdom his rule in pursuing that end, without asking leave or counsel of any." Freud, like Krutch, assumes that religion answers to the need for dependence, whereas Edwards speaks directly to those who proudly deny any such need—indeed, who find it galling to be reminded of their depen-dence on a power beyond their own control or at least beyond the control of humanity in general. Such people find it difficult to acknowledge the justice and goodness of this higher power when the world is so obviously full of evil. They find it difficult to reconcile their expectations of worldly success and happiness, so often undone by events, with the idea of a just, loving, and all-powerful creator. Unable to conceive of a God who does not regard human happiness as the be-all and end-all of creation, they cannot accept the central paradox of religious faith: that the secret of happiness lies in renouncing the right to be happy.

What makes the modern temper modern, then, is not that we have lost our childish sense of dependence but that the normal rebellion *against* dependence is more pervasive than it used to be. This rebellion is not new, as Flannery O'Conner reminds us when she observes that "there are long periods in the lives of all of us . . . when the truth as revealed by faith is hideous, emotionally disturbing, downright repulsive. Witness the dark night of the soul in individual saints." If the whole world now seems to be going through a dark night of the soul, it is because the normal rebellion against dependence appears to be sanctioned by our scientific control over nature, the same progress of science that has allegedly destroyed religious superstition.

Those wonderful machines that science has enabled us to construct have not eliminated drudgery, as Oscar Wilde and other false prophets so confidently predicted, but they have made it possible to imagine ourselves as masters of our fate. In an age that fancies itself as disillusioned, this is the one illusion—the illusion of mastery—that remains as tenacious as ever. But now that we are beginning to grasp the limits of our control over the natural world, it is an illusion—to invoke Freud once again—the future of which is very much in doubt, an illusion more problematical, certainly, than the future of religion.

Bibliography

Adams, Henry. *Democracy* (1879). New York, n.d.

Aldrich, Nelson W., Jr. *Old Money: The Mythology of America's Upper Class*. New York, 1988. Aldrich takes the position that the only alternative to old money is the market and that a hereditary upper class, accordingly, is the best defense against the market and the triumph of market values. This argument, persuasive as far as it goes, ignores the possibility of a populist alternative.

Arendt, Hannah. *The Human Condition*. Chicago, 1958.

Aronowitz, Stanley. *False Promises: The Shaping of American Working-Class Consciousness*. New York, 1973. The deception referred to in the title is the promise of upward mobility for all.

Bakke, E. Wight. *The Unemployed Worker*. New Haven, 1940.

Barr, Alwyn. "Occupational and Geographical Mobility in San Antonio, 1870–1890." *Social Science Quarterly* 51 (1970): 396–403.

Bellah, Robert, et al. *The Good Society*. New York, 1991. Like

Alan Wolfe, Bellah and his collaborators are looking for a communitarian alternative to the state and the market; like Wolfe, they are more critical of the market than of the state. The communitarian program, in this version, is not always easy to distinguish from the welfare state.

———. *Habits of the Heart*. Berkeley, 1985.

Bender, Thomas. "The Social Foundations of Professional Credibility." In *The Authority of Experts*, ed. Thomas Haskell. Bloomington, Ind., 1984.

Benedict, Ruth. *The Chrysanthemum and the Sword*. Boston, 1946. One of many anthropological studies that gave currency to the misleading distinction between shame cultures and guilt cultures.

Bennett, William J. *To Reclaim a Legacy: A Report on the Humanities in Higher Education*. Washington, D.C., 1984.

Berry, Wendell. *The Unsettling of America: Culture and Agriculture*. New York, 1977.

———. *Sex, Economy, Freedom, and Community: Eight Essays*. New York, 1993. "We have seen the emergence into power in this country," Berry writes, "of an economic elite who have invested their lives and loyalties in no locality and in no nation, whose ambitions are global, and who are so insulated by wealth and power that they feel no need to care about what happens to any place. . . . The global industrialists will go anywhere and destroy anything, so long as there is a market for the result."

Blau, Peter, and Otis D. Duncan. *The American Occupational Structure*. New York, 1967.

Bloom, Allan. *The Closing of the American Mind*. New York, 1987. The book liberals love to hate. Deserves closer attention than it has received from the academic left.

Blumin, Stuart. "The Historical Study of Vertical Mobility." *Historical Methods Newsletter* 1 (1968): 1–13.

Brownson, Orestes. Review of Horace Mann's Second Annual Report. *Boston Quarterly Review* (1839): 393–434.

———. "The Laboring Classes." *Boston Quarterly Review* (1840): 358–95.

———. "Our Future Policy." In *The Works of Orestes A. Brownson*, ed. Henry F. Brownson. Detroit, 1883.

Burke, Martin Joseph. "The Conundrum of Class: Public Discourse on the Social Order in America." Ph.D. dissertation, University of Michigan, 1987. Includes a wealth of material much of which supports my contention that nineteenth-century Americans did not conceive of society as a ladder or equate opportunity with upward mobility.

Burns, Rex. *Success in America: The Yeoman Dream and the Industrial Revolution*. Amherst, 1976. Contains a good deal of firsthand material showing that nineteenth-century Americans did not equate opportunity with upward mobility.

Cadbury, Henry J. *The Peril of Modernizing Jesus*. New York, 1937. A critique of the social gospel written from a neo-orthodox point of view.

Carey, James W. *Communication as Culture*. Boston, 1989. Sheds much-needed light on the Lippmann-Dewey debate.

Channing, Henry. "The Middle Class." *The Spirit of the Age* (September 15, 1849): 169–71.

Cheney, Lynn. *American Memory: A Report on the Humanities in the Nation's Public Schools*. Washington, D.C., 1987.

———. *Tyrannical Machines: A Report on Educational Practices Gone Wrong and Our Best Hopes for Setting Them Right*. Washington, D.C., 1990.

Chevalier, Michel. *Society, Manners, and Politics in the United States* (1838), ed. John William Ward. Garden City, 1961. Overshadowed by Tocqueville, Chevalier's account of equality is more penetrating. He was impressed by civic equality (as Mickey Kaus calls it) as opposed to equality of condition. The glory of America, as Chevalier saw it, was the "initiation" of the lower classes into the world's culture.

Chinoy, Ely. *Automobile Workers and the American Dream*. Garden City, N.Y., 1955. Following in the footsteps of Lloyd Warner, Chinoy equated the American dream with upward social mobility.

Chudacoff, Howard. *Mobile Americans: Residence and Social Mobility in Omaha, 1880–1920*. New York, 1972.

Clark, Christopher. *The Roots of Rural Capitalism: Western Massachusetts, 1780–1860*. Ithaca, N.Y., 1990.

Cmiel, Kenneth. *Democratic Eloquence: The Fight over Popular Speech in Nineteenth-Century America*. New York, 1990.

Colley, Linda. *Britons: Forging the Nation, 1707–1837*. New Haven, 1992.

Conant, James Bryant. "Education for a Classless Society: The Jeffersonian Tradition." *Atlantic* 165 (May 1940): 593–602. A key document, which illustrates the linkage between meritocracy and the concept of social mobility, as well as the steady impoverishment of the ideal of a classless society.

Cooley, Charles H. *Social Process*. Boston, 1907.

———. *Social Organization*. New York, 1909. Cooley was one of the first commentators of his generation to understand the distinction between democracy and social mobility, which, he explained, merely drained away talent from the working class.

Cox, Harvey. *The Secular City*. New York, 1965. The social gospel updated, with a therapeutic twist.

Croly, Herbert. *Progressive Democracy*. New York, 1914.

Dewey, John. *The Public and its Problems*. New York, 1927. A reply, in effect, to Lippmann's disparaging critique of public opinion.

Dionne, E. J. *Why Americans Hate Politics*. New York, 1991. The reason, Dionne concludes, is that the ideological politics advanced both by liberals and conservatives fails to address the issues that trouble people in their daily lives. Neither party represents the wishes of the electorate. Instead of a politics that would reflect the complexity of the economic, social, and moral issues that confront us, the public is asked to choose between rival ideologies that are equally lifeless and abstract.

Edwards, Jonathan. *The Nature of True Virtue*. Boston, 1765. Perhaps the most important book on ethics ever written by an American; repays many rereadings.

Emad, Parvis. "Max Scheler's Phenomenology of Shame." *Philosophy and Phenomenological Research* 32 (1972): 361–70.

Emerson, Ralph Waldo. "Society and Solitude" (1870). In *Selected Writings of Emerson*, ed. Donald McQuade. New York, 1981.

Etzioni, Amitai. *The Spirit of Community: Rights, Responsibilities, and the Communitarian Agenda.* New York, 1993. Exemplifies both the strengths and the weaknesses of communitarianism.

Follett, Mary Parker. *The New State.* New York, 1918. One of the best arguments for neighborhoods as the nursery of civic life.

Foner, Eric. *Free Soil, Free Labor, Free Men: The Ideology of the Republican Party before the Civil War.* New York, 1970. Misreads Lincoln as an exponent of upward social mobility.

Frank, Lawrence. *Society as the Patient: Essays on Culture and Personality.* New Brunswick, N.J., 1948. A landmark; instrumental in replacing moral and political with therapeutic categories.

Friedman, Milton. *Capitalism and Freedom.* (1962). Chicago, 1982. Friedman's willingness to leave everything to the market is qualified only by his acknowledgment that participation in the market requires at least a minimum of responsibility, foresight, and deferral of gratification—qualities, it might be added, that are increasingly notable by their absence.

Gates, Henry Louis, Jr. "Let Them Talk." *New Republic* (September 20–27, 1993): 37–49. A spirited critique, by a leading authority in black studies, of the movement to regulate "hate speech" and its intellectual roots in critical race theory, so called, which by "textualizing" everything seems to condemn not so much racism as the expression of racism. Noting the affinity between critical race theory and the "booming recovery industry," Gates concludes that "at the vital center of the hate speech movement is the seductive vision of the therapeutic state." As he says, "The recovery/survivor group paradigm leads to a puzzling contradiction. We are told that victims of racist speech are cured—that is, empowered—when they learn they are 'not alone' in their subordination, but subordinated as a group. But elsewhere we are told that what makes racist speech peculiarly wounding is that it conveys precisely the message that you are a member of a subordinated group. How can the suggestion of group subordination be the poison *and* the antidote?"

Geertz, Clifford. "Ideology as a Cultural System." *The Interpretation of Cultures.* New York, 1973. Ideologies are necessary, even useful, according to Geertz. Criticism of ideology rests on a naïve confidence in science, which allegedly promises to eradicate all traces of ideological thinking. Geertz argues that the assault on ideology is reminiscent of the positivist assault on religion. Religion, he reminds us, has proved equally resilient in the face of predictions of its demise.

Gleason, Philip. "Minorities (Almost) All: The Minority Concept in American Social Thought." *American Quarterly* 43 (1991): 392–424.

Goodrich, Samuel (Peter Parley). *Recollections of a Lifetime.* New York, 1856.

Gouldner, Alvin. *The Future of Intellectuals and the Rise of the New Class.* New York, 1979.

Green, Martin. *The Problem of Boston.* New York, 1966. Valuable for, among other things, its analysis of the gentry's withdrawal from civic concerns into the ironic detachment typified by Henry Adams, Charles Eliot Norton, and their friends.

Gregory, Frances W., and Irene D. Neu. "The American Industrial Elite in the 1870's." In *Men in Business,* ed. William Miller. Cambridge, 1952.

Griffen, Clyde. "Making It in America: Social Mobility in Mid-Nineteenth Century Poughkeepsie." *New York History* 51 (1970): 479–99.

———. "The Study of Occupational Mobility in Nineteenth-Century America; Problems and Possibilities." *Journal of Social History* 5 (1972): 310–30.

Hanson, F. Allan. *Testing Testing: Social Consequences of the Examined Life.* Berkeley, 1993. "Intelligence tests are designed in part to promote equal opportunity, but it happens that test scores are perfectly correlated with mean family income: those who score highest on tests have the highest family income, and those who score lowest come from families with the lowest average income." In other words, the examination system reinforces the existing distribution of wealth and power instead of promoting a real meritocracy. Like many others, Hanson contents himself with an attack on hereditary privilege instead of asking whether meritocracy isn't even worse.

Heller, Erich. "Man Ashamed." *Encounter* 42 (February 1974): 23–30.

Hobsbawm, E. J. *The Age of Revolution, 1789–1848.* New York, 1962. Contains useful material on the "career open to talent" and on middle-class nationalism.

Hofstadter, Richard. *The American Political Tradition.* New York, 1948. Hofstadter's view of Lincoln is evident in the title he chose for the essay in question: "Abraham Lincoln and the Self-Made Myth." Many others have followed Hofstadter in this, as in so much else.

Hopkins, Richard. "Occupational and Geographical Mobility in Atlanta, 1870–1890." *Journal of Southern History* 34 (1968): 200–13.

Horney, Karen. *The Neurotic Personality of Our Time.* New York, 1937.

Howe, Frederic C. *The City: Hope of Democracy.* New York, 1905.

Howe, Irving. *The World of Our Fathers.* New York, 1976.

Jacobs, Jane. *The Death and Life of Great American Cities.* New York, 1961. The health of a city, according to Jacobs, depends on the vitality of its neighborhoods, and the replacement of informal types of self-help by professional expertise undermines the ability of neighborhoods to take care of themselves.

Jacoby, Russell. *The Last Intellectuals.* New York, 1987. Traces the decline of public intellectuals and the rise of specialists who communicate only with each other.

———. *Dogmatic Wisdom: How the Culture Wars Have Misled America.* New York, 1994. Unlike most studies of higher education, this does not confine its attention to elite institutions, although it has plenty to say about the arrogance of those who work in such places.

James, William. *Varieties of Religious Experience.* New York, 1902. The best of all James's work, the one closest to his heart, this bears out his remark that religion was the central interest of his life. It bridges his early studies in psychology and his later formulation of the philosophy of pragmatism. Anyone who has mastered *Varieties* will no longer be puzzled by the meaning of James's seemingly philistine statement that ideas have to be judged by their "cash value."

Jay, Martin. "Class Struggle in the Classroom? The Myth of American 'Seminarmarxism.' " *Salmagundi* 85–86 (Winter–Spring 1990): 27–32.

Jung, C. G. *Modern Man in Search of a Soul.* New York, 1933. Like Freud, Jung was a moralist as well as a psychoanalyst; but his gnostic, esoteric religion had nothing in common with Freud's stoicism. Jung believed that by tapping into the collective unconscious, the hidden stream of thought preserved in mythology, folklore, and kabbalistic wisdom, modern man could achieve the comforts of religion without ceasing to be modern.

Kaelble, Hartmut. *Social Mobility in the Nineteenth and Twentieth Centuries.* Dover, N.H., 1985.

Karen, Robert. "Shame." *Atlantic* 269 (February 1992): 40–70.

Kaus, Mickey. *The End of Equality.* New York, 1992. Distinguishes between civic equality and "money equality" and pleads for more emphasis on the former.

Kazin, Alfred. *A Walker in the City.* New York, 1951.

Kerckhoff, Alan C. "The Current State of Social Mobility Research." *Sociological Quarterly* 25 (1984): 139–54.

Kimball, Roger. *Tenured Radicals: How Politics Has Corrupted Higher Education.* New York, 1990. A useful but one-sided polemic against the academic left, based on a defense of foundationalism.

Klein, Melanie. *Love, Guilt, and Reparation.* New York, 1975.

———. *Envy and Gratitude.* New York, 1975. Klein's work revealed the rich moral implications inherent in psychoanalytic concepts. For this reason it was difficult to assimilate into the therapeutic culture popularized by revisionists like Karen Horney and Lawrence Frank. Psychoanalysis bears much of the responsibility for the "triumph of the therapeutic," but it also contains insights, as we can see in the case of Klein, on the basis of which it is possible to arrive at a critical view of this same therapeutic culture.

Krutch, Joseph Wood. *The Modern Temper.* New York, 1929.

Krutch's lament for lost enchantment was based on the false premise that religion formerly provided a complete, comprehensive system of morals and that it sustained the flattering illusion that human beings are the center of the universe.

Lerner, Michael. *Surplus Powerlessness*. Oakland, 1986. An early formulation of Lerner's "politics of meaning"—that is, of compassion for victims.

Levine, George, ed. *Speaking for the Humanities*. New York, 1989.

Lewis, Helen Block. *Shame and Guilt in Neurosis*. New York, 1958.

Lewis, Michael. *Shame: The Exposed Self*. New York, 1992.

Liberator (March 19, March 26, July 9, October 1, 1847). Garrison and Phillips on "wages slavery."

Lincoln, Abraham. *Collected Works*, ed. Roy P. Basler. New Brunswick, N.J., 1953. The important address to the Wisconsin State Agriculture Society appears in vol. 3, pp. 471–82.

Lippmann, Walter. *Liberty and the News*. New York, 1920.

———. *Public Opinion*. New York, 1922. Here and in other studies of the same subject, Lippmann argued that public opinion was emotional and irrational—a poor guide to policy making.

———. *The Phantom Public*. New York, 1925.

———, and Charles Merz. "A Test of the News." *New Republic* 23 (supplement to Aug. 4, 1920).

Lipset, Seymour Martin, and Richard Bendix. *Social Mobility in Industrial Society*. Berkeley, 1959.

Lynd, Helen Merrell. *On Shame and the Search for Identity*. New York, 1958.

Lynd, Robert S., and Helen Merrell Lynd. *Middletown in Transition*. New York, 1937.

Mannheim, Karl. "The Democratization of Culture" (1932). In *From Karl Mannheim*, ed. Kurt H. Wolff. New York, 1971. The elimination of "vertical distance" leaves us with a flattened, disenchanted world, according to Mannheim, and gives rise to the "problem of ecstasy"—the inability to take an interest in anything beyond one's own immediate horizon. Mannheim thinks it may also make for more authentic, unmediated relationships between men and women, but this last-minute reassurance doesn't carry much conviction.

Mead, Margaret. *Cooperation and Competition among Primitive Peoples*. New York, 1937.

Meyrowitz, Joshua. *No Sense of Place*. New York, 1985. One of the best studies of television and its influence in undermining the sense of place.

Miller, Mark Crispin. *Boxed In: The Culture of TV*. Evanston, Ill., 1988.

Miller, William. "American Historians and the American Business Elite in the 1870s." In *Men in Business*, ed. William Miller. Cambridge, 1952.

Mills, C. Wright. "The American Business Elite: A Collective Portrait." *Journal of Economic History* (December 1945), supplement 5, *The Task of Economic History:* 20–44.

Morris, Herbert, ed. *Guilt and Shame*. Belmont, Calif., 1971.

Nathanson, Donald L. *Shame and Pride: Affect, Sex, and the Birth of the Self*. New York, 1992. Exemplifies the secularization of shame, an affect here stripped of all its moral and religious associations and reduced to a deficiency of self-esteem.

Newman, Charles. *The Post-Modern Aura*. Evanston, Ill., 1985.

Nichols, Michael P. *No Place to Hide: Facing Shame So We Can Find Self-Respect*. New York, 1991.

Nietzsche, Friedrich. *Human, All Too Human*. (1886). Munich, 1981.

O'Connor, Flannery. *Collected Works*, ed. Sally Fitzgerald. New York, 1988. In a letter of September 6, 1955, O'Connor observes that "the whole world seems to be going through a dark night of the soul."

Oldenburg, Ray. *The Great Good Place: Cafés, Coffee Shops, Community Centers, Beauty Parlors, General Stores, Bars, Hangouts and How They Get You through the Day*. New York, 1989.

Ortega y Gasset, José. *The Revolt of the Masses*. New York, 1932.

Packard, Vance. *The Hidden Persuaders*. New York, 1957.

Parker, William Belmont. *The Life and Public Services of Justin Smith Morrill*. Boston, 1924.

Pessen, Edward, ed. *Three Centuries of Social Mobility in America*. Lexington, Mass., 1974.

Phillips, Kevin. *The Politics of Rich and Poor*. New York, 1991. ←

Piers, Gerhart, and Milton B. Singer. *Shame and Guilt: A Psychoanalytic Study*. New York, 1953.

Podhoretz, Norman. *Making It*. New York, 1967.

Rantoul, Robert. "An Address to the Workingmen of the United States of America." In *Memoirs, Speeches, and Writings of Robert Rantoul, Jr.*, ed. Luther Hamilton. Boston, 1854.

Reich, Robert B. *The Work of Nations*. New York, 1992. Valuable for its analysis of the "secession" of the knowledge class, Reich's book is vitiated by its excessively rosy, almost fawning portrait of this same class.

Rieff, David. *Los Angeles: Capital of the Third World*. New York, 1991. A persuasive analysis of the permeability of national boundaries and the disturbing implications of this development, including the loss of a sense of place.

———. "Multiculturalism's Silent Partner." *Harper's* (August 1993): 62–72. "Both sides have misconstrued the power of multiculturalism in precisely the same way: as a threat to the capitalist system." In fact, Rieff maintains, it is an ideology well suited to the requirements of capitalism in a world without boundaries. Specifically it represents the "abdication of judgment," moral and aesthetic, in favor of the "rules of the market."

Rieff, Philip. *Freud: The Mind of the Moralist* (1959). Chicago, 1979. To call Freud a moralist places him in a long tradition of moral and religious inquiry—the very humanistic tradition, as Rieff shows here and elsewhere, that psychoanalysis did so much to subvert.

———. *The Triumph of the Therapeutic*. New York, 1966.

———. *Fellow Teachers* (1973). Chicago, 1985.

———. *The Feeling Intellect: Selected Writings*, ed. Jonathan Imber. Chicago, 1990. Certain persistent themes run through Rieff's work over the years: the decline of religion; the replacement of a religious by a therapeutic world view; the intellectual and moral bankruptcy of the latter. Before the Enlightenment the essence of Western culture found its material and symbolic embodiment in the cathedral, according to Rieff; in the nineteenth century, in the statehouse; and in our own time, in the hospital.

Riezler, Kurt. "Shame and Awe." *Man: Mutable and Immutable.* New York, 1951.

Rorty, Richard. "Post-Modernist Bourgeois Liberalism." *Journal of Philosophy* 80 (1983): 583–89. The world as a "Kuwaiti bazaar."

Ross, Edward Alsworth. *Social Control: A Survey of the Foundations of Order.* New York, 1901.

Rotenstreich, Nathan. "On Shame." *Review of Metaphysics* 19 (1965): 55–86.

Ryan, William. *Blaming the Victim.* New York, 1971.

Schneider, Carl D. *Shame, Exposure, and Privacy.* Boston, 1977.

Siracusa, Carl. *A Mechanical People: Perceptions of the Industrial Order in Massachusetts, 1815–1880.* Middletown, Conn., 1979. Projects back into the nineteenth century the current tendency to confuse opportunity with mobility. Siracusa assumes that nineteenth-century Americans equated the two, just as we do.

Sleeper, Jim. *The Closest of Strangers: Liberalism and The Politics of Race in New York.* New York, 1990. The politics of identity, Sleeper maintains, has encouraged racial and ideological posturing and created a stalemate in which the privileged classes maintain their power at the expense of ordinary people of all races.

———. "The End of the Rainbow." *New Republic* (November 1, 1993): 20–25. Further reflections on the politics of racial identity and the Rainbow Coalition's program, which "presumes victimization by white racism." The new immigration, by changing the racial makeup of cities, may lead to a more genuinely multiracial politics, Sleeper thinks, a politics no longer dominated by the polarized opposition between blacks and whites. "Most newcomers are wary of the stigma and polarization that often accompany race-based politics and programs such as all-black schools, racial redistricting, municipal affirmative action quotas and multiracial curricula."

"A Sociologist Looks at an American Community," *Life* (September 12, 1949). Based on the work of W. Lloyd Warner, this profile of Rockford, Illinois, helped to popularize the concept of social mobility.

Steinem, Gloria. *Revolution from Within: A Book of Self-Esteem.* Boston, 1992. Criticized by some feminists as a retreat from politics, Steinem's new program is equally vulnerable to the criticism that it trivializes the concept of shame and substitutes a therapeutic for a moral and religious framework—the only framework that will enable us to make sense of such matters as guilt and shame.

Tawney, R. H. *Equality.* New York, 1931. One of the few works to grasp the difference between equality and meritocracy.

Thernstrom, Stephan. *Poverty and Progress: Social Mobility in a Nineteenth-Century City.* Cambridge, 1964. Historicizes Lloyd Warner's theory of social mobility.

———. "Working Class Social Mobility in Industrial America." In *Essays in Theory and History,* ed. Melvin Richter. Cambridge, 1970.

———. *The Other Bostonians.* Cambridge, 1973.

Turner, Frederick Jackson. *The Frontier in American History.* New York, 1958. This collection includes the essay "Contributions of the West to American Democracy" (1903) in which the term "social mobility" (so far as I have been able to determine) makes its first appearance in American social science.

Walsh, W. W. "Pride, Shame, and Responsibility." *Philosophical Quarterly* 20 (1970): 1–13.

Warner, W. Lloyd. *American Life: Dream and Reality.* (1953). Chicago, 1962. Warner's studies of social mobility were extremely influential, contributing to the misunderstanding that equates mobility with democracy—a fateful mistake with far-reaching repercussions.

———, Marcia Meeker, and Kenneth Eels. *Social Class in America.* Chicago, 1949. Here and in other works Warner advanced his thesis that "education is now competing with economic [i.e., occupational] mobility as the principal route to success. . . . The prudent mobile man today must prepare himself by education if he wishes to fill an important job and provide his family with the money and prestige necessary to get 'the better things of life'."

——, et al. *Democracy in Jonesville*. New York, 1949.

Weber, Max. *The Protestant Ethic and the Spirit of Capitalism*. (1904). New York, 1958.

Westbrook, Robert. *John Dewey and American Democracy*. Ithaca, N.Y., 1991.

Whitman, Walt. *Democratic Vistas*. Washington, D.C., 1871.

Wilde, Oscar. *De Profundis*. London, 1905.

——. "The Soul of Man under Socialism." *Intentions and the Soul of Man*. London, 1911.

Wolfe, Alan. *Whose Keeper?: Social Science and Moral Obligation*. Berkeley, 1989. Groping for an alternative alike to the market and to the superstate, Wolfe attempts, not always successfully, to breathe new life into the concept of "civil society."

Wood, Gordon S. *The Creation of the American Republic, 1776–1787*. Chapel Hill, 1968.

——. *The Radicalism of the American Revolution*. New York, 1992.

Wriston, Walter. *The Twilight of Sovereignty*. New York, 1992. "Those who fully participate in the information economy benefit most from it. . . . They will feel more affinity to their fellow global conversationalists than to those of their countrymen who are not yet part of the global conversation."

Wurmser, Leon. *The Mask of Shame*. Baltimore, 1981. The best of the many psychoanalytic studies of this subject.

Young, Michael. *The Revolt of the Meritocracy*. London, 1958; New York, 1959. A dystopian novel, this is still the best account of a strangely neglected subject, one that brings out the deeply antidemocratic implications of the meritocratic ideal.

Index